Mometrix
TEST PREPARATION

I0892017

CSET®

Biology/Life Science Exam Secrets Study Guide

DEAR FUTURE EXAM SUCCESS STORY

First of all, **THANK YOU** for purchasing Mometrix study materials!

Second, congratulations! You are one of the few determined test-takers who are committed to doing whatever it takes to excel on your exam. **You have come to the right place.** We developed these study materials with one goal in mind: to deliver you the information you need in a format that's concise and easy to use.

In addition to optimizing your guide for the content of the test, we've outlined our recommended steps for breaking down the preparation process into small, attainable goals so you can make sure you stay on track.

We've also analyzed the entire test-taking process, identifying the most common pitfalls and showing how you can overcome them and be ready for any curveball the test throws you.

Standardized testing is one of the biggest obstacles on your road to success, which only increases the importance of doing well in the high-pressure, high-stakes environment of test day. Your results on this test could have a significant impact on your future, and this guide provides the information and practical advice to help you achieve your full potential on test day.

Your success is our success

We would love to hear from you! If you would like to share the story of your exam success or if you have any questions or comments in regard to our products, please contact us at **800-673-8175** or **support@mometrix.com**.

Thanks again for your business and we wish you continued success!

Sincerely,
The Mometrix Test Preparation Team

Need more help? Check out our flashcards at:
http://MometrixFlashcards.com/CSET

Table of Contents

Introduction

Thank you for purchasing this resource! You have made the choice to prepare yourself for a test that could have a huge impact on your future, and this guide is designed to help you be fully ready for test day. Obviously, it's important to have a solid understanding of the test material, but you also need to be prepared for the unique environment and stressors of the test, so that you can perform to the best of your abilities.

For this purpose, the first section that appears in this guide is the **Secret Keys**. We've devoted countless hours to meticulously researching what works and what doesn't, and we've boiled down our findings to the five most impactful steps you can take to improve your performance on the test. We start at the beginning with study planning and move through the preparation process, all the way to the testing strategies that will help you get the most out of what you know when you're finally sitting in front of the test.

We recommend that you start preparing for your test as far in advance as possible. However, if you've bought this guide as a last-minute study resource and only have a few days before your test, we recommend that you skip over the first two Secret Keys since they address a long-term study plan.

If you struggle with **test anxiety**, we strongly encourage you to check out our recommendations for how you can overcome it. Test anxiety is a formidable foe, but it can be beaten, and we want to make sure you have the tools you need to defeat it.

Secret Key #1 – Plan Big, Study Small

There's a lot riding on your performance. If you want to ace this test, you're going to need to keep your skills sharp and the material fresh in your mind. You need a plan that lets you review everything you need to know while still fitting in your schedule. We'll break this strategy down into three categories.

Information Organization

Start with the information you already have: the official test outline. From this, you can make a complete list of all the concepts you need to cover before the test. Organize these concepts into groups that can be studied together, and create a list of any related vocabulary you need to learn so you can brush up on any difficult terms. You'll want to keep this vocabulary list handy once you actually start studying since you may need to add to it along the way.

Time Management

Once you have your set of study concepts, decide how to spread them out over the time you have left before the test. Break your study plan into small, clear goals so you have a manageable task for each day and know exactly what you're doing. Then just focus on one small step at a time. When you manage your time this way, you don't need to spend hours at a time studying. Studying a small block of content for a short period each day helps you retain information better and avoid stressing over how much you have left to do. You can relax knowing that you have a plan to cover everything in time. In order for this strategy to be effective though, you have to start studying early and stick to your schedule. Avoid the exhaustion and futility that comes from last-minute cramming!

Study Environment

The environment you study in has a big impact on your learning. Studying in a coffee shop, while probably more enjoyable, is not likely to be as fruitful as studying in a quiet room. It's important to keep distractions to a minimum. You're only planning to study for a short block of time, so make the most of it. Don't pause to check your phone or get up to find a snack. It's also important to **avoid multitasking**. Research has consistently shown that multitasking will make your studying dramatically less effective. Your study area should also be comfortable and well-lit so you don't have the distraction of straining your eyes or sitting on an uncomfortable chair.

The time of day you study is also important. You want to be rested and alert. Don't wait until just before bedtime. Study when you'll be most likely to comprehend and remember. Even better, if you know what time of day your test will be, set that time aside for study. That way your brain will be used to working on that subject at that specific time and you'll have a better chance of recalling information.

Finally, it can be helpful to team up with others who are studying for the same test. Your actual studying should be done in as isolated an environment as possible, but the work of organizing the information and setting up the study plan can be divided up. In between study sessions, you can discuss with your teammates the concepts that you're all studying and quiz each other on the details. Just be sure that your teammates are as serious about the test as you are. If you find that your study time is being replaced with social time, you might need to find a new team.

Secret Key #2 – Make Your Studying Count

You're devoting a lot of time and effort to preparing for this test, so you want to be absolutely certain it will pay off. This means doing more than just reading the content and hoping you can remember it on test day. It's important to make every minute of study count. There are two main areas you can focus on to make your studying count.

Retention

It doesn't matter how much time you study if you can't remember the material. You need to make sure you are retaining the concepts. To check your retention of the information you're learning, try recalling it at later times with minimal prompting. Try carrying around flashcards and glance at one or two from time to time or ask a friend who's also studying for the test to quiz you.

To enhance your retention, look for ways to put the information into practice so that you can apply it rather than simply recalling it. If you're using the information in practical ways, it will be much easier to remember. Similarly, it helps to solidify a concept in your mind if you're not only reading it to yourself but also explaining it to someone else. Ask a friend to let you teach them about a concept you're a little shaky on (or speak aloud to an imaginary audience if necessary). As you try to summarize, define, give examples, and answer your friend's questions, you'll understand the concepts better and they will stay with you longer. Finally, step back for a big picture view and ask yourself how each piece of information fits with the whole subject. When you link the different concepts together and see them working together as a whole, it's easier to remember the individual components.

Finally, practice showing your work on any multi-step problems, even if you're just studying. Writing out each step you take to solve a problem will help solidify the process in your mind, and you'll be more likely to remember it during the test.

Modality

Modality simply refers to the means or method by which you study. Choosing a study modality that fits your own individual learning style is crucial. No two people learn best in exactly the same way, so it's important to know your strengths and use them to your advantage.

For example, if you learn best by visualization, focus on visualizing a concept in your mind and draw an image or a diagram. Try color-coding your notes, illustrating them, or creating symbols that will trigger your mind to recall a learned concept. If you learn best by hearing or discussing information, find a study partner who learns the same way or read aloud to yourself. Think about how to put the information in your own words. Imagine that you are giving a lecture on the topic and record yourself so you can listen to it later.

For any learning style, flashcards can be helpful. Organize the information so you can take advantage of spare moments to review. Underline key words or phrases. Use different colors for different categories. Mnemonic devices (such as creating a short list in which every item starts with the same letter) can also help with retention. Find what works best for you and use it to store the information in your mind most effectively and easily.

Secret Key #3 – Practice the Right Way

Your success on test day depends not only on how many hours you put into preparing, but also on whether you prepared the right way. It's good to check along the way to see if your studying is paying off. One of the most effective ways to do this is by taking practice tests to evaluate your progress. Practice tests are useful because they show exactly where you need to improve. Every time you take a practice test, pay special attention to these three groups of questions:

- The questions you got wrong
- The questions you had to guess on, even if you guessed right
- The questions you found difficult or slow to work through

This will show you exactly what your weak areas are, and where you need to devote more study time. Ask yourself why each of these questions gave you trouble. Was it because you didn't understand the material? Was it because you didn't remember the vocabulary? Do you need more repetitions on this type of question to build speed and confidence? Dig into those questions and figure out how you can strengthen your weak areas as you go back to review the material.

Additionally, many practice tests have a section explaining the answer choices. It can be tempting to read the explanation and think that you now have a good understanding of the concept. However, an explanation likely only covers part of the question's broader context. Even if the explanation makes perfect sense, **go back and investigate** every concept related to the question until you're positive you have a thorough understanding.

As you go along, keep in mind that the practice test is just that: practice. Memorizing these questions and answers will not be very helpful on the actual test because it is unlikely to have any of the same exact questions. If you only know the right answers to the sample questions, you won't be prepared for the real thing. **Study the concepts** until you understand them fully, and then you'll be able to answer any question that shows up on the test.

It's important to wait on the practice tests until you're ready. If you take a test on your first day of study, you may be overwhelmed by the amount of material covered and how much you need to learn. Work up to it gradually.

On test day, you'll need to be prepared for answering questions, managing your time, and using the test-taking strategies you've learned. It's a lot to balance, like a mental marathon that will have a big impact on your future. Like training for a marathon, you'll need to start slowly and work your way up. When test day arrives, you'll be ready.

Start with the strategies you've read in the first two Secret Keys—plan your course and study in the way that works best for you. If you have time, consider using multiple study resources to get different approaches to the same concepts. It can be helpful to see difficult concepts from more than one angle. Then find a good source for practice tests. Many times, the test website will suggest potential study resources or provide sample tests.

Practice Test Strategy

If you're able to find at least three practice tests, we recommend this strategy:

UNTIMED AND OPEN-BOOK PRACTICE

Take the first test with no time constraints and with your notes and study guide handy. Take your time and focus on applying the strategies you've learned.

TIMED AND OPEN-BOOK PRACTICE

Take the second practice test open-book as well, but set a timer and practice pacing yourself to finish in time.

TIMED AND CLOSED-BOOK PRACTICE

Take any other practice tests as if it were test day. Set a timer and put away your study materials. Sit at a table or desk in a quiet room, imagine yourself at the testing center, and answer questions as quickly and accurately as possible.

Keep repeating timed and closed-book tests on a regular basis until you run out of practice tests or it's time for the actual test. Your mind will be ready for the schedule and stress of test day, and you'll be able to focus on recalling the material you've learned.

Secret Key #4 – Pace Yourself

Once you're fully prepared for the material on the test, your biggest challenge on test day will be managing your time. Just knowing that the clock is ticking can make you panic even if you have plenty of time left. Work on pacing yourself so you can build confidence against the time constraints of the exam. Pacing is a difficult skill to master, especially in a high-pressure environment, so **practice is vital**.

Set time expectations for your pace based on how much time is available. For example, if a section has 60 questions and the time limit is 30 minutes, you know you have to average 30 seconds or less per question in order to answer them all. Although 30 seconds is the hard limit, set 25 seconds per question as your goal, so you reserve extra time to spend on harder questions. When you budget extra time for the harder questions, you no longer have any reason to stress when those questions take longer to answer.

Don't let this time expectation distract you from working through the test at a calm, steady pace, but keep it in mind so you don't spend too much time on any one question. Recognize that taking extra time on one question you don't understand may keep you from answering two that you do understand later in the test. If your time limit for a question is up and you're still not sure of the answer, mark it and move on, and come back to it later if the time and the test format allow. If the testing format doesn't allow you to return to earlier questions, just make an educated guess; then put it out of your mind and move on.

On the easier questions, be careful not to rush. It may seem wise to hurry through them so you have more time for the challenging ones, but it's not worth missing one if you know the concept and just didn't take the time to read the question fully. Work efficiently but make sure you understand the question and have looked at all of the answer choices, since more than one may seem right at first.

Even if you're paying attention to the time, you may find yourself a little behind at some point. You should speed up to get back on track, but do so wisely. Don't panic; just take a few seconds less on each question until you're caught up. Don't guess without thinking, but do look through the answer choices and eliminate any you know are wrong. If you can get down to two choices, it is often worthwhile to guess from those. Once you've chosen an answer, move on and don't dwell on any that you skipped or had to hurry through. If a question was taking too long, chances are it was one of the harder ones, so you weren't as likely to get it right anyway.

On the other hand, if you find yourself getting ahead of schedule, it may be beneficial to slow down a little. The more quickly you work, the more likely you are to make a careless mistake that will affect your score. You've budgeted time for each question, so don't be afraid to spend that time. Practice an efficient but careful pace to get the most out of the time you have.

Secret Key #5 – Have a Plan for Guessing

When you're taking the test, you may find yourself stuck on a question. Some of the answer choices seem better than others, but you don't see the one answer choice that is obviously correct. What do you do?

The scenario described above is very common, yet most test takers have not effectively prepared for it. Developing and practicing a plan for guessing may be one of the single most effective uses of your time as you get ready for the exam.

In developing your plan for guessing, there are three questions to address:

- When should you start the guessing process?
- How should you narrow down the choices?
- Which answer should you choose?

When to Start the Guessing Process

Unless your plan for guessing is to select C every time (which, despite its merits, is not what we recommend), you need to leave yourself enough time to apply your answer elimination strategies. Since you have a limited amount of time for each question, that means that if you're going to give yourself the best shot at guessing correctly, you have to decide quickly whether or not you will guess.

Of course, the best-case scenario is that you don't have to guess at all, so first, see if you can answer the question based on your knowledge of the subject and basic reasoning skills. Focus on the key words in the question and try to jog your memory of related topics. Give yourself a chance to bring the knowledge to mind, but once you realize that you don't have (or you can't access) the knowledge you need to answer the question, it's time to start the guessing process.

It's almost always better to start the guessing process too early than too late. It only takes a few seconds to remember something and answer the question from knowledge. Carefully eliminating wrong answer choices takes longer. Plus, going through the process of eliminating answer choices can actually help jog your memory.

Summary: Start the guessing process as soon as you decide that you can't answer the question based on your knowledge.

How to Narrow Down the Choices

The next chapter in this book (**Test-Taking Strategies**) includes a wide range of strategies for how to approach questions and how to look for answer choices to eliminate. You will definitely want to read those carefully, practice them, and figure out which ones work best for you. Here though, we're going to address a mindset rather than a particular strategy.

Your odds of guessing an answer correctly depend on how many options you are choosing from.

Number of options left	5	4	3	2	1
Odds of guessing correctly	20%	25%	33%	50%	100%

You can see from this chart just how valuable it is to be able to eliminate incorrect answers and make an educated guess, but there are two things that many test takers do that cause them to miss out on the benefits of guessing:

- Accidentally eliminating the correct answer
- Selecting an answer based on an impression

We'll look at the first one here, and the second one in the next section.

To avoid accidentally eliminating the correct answer, we recommend a thought exercise called **the $5 challenge**. In this challenge, you only eliminate an answer choice from contention if you are willing to bet $5 on it being wrong. Why $5? Five dollars is a small but not insignificant amount of money. It's an amount you could afford to lose but wouldn't want to throw away. And while losing $5 once might not hurt too much, doing it twenty times will set you back $100. In the same way, each small decision you make—eliminating a choice here, guessing on a question there—won't by itself impact your score very much, but when you put them all together, they can make a big difference. By holding each answer choice elimination decision to a higher standard, you can reduce the risk of accidentally eliminating the correct answer.

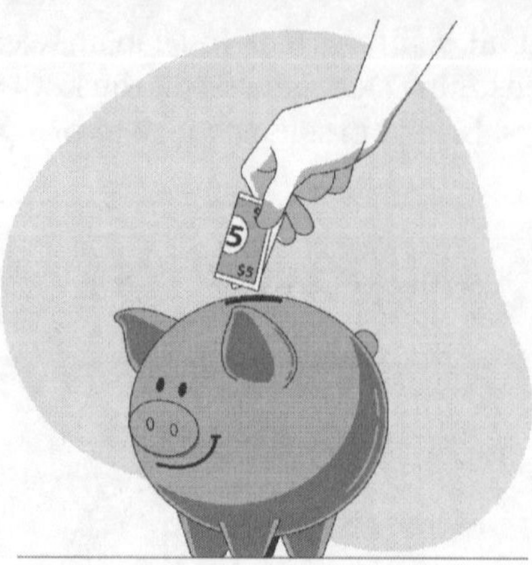

The $5 challenge can also be applied in a positive sense: If you are willing to bet $5 that an answer choice *is* correct, go ahead and mark it as correct.

Summary: Only eliminate an answer choice if you are willing to bet $5 that it is wrong.

Which Answer to Choose

You're taking the test. You've run into a hard question and decided you'll have to guess. You've eliminated all the answer choices you're willing to bet $5 on. Now you have to pick an answer. Why do we even need to talk about this? Why can't you just pick whichever one you feel like when the time comes?

The answer to these questions is that if you don't come into the test with a plan, you'll rely on your impression to select an answer choice, and if you do that, you risk falling into a trap. The test writers know that everyone who takes their test will be guessing on some of the questions, so they intentionally write wrong answer choices to seem plausible. You still have to pick an answer though, and if the wrong answer choices are designed to look right, how can you ever be sure that you're not falling for their trap? The best solution we've found to this dilemma is to take the decision out of your hands entirely. Here is the process we recommend:

Once you've eliminated any choices that you are confident (willing to bet $5) are wrong, select the first remaining choice as your answer.

Whether you choose to select the first remaining choice, the second, or the last, the important thing is that you use some preselected standard. Using this approach guarantees that you will not be enticed into selecting an answer choice that looks right, because you are not basing your decision on how the answer choices look.

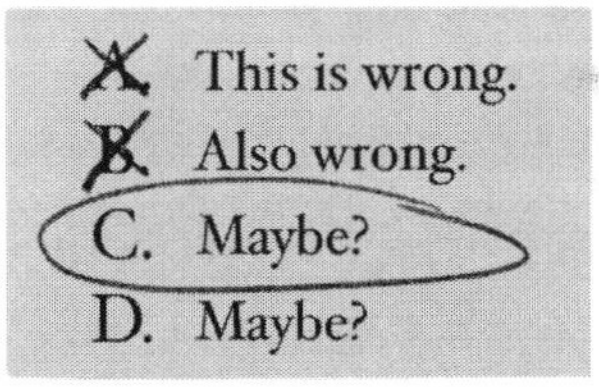

This is not meant to make you question your knowledge. Instead, it is to help you recognize the difference between your knowledge and your impressions. There's a huge difference between thinking an answer is right because of what you know, and thinking an answer is right because it looks or sounds like it should be right.

Summary: To ensure that your selection is appropriately random, make a predetermined selection from among all answer choices you have not eliminated.

Test-Taking Strategies

This section contains a list of test-taking strategies that you may find helpful as you work through the test. By taking what you know and applying logical thought, you can maximize your chances of answering any question correctly!

It is very important to realize that every question is different and every person is different: no single strategy will work on every question, and no single strategy will work for every person. That's why we've included all of them here, so you can try them out and determine which ones work best for different types of questions and which ones work best for you.

Question Strategies

⊘ Read Carefully

Read the question and the answer choices carefully. Don't miss the question because you misread the terms. You have plenty of time to read each question thoroughly and make sure you understand what is being asked. Yet a happy medium must be attained, so don't waste too much time. You must read carefully and efficiently.

⊘ Contextual Clues

Look for contextual clues. If the question includes a word you are not familiar with, look at the immediate context for some indication of what the word might mean. Contextual clues can often give you all the information you need to decipher the meaning of an unfamiliar word. Even if you can't determine the meaning, you may be able to narrow down the possibilities enough to make a solid guess at the answer to the question.

⊘ Prefixes

If you're having trouble with a word in the question or answer choices, try dissecting it. Take advantage of every clue that the word might include. Prefixes can be a huge help. Usually, they allow you to determine a basic meaning. *Pre-* means before, *post-* means after, *pro-* is positive, *de-* is negative. From prefixes, you can get an idea of the general meaning of the word and try to put it into context.

⊘ Hedge Words

Watch out for critical hedge words, such as *likely, may, can, often, almost, mostly, usually, generally, rarely,* and *sometimes.* Question writers insert these hedge phrases to cover every possibility. Often an answer choice will be wrong simply because it leaves no room for exception. Be on guard for answer choices that have definitive words such as *exactly* and *always.*

⊘ Switchback Words

Stay alert for *switchbacks.* These are the words and phrases frequently used to alert you to shifts in thought. The most common switchback words are *but, although,* and *however.* Others include *nevertheless, on the other hand, even though, while, in spite of, despite,* and *regardless of.* Switchback words are important to catch because they can change the direction of the question or an answer choice.

✓ FACE VALUE

When in doubt, use common sense. Accept the situation in the problem at face value. Don't read too much into it. These problems will not require you to make wild assumptions. If you have to go beyond creativity and warp time or space in order to have an answer choice fit the question, then you should move on and consider the other answer choices. These are normal problems rooted in reality. The applicable relationship or explanation may not be readily apparent, but it is there for you to figure out. Use your common sense to interpret anything that isn't clear.

Answer Choice Strategies

✓ ANSWER SELECTION

The most thorough way to pick an answer choice is to identify and eliminate wrong answers until only one is left, then confirm it is the correct answer. Sometimes an answer choice may immediately seem right, but be careful. The test writers will usually put more than one reasonable answer choice on each question, so take a second to read all of them and make sure that the other choices are not equally obvious. As long as you have time left, it is better to read every answer choice than to pick the first one that looks right without checking the others.

✓ ANSWER CHOICE FAMILIES

An answer choice family consists of two (in rare cases, three) answer choices that are very similar in construction and cannot all be true at the same time. If you see two answer choices that are direct opposites or parallels, one of them is usually the correct answer. For instance, if one answer choice says that quantity *x* increases and another either says that quantity *x* decreases (opposite) or says that quantity *y* increases (parallel), then those answer choices would fall into the same family. An answer choice that doesn't match the construction of the answer choice family is more likely to be incorrect. Most questions will not have answer choice families, but when they do appear, you should be prepared to recognize them.

✓ ELIMINATE ANSWERS

Eliminate answer choices as soon as you realize they are wrong, but make sure you consider all possibilities. If you are eliminating answer choices and realize that the last one you are left with is also wrong, don't panic. Start over and consider each choice again. There may be something you missed the first time that you will realize on the second pass.

✓ AVOID FACT TRAPS

Don't be distracted by an answer choice that is factually true but doesn't answer the question. You are looking for the choice that answers the question. Stay focused on what the question is asking for so you don't accidentally pick an answer that is true but incorrect. Always go back to the question and make sure the answer choice you've selected actually answers the question and is not merely a true statement.

✓ EXTREME STATEMENTS

In general, you should avoid answers that put forth extreme actions as standard practice or proclaim controversial ideas as established fact. An answer choice that states the "process should be used in certain situations, if..." is much more likely to be correct than one that states the "process should be discontinued completely." The first is a calm rational statement and doesn't even make a definitive, uncompromising stance, using a hedge word *if* to provide wiggle room, whereas the second choice is far more extreme.

⊘ Benchmark

As you read through the answer choices and you come across one that seems to answer the question well, mentally select that answer choice. This is not your final answer, but it's the one that will help you evaluate the other answer choices. The one that you selected is your benchmark or standard for judging each of the other answer choices. Every other answer choice must be compared to your benchmark. That choice is correct until proven otherwise by another answer choice beating it. If you find a better answer, then that one becomes your new benchmark. Once you've decided that no other choice answers the question as well as your benchmark, you have your final answer.

⊘ Predict the Answer

Before you even start looking at the answer choices, it is often best to try to predict the answer. When you come up with the answer on your own, it is easier to avoid distractions and traps because you will know exactly what to look for. The right answer choice is unlikely to be word-for-word what you came up with, but it should be a close match. Even if you are confident that you have the right answer, you should still take the time to read each option before moving on.

General Strategies

⊘ Tough Questions

If you are stumped on a problem or it appears too hard or too difficult, don't waste time. Move on! Remember though, if you can quickly check for obviously incorrect answer choices, your chances of guessing correctly are greatly improved. Before you completely give up, at least try to knock out a couple of possible answers. Eliminate what you can and then guess at the remaining answer choices before moving on.

⊘ Check Your Work

Since you will probably not know every term listed and the answer to every question, it is important that you get credit for the ones that you do know. Don't miss any questions through careless mistakes. If at all possible, try to take a second to look back over your answer selection and make sure you've selected the correct answer choice and haven't made a costly careless mistake (such as marking an answer choice that you didn't mean to mark). This quick double check should more than pay for itself in caught mistakes for the time it costs.

⊘ Pace Yourself

It's easy to be overwhelmed when you're looking at a page full of questions; your mind is confused and full of random thoughts, and the clock is ticking down faster than you would like. Calm down and maintain the pace that you have set for yourself. Especially as you get down to the last few minutes of the test, don't let the small numbers on the clock make you panic. As long as you are on track by monitoring your pace, you are guaranteed to have time for each question.

⊘ Don't Rush

It is very easy to make errors when you are in a hurry. Maintaining a fast pace in answering questions is pointless if it makes you miss questions that you would have gotten right otherwise. Test writers like to include distracting information and wrong answers that seem right. Taking a little extra time to avoid careless mistakes can make all the difference in your test score. Find a pace that allows you to be confident in the answers that you select.

✅ KEEP MOVING

Panicking will not help you pass the test, so do your best to stay calm and keep moving. Taking deep breaths and going through the answer elimination steps you practiced can help to break through a stress barrier and keep your pace.

Final Notes

The combination of a solid foundation of content knowledge and the confidence that comes from practicing your plan for applying that knowledge is the key to maximizing your performance on test day. As your foundation of content knowledge is built up and strengthened, you'll find that the strategies included in this chapter become more and more effective in helping you quickly sift through the distractions and traps of the test to isolate the correct answer.

Now that you're preparing to move forward into the test content chapters of this book, be sure to keep your goal in mind. As you read, think about how you will be able to apply this information on the test. If you've already seen sample questions for the test and you have an idea of the question format and style, try to come up with questions of your own that you can answer based on what you're reading. This will give you valuable practice applying your knowledge in the same ways you can expect to on test day.

Good luck and good studying!

From Molecules to Organisms: Structures and Processes

Transform passive reading into active learning! After immersing yourself in this chapter, put your comprehension to the test by taking a quiz. The insights you gained will stay with you longer this way. Scan the QR code to go directly to the chapter quiz interface for this study guide. If you're using a computer, simply visit the online resources page at **mometrix.com/resources719/csetbiolifesci** and click the Chapter Quizzes link.

Chemical Structures and Properties of Biologically Important Molecules

Chemical Bonding Properties of Carbon

Carbon is considered to be the central atom of organic compounds. Carbon atoms each have four valence electrons and require four more electrons to have a stable outer shell. Due to the repulsion between the valence electrons, the bond sites are all equidistant from each other. This enables carbon to form longs chains and rings. Carbon atoms can form four single covalent bonds with other atoms. For example, methane (CH_4) consists of one carbon atom singly bonded to four separate hydrogen atoms. Carbon atoms can also form double or triple covalent bonds. For example, an oxygen atom can form a double bond with a carbon atom, and a nitrogen atom can form a triple bond with a carbon atom.

Organic and Inorganic Molecules

Organic molecules contain carbon and hydrogen. Because carbon can form four covalent bonds, organic molecules can be very complex structures. Organic molecules can have carbon backbones that form long chains, branched chains, or even rings. Organic compounds tend to be less soluble in water than inorganic compounds. Organic compounds are often classified as either natural (found in plants and animals) or as synthetic (made via laboratory or industrial processes). **Inorganic molecules** generally do not contain carbon-carbon or carbon-hydrogen bonds, but there are some exceptions. Inorganic compounds include salts and metals. Specific examples of inorganic molecules include sodium chloride, oxygen, and carbon dioxide.

Covalent Bonds

Chemical bonds are the attractive forces that bind atoms together to form molecules. Chemical bonds include covalent bonds, ionic bonds, and metallic bonds. **Covalent bonds** are formed from the sharing of electron pairs between two atoms in a molecule. In organic molecules, carbon atoms form single, double, or triple covalent bonds. Organic compounds including proteins, carbohydrates, lipids, and nucleic acids are molecular compounds formed by covalent bonds.

Review Video: Covalent Bonds
Visit mometrix.com/academy and enter code: 482899

Hydrogen Bonds

Intermolecular forces are the attractive forces between molecules. Intermolecular forces include hydrogen bonds, London or dispersion forces, and dipole-dipole forces. **Hydrogen bonds** are the attractive forces between molecules containing hydrogen atoms covalently bonded to oxygen, fluorine, or nitrogen. Hydrogen bonds bind the two strands of a DNA molecule to each other. Two hydrogen bonds join each adenosine and thymine, and three hydrogen bonds join each cytosine and guanine.

ATP

Adenosine triphosphate (ATP) is the energy source for most cellular functions. Each ATP molecule is a nucleotide consisting of a central ribose sugar flanked by a purine base and a chain of three phosphate groups. The purine base is adenine, and when adenine is joined to ribose, an adenosine is formed, explaining the name adenosine triphosphate. If one phosphate is removed from the end of the molecule, adenosine diphosphate (ADP) is formed.

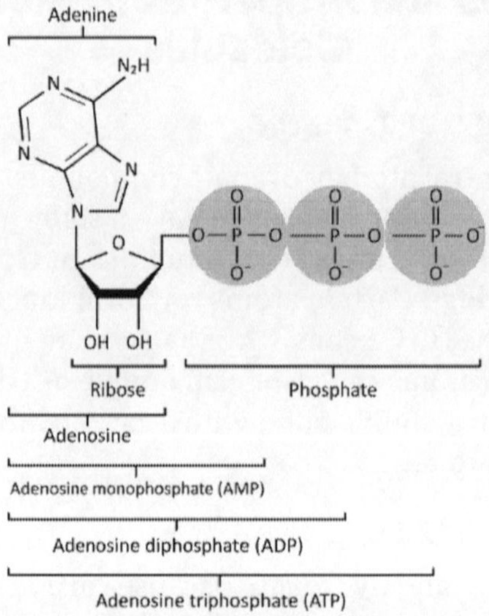

Properties of Water

Water exhibits numerous properties. Water has a high surface tension due to the cohesion between water molecules from the hydrogen bonds between the molecules. The capillary action of water is also due to this cohesion, and the adhesion of water is due to its polarity. Water is an excellent solvent due to its polarity and is considered the universal solvent. Water exists naturally as a solid, liquid, and gas. The density of water decreases as ice freezes and forms crystals in the solid phase. Water is most dense at 4 °C. Water can act as an acid or base in chemical reactions. Pure water is an insulator because it has virtually no ions. Water has a high specific heat capacity due to its low molecular mass and bent molecular shape.

Review Video: Properties of Water
Visit mometrix.com/academy and enter code: 279526

Biological Macromolecules

Macromolecules are large molecules made up of smaller organic molecules. Four classes of macromolecules include carbohydrates, nucleic acids, proteins, and lipids. Carbohydrates, proteins, and nucleic acids are polymers that are formed when the monomers are joined together in a dehydration process. In this dehydration process, the monomers are joined by a covalent bond and a water molecule is released. The monomers in carbohydrates are simple sugars such as glucose, while polysaccharides are polymers of carbohydrates. The monomers in proteins are amino acids. The amino acids form polypeptide chains, which are folded into proteins. The monomers in nucleic acids are nucleotides. Lipids are not actually considered to be polymers. Lipids typically are classified as fats, phospholipids, or steroids.

Review Video: Macromolecules
Visit mometrix.com/academy and enter code: 220156

Biological Processes Dependent on Chemical Principles

Biochemical Pathways

Autotrophs that use light to produce energy use **photosynthesis** as a biochemical pathway. In eukaryotic autotrophs photosynthesis takes place in chloroplasts. Prokaryotic autotrophs that use inorganic chemical reactions to produce energy use **chemosynthesis** as a biochemical pathway. Heterotrophs require food and use **cellular respiration** to release energy from chemical bonds in the food. All organisms use cellular respiration to release energy from stored food. Cellular respiration can be aerobic or anaerobic. Most eukaryotes use cellular respiration that takes place in the mitochondria.

Photosynthesis

Photosynthesis is a food-making process that occurs in three processes: light-capturing events, light-dependent reactions, and light-independent reactions. In light-capturing events, the thylakoids of the chloroplasts, which contain chlorophyll and accessory pigments, absorb light energy and produce excited electrons. Thylakoids also contain enzymes and electron-transport molecules. Molecules involved in this process are arranged in groups called photosystems. In light-dependent reactions, the excited electrons from the light-capturing events are moved by electron transport in a series of steps in which they are used to split water into hydrogen and oxygen ions. The oxygen is released, and the $NADP^+$ bonds with the hydrogen atoms and forms NADPH. ATP is produced from the excited elections. The light-independent reactions use this ATP, NADPH, and carbon dioxide to produce sugars.

Review Video: Photosynthesis
Visit mometrix.com/academy and enter code: 227035

C_3 and C_4 Photosynthesis

Plants undergo an additional process during photosynthesis that is known as photorespiration. Photorespiration is a wasteful process that uses energy and decreases sugar synthesis. This process occurs when the enzyme rubisco binds to oxygen rather than atmospheric carbon dioxide. There are three different processes that plants use to fix carbon during photosynthesis and these include C_3, C_4, and crassulacean acid metabolism (CAM). Some plants, such as C_4 and CAM plants, can decrease photorespiration and therefore minimize energy lost while C_3 plants, which make up more than 85% of plants, have no special adaptations to stop photorespiration from occuring. C_3 and C_4 plants are named for the type of carbon molecule (three-carbon or four-carbon) that is made during the first step of the reaction. The first step of the C_3 process involves the formation of two three-carbon molecules (3-phosphoglycerate; 3-PGA) from carbon dioxide being fixed by the enzyme. The first step of C_4 photosynthesis is carbon dioxide beign fixed by the enzyme PEP carboxylase, which unlike rubisco does not have the ability to bind to oxygen. This fixation forms a four-carbon molecule (oxaloaceate) and these initial steps occur in the mesophyll cell. Next, oxaloacetate is converted into a malate, a molecule that can enter the bundle sheath cells, and then is broken down to release carbon dioxide. From there, the carbon dioxide is fixed by rubisco as it undergoes the Calvin cycle seen in C_3 photosynthesis. Because C_4 plants undergo an initial step that allows carbon dioxide to be more readily available, with the use of malate, photorespiration is minimized.

Crassulacean Acid Metabolism

Crassulacean acid metabolism (CAM) is a form of photosynthesis adapted to dry environments. While C_4 plants separate the Calvin cycle via space, or by having different cells for different functions and processes, CAM plants separate the processes by time of day. During the night, pores of the plant leaves, called stomata, open to receive carbon dioxide, which combines with PEP carboxylase to form oxaloacetate. Oxaloacetate is eventually converted into malate, which is stored in vacuoles until the next day. During the following day, the stomata are closed and the malate is transported to chloroplasts, where malate is broken down into pyruvate (three-carbon molecule) and carbon dioxide. The carbon dioxide released from malate is used in photosynthesis during the daytime. One advantage of the CAM cycle is that it minimizes loss of water through the stomata during the daytime. A second advantage is that concentrating carbon dioxide in the chloroplasts in this manner increases the efficiency of the enzyme rubisco to fix carbon dioxide and complete the Calvin cycle.

Aerobic Respiration

Aerobic cellular respiration is a series of enzyme-controlled chemical reactions in which oxygen reacts with glucose to produce carbon dioxide and water, releasing energy in the form of adenosine triphosphate (ATP). Cellular respiration occurs in a series of three processes: glycolysis, the Krebs cycle, and the electron-transport system.

Review Video: Aerobic Respiration
Visit mometrix.com/academy and enter code: 770290

Glycolysis

Glycolysis is a series of enzyme-controlled chemical reactions that occur in the cell's cytoplasm. Each glucose molecule is split in half to produce two pyruvic acid molecules, four ATP molecules, and two NADH molecules. Because two ATP molecules are used to split the glucose molecule, the net ATP yield for glycolysis is two ATP molecules.

Review Video: Glycolysis
Visit mometrix.com/academy and enter code: 466815

Krebs Cycle

The **Krebs cycle** is also called the citric acid cycle or the tricarboxylic acid cycle (TCA). It is a **catabolic pathway** in which the bonds of glucose and occasionally fats or lipids are broken down and reformed into ATP. It is a respiration process that uses oxygen and produces carbon dioxide, water, and ATP. Cells require energy from ATP to synthesize proteins from amino acids and replicate DNA. The cycle is acetyl CoA, citric acid, isocitric acid, ketoglutaric acid (products are amino acids and CO_2), succinyl CoA, succinic acid, fumaric acid, malic acid, and oxaloacetic acid. One of the products of the Krebs cycle is NADH, which is then used in the electron chain transport system to manufacture ATP. From glycolysis, pyruvate is oxidized in a step linking to the Krebs cycle. After the Krebs cycle, NADH and succinate are oxidized in the electron transport chain.

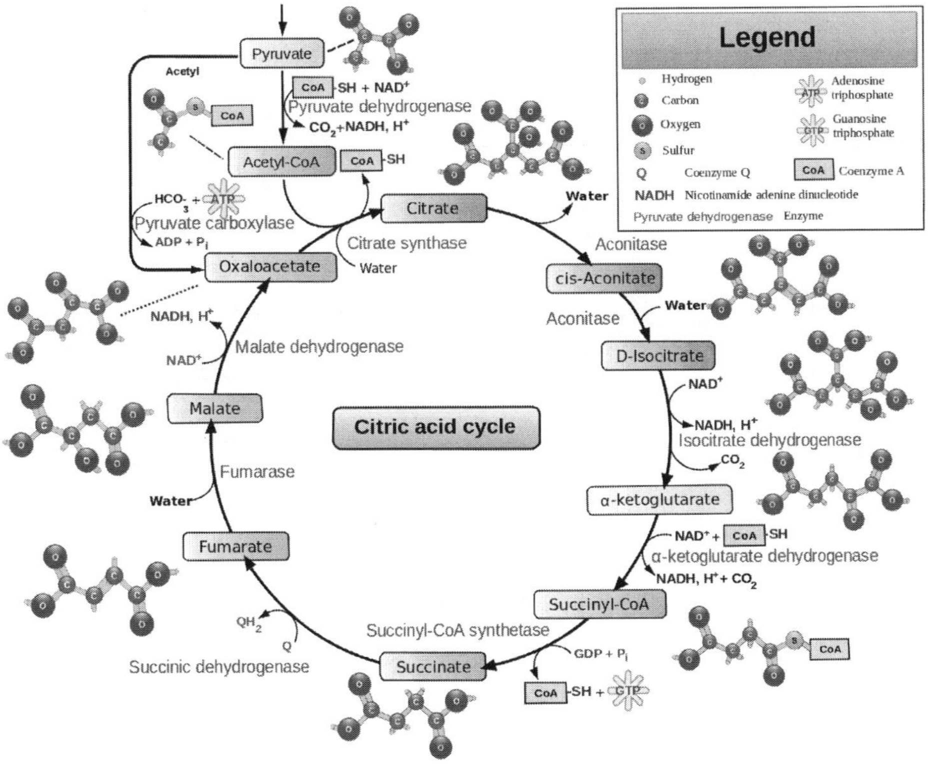

Electron Transport Chain

The **electron transport chain** is part of phosphorylation, whereby electrons are transported from enzyme to enzyme until they reach a final acceptor. The electron transport chain includes a series of oxidizing and reducing molecules involved in the release of energy. In **redox reactions**, electrons are removed from a substrate (oxidative) and H^+ (protons) can also be simultaneously removed. A substrate gains electrons during reduction. For example, when glucose is oxidized, electrons are lost and energy is released. There are enzymes in the membranes of mitochondria. The electrons are carried from one enzyme to another by a co-enzyme. Protons are also released to the other side of the membrane. For example, FAD and $FADH_2$ are used in oxidative phosphorylation. FAD is reduced to $FADH_2$. Electrons are stored there and then sent onward, and the $FADH_2$ becomes FAD again. In aerobic respiration, the final electron acceptor is O_2. In anaerobic respiration, it is something other than O_2.

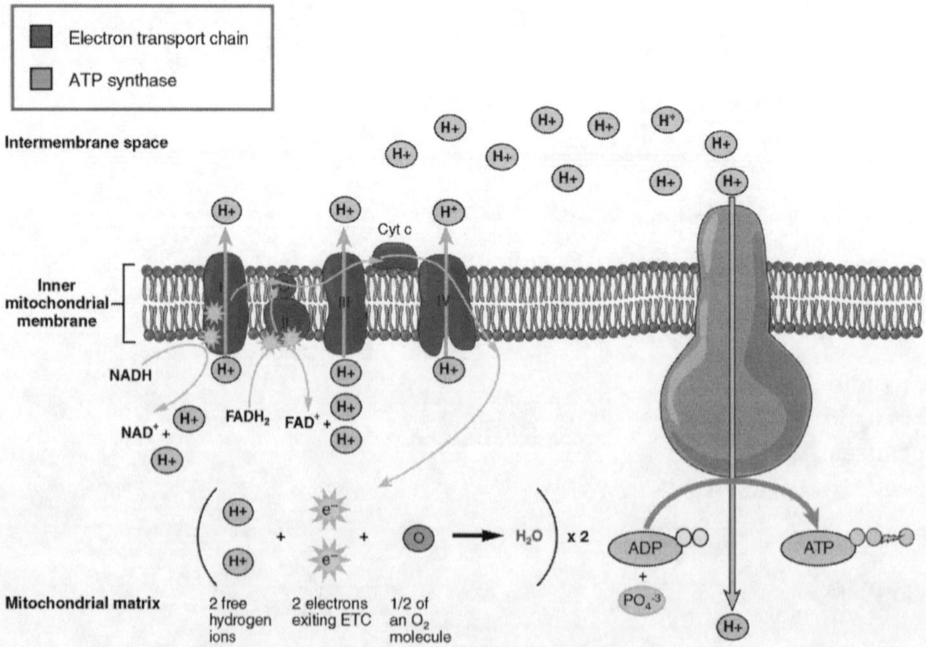

Fermentation

Fermentation is an anaerobic reaction in which glucose is only partially broken down. It releases energy through the oxidation of sugars or other types of organic molecules. Oxygen is sometimes involved, but not always. It is different from respiration in that it uses neither the Krebs cycle nor the electron transport chain and the final electron acceptor is an organic molecule. It uses **substrate-level phosphorylation** to form ATP. NAD^+ is reduced to NADH and NADH further reduces pyruvic acid to various end products. Fermentation can lead to excess waste products and is less efficient than aerobic respiration. **Homolactic fermentation** refers to lactic acid fermentation in which the sugars are converted to lactic acid only (there is one end product). In **heterolactic fermentation**, the sugars are converted to a range of products.

Examples of Fermentation

Lactic acid fermentation is the breakdown of glucose and six-carbon sugars into lactic acid to release energy. It is an anaerobic process, meaning that it does not require oxygen. It can occur in muscle cells and is also performed by streptococcus and lactobacillus bacteria. It can also be used to making yogurt and other food products.

Alcohol fermentation is the breakdown of glucose and six-carbon sugars into ethanol and carbon dioxide to release energy. It is an anaerobic process. It is performed by yeast and used in the production of alcoholic beverages.

Chemosynthesis

Chemosynthesis is the food-making process of chemoautotrophs in extreme environments such as deep-sea-vents, or hydrothermal vents. Unlike photosynthesis, chemosynthesis does not require light. In general, chemosynthesis involves the oxidation of inorganic substances to make a sugar, but there are several species that use different pathways or processses. For example, sulfur bacteria live near or in deep-sea vents and oxidize hydrogen sulfide released from those vents to make a sugar. Instead of sunlight, chemosynthesis uses the energy stored in the chemical bonds of chemicals such as hydrogen sulfide to produce food. During chemosynthesis, the electrons that are removed from the inorganic molecules are combined with carbon dioxide and oxygen to produce sugar, sulfur, and water. Some bacteria use metal ions such as iron and magnesium to obtain the needed electrons. For example, methanobacteria such as those found in human intestines combine carbon dioxide and hydrogen gas and release methane as a waste product. Nitrogen bacteria such as nitrogen-fixing bacteria in the nodules of legumes convert atmospheric nitrogen into nitrates.

Structure and Function of Enzymes

Active Site Structure and Substrate Binding

Each enzyme has a complex three-dimensional shape that is specifically designed to fit to a particular reactant, which is called the **substrate**. The enzyme and the substrate join temporarily forming the enzyme-substrate complex. This complex is unstable, and the chemical bonds are likely to be altered to produce a new molecule or molecules. Each enzyme can only combine with specific substrates because of this "lock-and-key" fit. Each enzyme has a designated binding site on the surface that binds to the substrate. Often, the binding site and the active site are at the same location. The enzyme and the substrate are specifically designed for each other, and as the substrate binds to the active site of the enzyme, that active site can bend and fold to form around the substrate. This concept of the active site slightly altering its shape is the **induced fit hypothesis**. The active site of the enzyme with return to its original shape after the products are released.

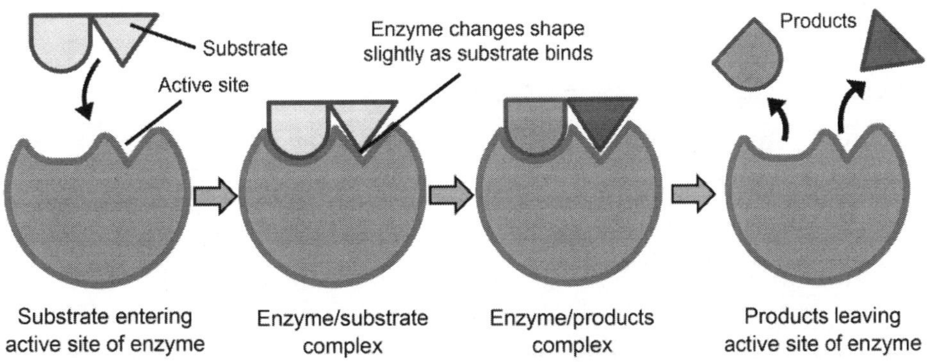

Effects of Temperature, pH, and Inhibitors on Enzyme Activity

The rate of an enzyme-controlled reaction is affected by factors such as temperature, pH, and inhibitors. According to kinetic-molecular theory, increasing the temperature increases the rate of molecular motion. Typically, increasing the temperature increases the rate of these reactions. The optimum temperature is the temperature at which the rate is the fastest and the most product is formed. Increasing the temperature above the optimum temperature actually decreases the reaction rate due to changes on the enzyme's structure that affect substrate binding. The pH also affects enzyme activity due to hydrogen ions binding to the enzyme's surface and changing the enzyme's surface shape. Because enzymes must have a specific shape for their specific substrate, enzymes have a certain pH range in which they can function. Inhibitors are molecules that attach to the enzymes and interfere with substrate binding, thus decreasing or even halting enzyme-controlled reactions.

Regulation of Enzymes by Feedback Inhibition

Enzyme-controlled reactions can be regulated by feedback inhibition, or negative feedback. **Feedback inhibition** can be illustrated by a furnace and thermostat. The inhibitor in this system is the heat. When the furnace runs, the temperature increases. When the temperature reaches a specific level, the thermostat switches the furnace off. When the temperature decreases below a specific level, the thermostat switches the furnace back on, and the cycle begins again. In enzyme-controlled reactions, the end products of a metabolic pathway bind to the enzymes that initiate the metabolic pathway. This causes the reaction rate to decrease. The more product there is, the less product is produced. The less product there is, the more product is produced. This process of feedback inhibition enables a stable range of concentrations that are necessary for homeostasis.

Biochemical Processes Within an Organism

Concentration Gradients

Concentration gradients, also called diffusion gradients, are differences in the concentration (i.e., the number of molecules of solutes in a solution) between two regions. A gradient can also result from an unequal distribution of ions across a cell membrane. Solutes move along a concentration gradient by random motion from the region of high concentration toward the region of low concentration in a process called diffusion. In other words, **diffusion** is the movement of molecules or ions down a concentration gradient. Diffusion is the method by which oxygen, carbon dioxide, and other nonpolar molecules cross a cell membrane. The steepness of the concentration gradient affects the rate of diffusion. **Passive transport** makes use of concentration gradients as well as electric gradients to move substances across the cell membrane, while **active transport** can move a substance against its concentration gradient.

Laws of Thermodynamics and Gibbs Free Energy

The **first law of thermodynamics** states that energy can neither be created nor destroyed. Energy may change forms, but the energy in a closed system is constant. The **second law of thermodynamics** states that systems tend toward a state of lower energy and greater disorder. This disorder is called **entropy**. According to the second law of thermodynamics, entropy is increasing. **Gibbs free energy** is the energy a system that is available or "free" to be released to perform work at a constant temperature. Organisms must be able to use energy to survive, and biological processes such as the chemical reactions involved in metabolism are governed by these laws.

Anabolic and Catabolic Reactions

Anabolism and catabolism are metabolic processes. **Anabolism** is essentially the synthesis of large molecules from monomers, whereas **catabolism** is the decomposition of large molecules into their component monomers. Anabolism uses energy, whereas catabolism produces energy. Anabolism typically builds and repair tissues, and catabolism typically burns stored food to produce energy. Protein synthesis, which is the polymerization of amino acids to form proteins, is an anabolic reaction. Another anabolic process is the mineralization of bones. An example of a catabolic reaction is hydrolysis, which is the decomposition of polymers into monomers that releases a water molecule and energy. Cellular respiration is a catabolic process in which typically glucose combines with oxygen to release energy in the form of adenosine triphosphate (ATP).

Oxidation-Reduction Reactions

Oxidation-reduction reactions, or redox reactions, involve the transfer of electrons from one substance to another. Reduction occurs in the substance that gains the electrons. Oxidation occurs in the substance that loses the electrons. Cellular respiration and photosynthesis are examples of redox reactions. During cellular respiration, glucose molecules are oxidized and oxygen molecules are reduced. Because electrons lose energy when being transferred to oxygen, the electrons are usually first transferred to the coenzyme NAD^+, which is reduced to NADH. The NADH then releases the energy to oxygen. During photosynthesis, water molecules are split and oxidized and carbon dioxide molecules are reduced. When the water molecules are split, electrons are transferred with the hydrogen ions to the carbon dioxide molecules.

Differences Between Prokaryotic and Eukaryotic Cells

PROKARYOTES AND EUKARYOTES

SIZES AND METABOLISM

Cells of the domains of Bacteria and Archaea are **prokaryotes**. Bacteria cells and Archaea cells are much smaller than cells of eukaryotes. Prokaryote cells are usually only 1 to 2 micrometers in diameter, but eukaryotic cells are usually at least 10 times and possibly 100 times larger than prokaryotic cells. Eukaryotic cells are usually 10 to 100 micrometers in diameter. Most prokaryotes are unicellular organisms, although some prokaryotes live in colonies. Because of their large surface-area-to-volume ratios, prokaryotes have a very high metabolic rate. **Eukaryotic cells** are much larger than prokaryotic cells. Due to their larger sizes, they have a much smaller surface-area-to-volume ratio and consequently have much lower metabolic rates.

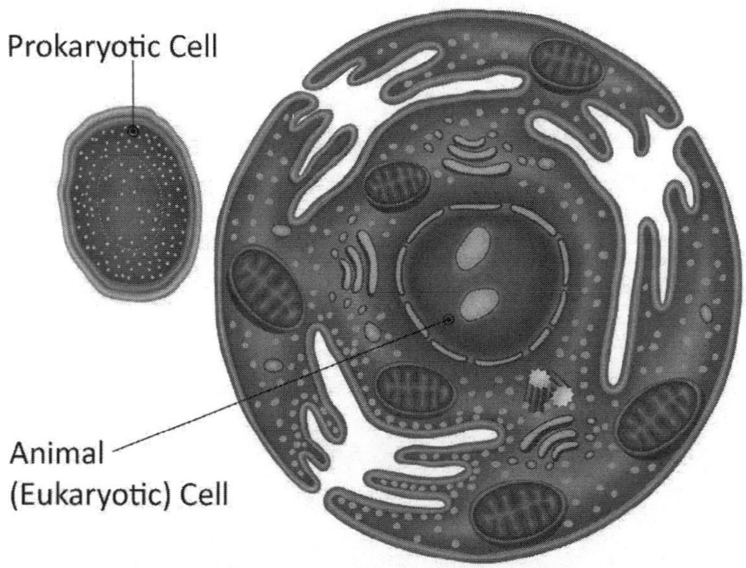

Review Video: Eukaryotic and Prokaryotic Cells
Visit mometrix.com/academy and enter code: 231438

Review Video: Cell Structure
Visit mometrix.com/academy and enter code: 591293

MEMBRANE-BOUND ORGANELLES

Prokaryotic cells are much simpler than eukaryotic cells. Prokaryote cells do not have a nucleus due to their small size and their DNA is located in the center of the cell in a region referred to as a **nucleoid**. Eukaryote cells have a **nucleus** bound by a double membrane. Eukaryotic cells typically have hundreds or thousands of additional **membrane-bound organelles** that are independent of the cell membrane. Prokaryotic cells do not have any membrane-bound organelles that are independent of the cell membrane. Once again, this is probably due to the much larger size of the eukaryotic cells. The organelles of eukaryotes give them much higher levels of intracellular division than is possible in prokaryotic cells.

Cell Walls

Not all cells have cell walls, but most prokaryotes have cell walls. The cell walls of organisms from the domain Bacteria differ from the cell walls of the organisms from the domain Archaea. Some eukaryotes, such as some fungi, some algae, and plants, have cell walls that differ from the cell walls of the Bacteria and Archaea domains. The main difference between the cell walls of different domains or kingdoms is the composition of the cell walls. For example, most bacteria have cell walls outside of the plasma membrane that contains the molecule peptidoglycan. **Peptidoglycan** is a large polymer of amino acids and sugars. The peptidoglycan helps maintain the strength of the cell wall. Some of the Archaea cells have cell walls containing the molecule pseudopeptidoglycan, which differs in chemical structure from the peptidoglycan but basically provides the same strength to the cell wall. Some fungi cell walls contain **chitin**. The cell walls of diatoms, a type of yellow algae, contain silica. Plant cell walls contain cellulose, and woody plants are further strengthened by lignin. Some algae also contain lignin. Animal cells do not have cell walls.

Chromosome Structure

Prokaryote cells have DNA arranged in a **circular structure** that should not be referred to as a chromosome. Due to the small size of a prokaryote cell, the DNA material is simply located near the center of the cell in a region called the nucleoid. A prokaryotic cell may also contain tiny rings of DNA called plasmids. Prokaryote cells lack histone proteins, and therefore the DNA is not actually packaged into chromosomes. Prokaryotes reproduce by binary fission, while eukaryotes reproduce by mitosis with the help of **linear chromosomes** and histone proteins. During mitosis, the chromatin is tightly wound on the histone proteins and packaged as a chromosome. The DNA in a eukaryotic cell is located in the membrane-bound nucleus.

Review Video: Chromosomes
Visit mometrix.com/academy and enter code: 132083

Structure and Function of Cells and Organelles

Cells and Organelles of Plant Cells and Animal Cells

Plant cells and animal cells both have a nucleus, cytoplasm, cell membrane, ribosomes, mitochondria, endoplasmic reticulum, Golgi apparatus, and vacuoles. Plant cells have only one or two extremely large vacuoles. Animal cells typically have several small vacuoles. Plant cells have chloroplasts for photosynthesis and use this process to produce their own food, distinguishing plants as **autotrophs**. Animal cells do not have chloroplasts and therefore cannot use photosynthesis to produce their own food. Instead animal cells rely on other sources for food, which classifies them as **heterotrophs**. Animal cells have centrioles, which are used to help organize microtubules and in in cell division, but only some plant cells have centrioles. Additionally, plant cells have a rectangular and more rigid shape due to the cell wall, while animal cells have more of a circular shape because they lack a cell wall.

Review Video: Difference Between Plant and Animal Cells
Visit mometrix.com/academy and enter code: 115568

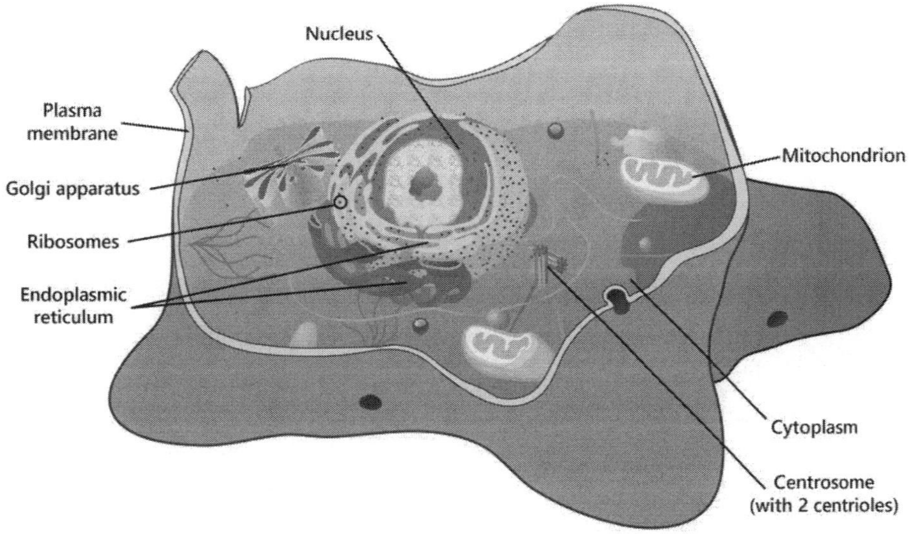

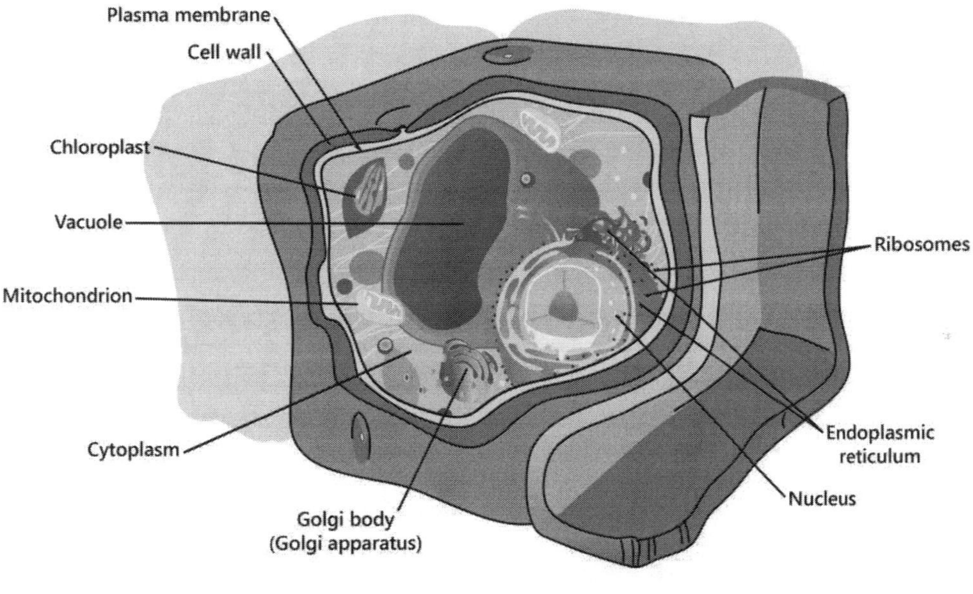

Cell Membranes

The **cell membrane**, also referred to as the plasma membrane, is a thin semipermeable membrane of lipids and proteins. The cell membrane isolates the cell from its external environment while still enabling the cell to communicate with that outside environment. It consists of a phospholipid bilayer, or double layer, with the hydrophilic ("water-loving") ends of the outer layer facing the external environment, the inner layer facing the inside of the cell, and the hydrophobic ("water-fearing") ends facing each other. Cholesterol in the cell membrane adds stiffness and flexibility. Glycolipids help the cell to recognize other cells of the organisms. The proteins in the cell membrane help give the cells shape. Special proteins help the cell communicate with its external environment, while other proteins transport molecules across the cell membrane.

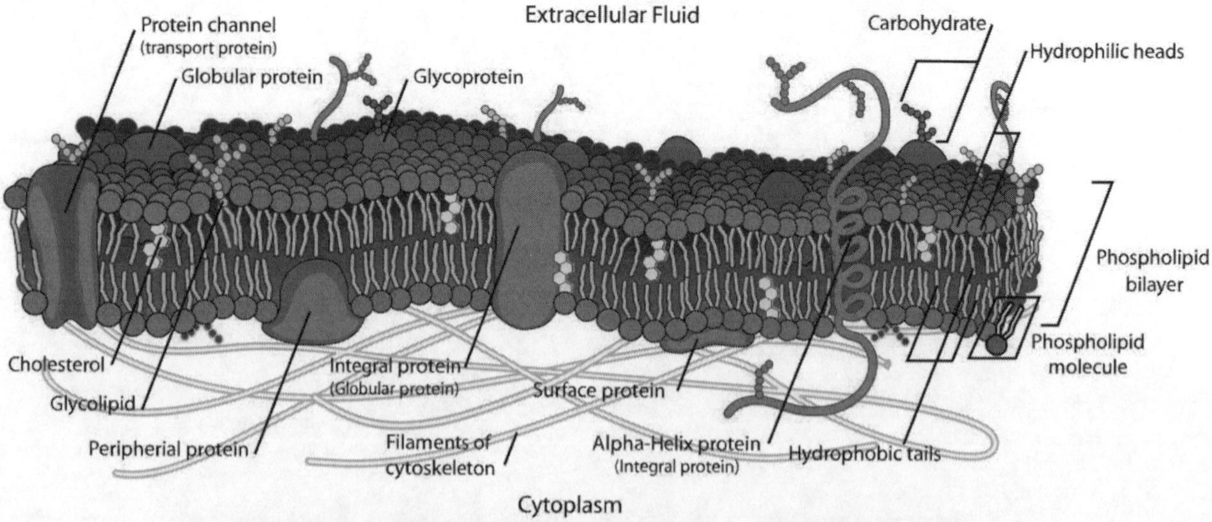

Review Video: Function of the Plasma Membrane
Visit mometrix.com/academy and enter code: 943095

NUCLEUS

Typically, a eukaryote has a single nucleus that takes up approximately 10% of the volume of the cell. Components of the nucleus include the nuclear envelope, nucleoplasm, chromatin, and nucleolus. The **nuclear envelope** is a double-layered membrane with the outer layer connected to the endoplasmic reticulum. The nucleus can communicate with the rest of the cell through several nuclear pores. The chromatin consists of deoxyribonucleic acid (DNA) and histones that are packaged into chromosomes during mitosis. The **nucleolus**, which is the dense central portion of the nucleus, produced and assembles ribosomes with the help of ribosomal RNA and proteins.

Functions of the nucleus include the storage of genetic material, production of ribosomes, and transcription of ribonucleic acid (RNA).

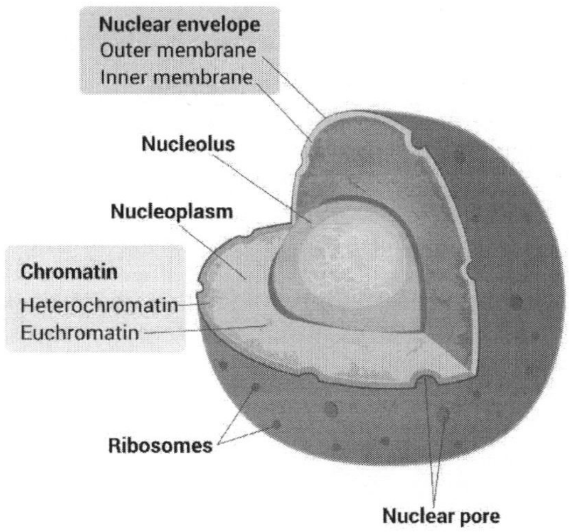

Review Video: Nucleic Acids
Visit mometrix.com/academy and enter code: 503931

CHLOROPLASTS

Chloroplasts are large organelles that are enclosed in a double membrane. Just as cells contain a fluid called cytoplasm, chloroplasts contain a fluid called the **stroma**. Within the stroma, there are discs called **thylakoids**, which are arranged in stacks called **grana** (singular: granum). The thylakoids have chlorophyll molecules on their surfaces. **Stromal lamellae** separate the thylakoid stacks. Chloroplasts perform photosynthesis and make food (in the form of sugars) for the plant. The light reaction stage of photosynthesis occurs in the grana, and the dark reaction stage of photosynthesis occurs in the stroma. Sugars are formed in the stroma. Chloroplasts have their own DNA and can reproduce by fission independently.

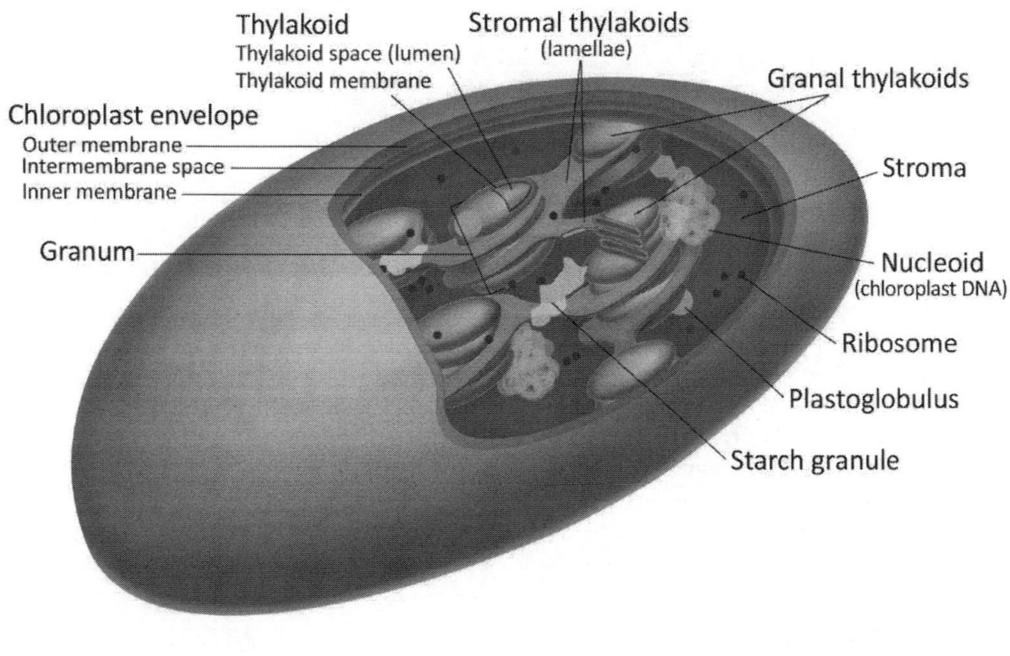

Plastids

Plastids are major organelles found in plants and algae that are used to synthesize and store food. Because plastids can differentiate, there are many forms of plastids. Specialized plastids can store pigments, starches, fats, or proteins. Two examples of plastids are amyloplasts and chloroplasts. **Amyloplasts** are the plastids that store the starch formed from long chains of glucose produced during photosynthesis. Amyloplasts synthesize and store the starch granules through the polymerization of glucose. When needed, amyloplasts also convert these starch granules back into sugar. Fruits and potato tubers have large numbers of amyloplasts. **Chloroplasts** can synthesize and store starch. Interestingly, amyloplasts can redifferentiate and transform into chloroplasts.

Mitochondria

Mitochondria break down sugar molecules and produce energy in the form of molecules of adenosine triphosphate (ATP). Both plant and animal cells contain mitochondria. Mitochondria are enclosed in a bilayer semi-membrane of phospholipids and proteins. The intermembrane space is the space between the two layers. The outer membrane has proteins called porins, which allow small molecules through. The inner membrane contains proteins that aid in the synthesis of ATP. The matrix consists of enzymes that help synthesize ATP. Mitochondria have their own DNA and can reproduce by fission independently. Mitochondria also help to maintain calcium concentrations, form blood components and hormones, and are involved in activating cell death pathways.

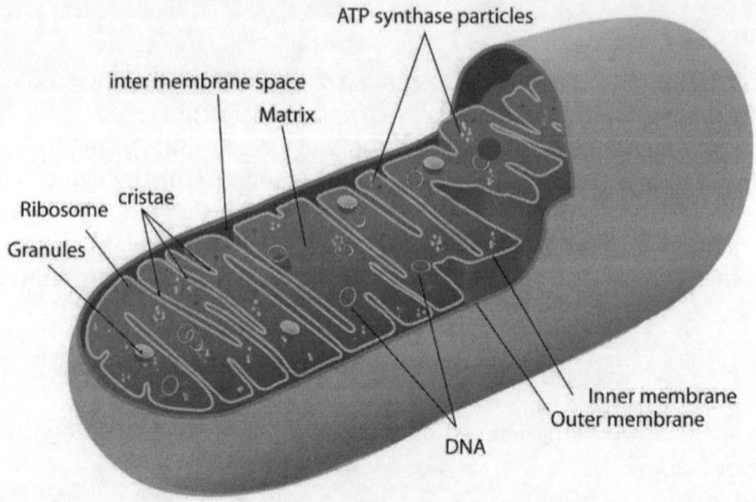

Review Video: Mitochondria
Visit mometrix.com/academy and enter code: 444287

Ribosomes

A **ribosome** consists of RNA and proteins. The RNA component of the ribosome is known as ribosomal RNA (rRNA). Ribosomes consist of two subunits, a large subunit and a small subunit. Few ribosomes are free in the cell. Most of the ribosomes in the cell are embedded in the rough endoplasmic reticulum located near the nucleus. Ribosomes are protein factories and translate the code of DNA into proteins by assembling long chains of amino acids. **Messenger RNA** (mRNA) is used by the ribosome to generate a specific protein sequence, while **transfer RNA** (tRNA) collects the needed amino acids and delivers them to the ribosome.

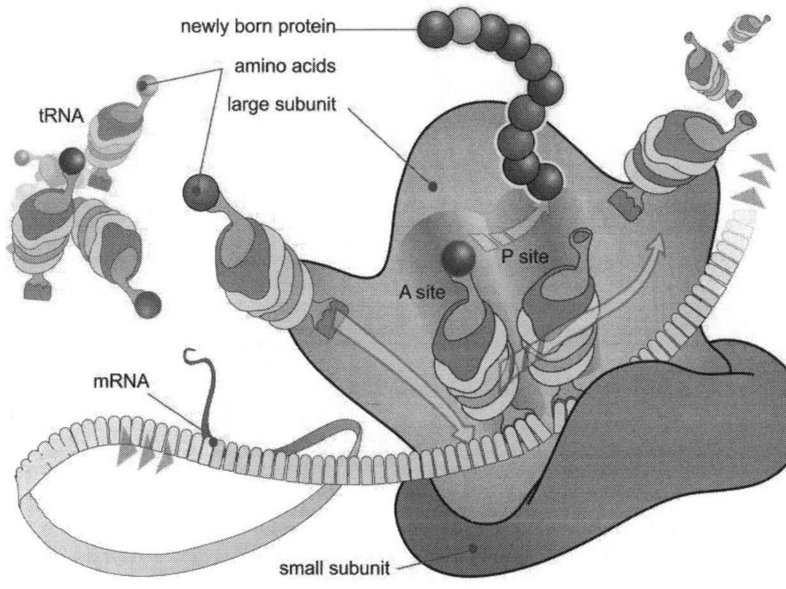

Golgi Apparatus

The **Golgi apparatus**, also called the Golgi body or Golgi complex, is a stack of flattened membranes called **cisternae** that package, ship, and distribute macromolecules such as carbohydrates, proteins, and lipids in shipping containers called **vesicles**. It also helps modify proteins and lipids before they are shipped. Most Golgi apparatuses have six to eight cisternae. Each Golgi apparatus has four regions: the cis region, the endo region, the medial region, and the trans region. Transfer vesicles from the rough endoplasmic reticulum (ER) enter at the cis region, and secretory vesicles leave the Golgi apparatus from the trans region.

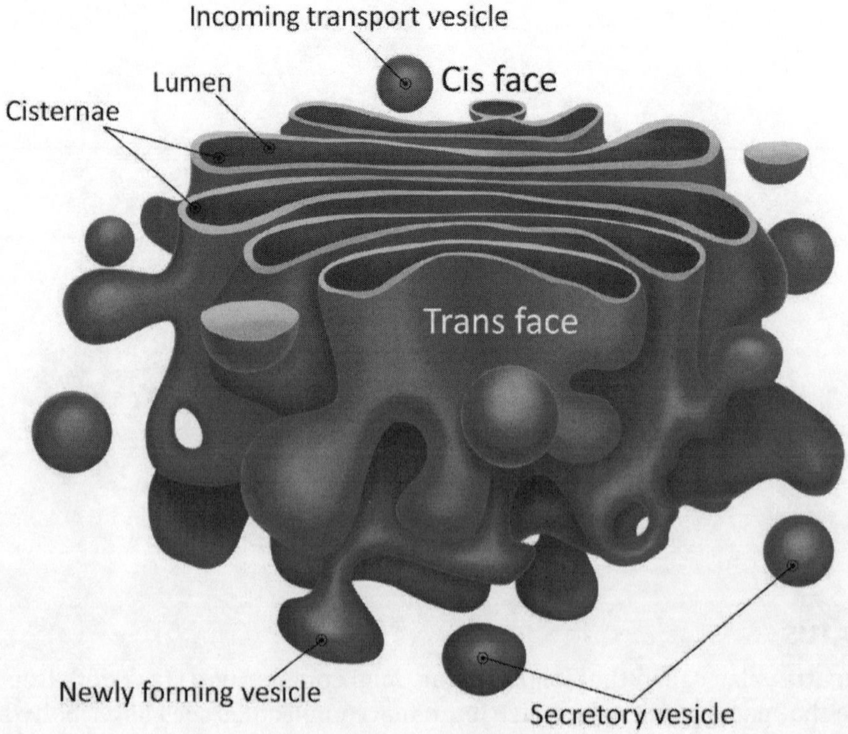

CYTOSKELETON

The **cytoskeleton** is a scaffolding system located in the cytoplasm. The cytoskeleton consists of elongated organelles made of proteins called microtubules, microfilaments, and intermediate filaments. These organelles provide shape, support, and the ability to move. These structures also assist in moving the chromosomes during mitosis. Microtubules and microfilaments help transport materials throughout the cell and are the major components in cilia and flagella.

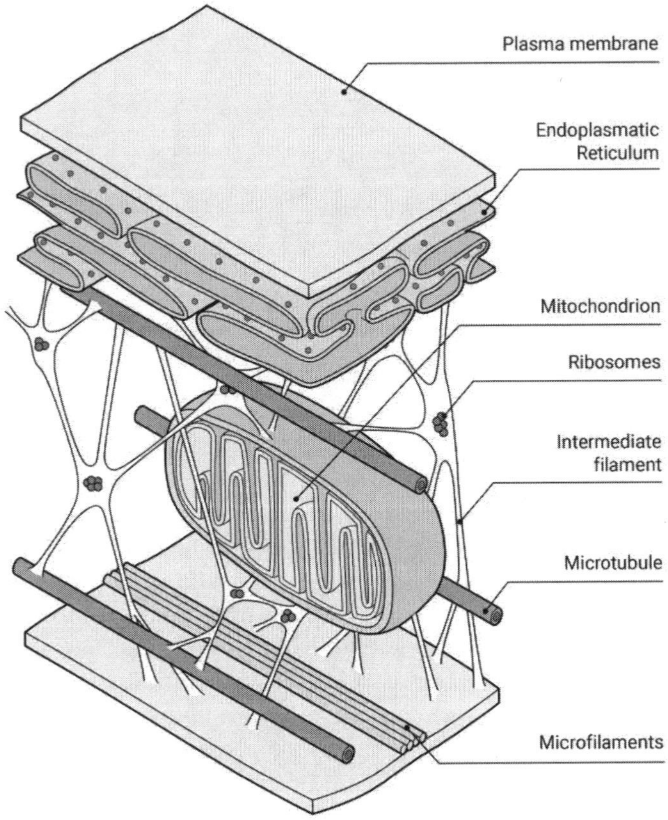

Cellular Homeostasis

Selective Permeability

The cell membrane, or plasma membrane, has selective permeability with regard to size, charge, and solubility. With regard to molecule size, the cell membrane allows only small molecules to diffuse through it. Oxygen and water molecules are small and typically can pass through the cell membrane. The charge of the ions on the cell's surface also either attracts or repels ions. Ions with like charges are repelled, and ions with opposite charges are attracted to the cell's surface. Molecules that are soluble in phospholipids can usually pass through the cell membrane. Many molecules are not able to diffuse the cell membrane, but, if needed, those molecules must be moved through by active transport and vesicles.

ACTIVE AND PASSIVE TRANSPORT

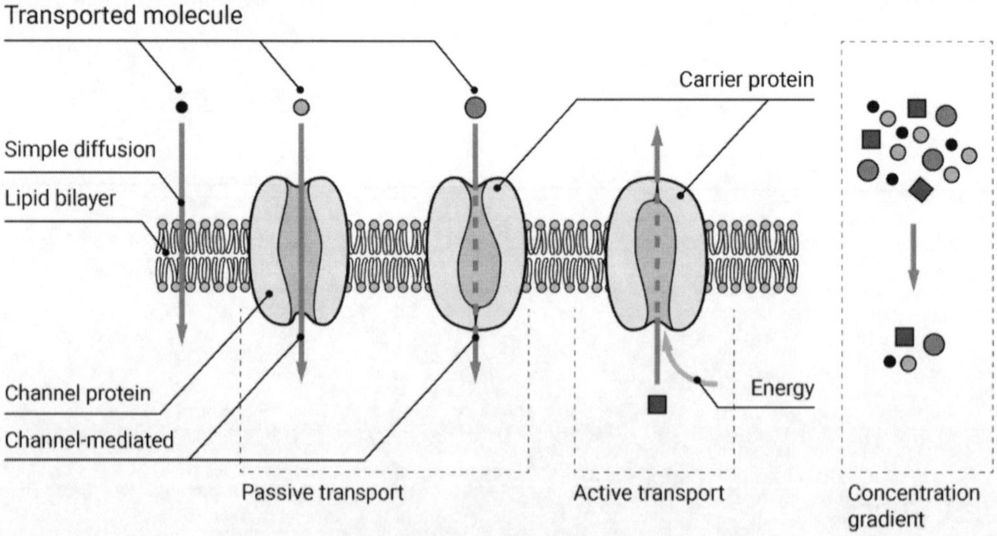

Cells can move materials in and out through the cell membrane by active and passive transport. In **passive transport**, the molecules diffuse across the cell membrane by osmosis. These molecules are moving from a region where they have a high concentration to a region where the concentration is lower. In passive transport, the molecules move across the cell membrane without the cell expending any extra energy. Diffusion and facilitated diffusion are considered passive transport. **Facilitated diffusion** occurs when molecules are helped across the membrane by certain proteins called channel proteins or carrier proteins. Because facilitated diffusion is still from a region of high to low concentration, it does not require additional energy and is therefore a type of passive transport. In active transport, molecules are forcibly moved from regions where the concentration is low into a region where the concentration is higher. Carrier proteins must carry these ions and molecules, and this requires an expenditure of energy. Some ions are actively pumped across the cell membrane by proteins. Sodium ions are pumped out of the cell and potassium ions are pumped into the cell in this manner.

Review Video: Passive Transport: Diffusion and Osmosis
Visit mometrix.com/academy and enter code: 642038

WATER MOVEMENT TO MAINTAIN INTERNAL ENVIRONMENTS OF CELLS

Cells must maintain their water balance for **homeostasis**. If cells have too little water, wastes and poisons can build up in the cells. If cells have too much water, the chemicals in the cells may be diluted. Water is moved in and out of cells by **osmosis**. Because osmosis is a type of passive transport, the cell cannot actually control this diffusion of water in and out of the cells. The amount of water that diffuses into or out of cells depends on the cell's environment. When the cell's concentration of water and dissolved solids equals that of its environment, the cells are **isotonic** with their environment. Cells with a lower concentration of water than their environment tend to rapidly gain water by osmosis. These cells are **hypotonic** with their environment. Cells with a higher concentration of water than their environment tend to rapidly lose water by osmosis. The cells are **hypertonic** with their environment. If cells are hypotonic or hypertonic, they must expend energy to maintain the proper water balance.

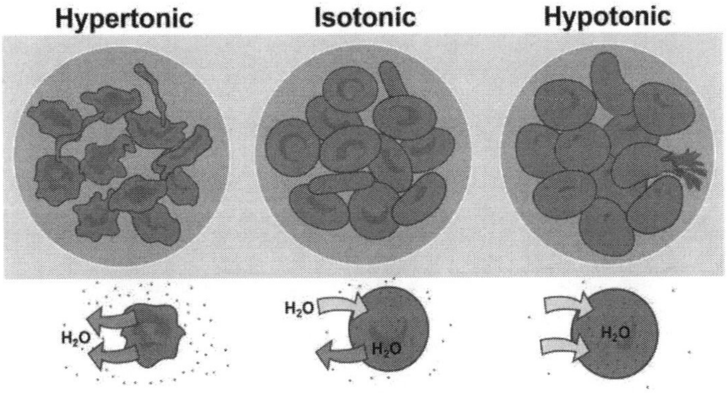

Use of Cell Surface Proteins and Cell Communication

In order to maintain a stable internal environment, cells need to send and receive signals from the external environment. Cells have specialized surface proteins called **receptors** embedded in the cell membrane that allow them to communicate with this external environment. Surface proteins are exposed to the external side of the membrane. Some surface proteins allow entry to specific materials, and others trigger chemical signals inside the cell. Because these proteins have attached carbohydrates, they are called **glycoproteins**. Due to the cholesterol in the cell membrane, fat-soluble materials can pass straight through the membrane, but water-soluble materials cannot diffuse. Sodium, calcium, and potassium must use these specialized surface proteins to gain entry to the cell. These surface proteins bind to specific chemicals in the materials seeking access to the cell. This triggers a chemical signal to the interior of the cell.

Exocytosis and Endocytosis

Larger particles or groups of particles can be transported whole across the cell membrane by being packaged in a piece of cell membrane. **Endocytosis** is the process by which large particles are moved into the cell, and **exocytosis** is the process by which large molecules are moved out of the cell. The three main types of endocytosis are phagocytosis, pinocytosis, and receptor-mediated endocytosis. **Phagocytosis**, or "cell eating," is the process by which large solid particles are engulfed. **Pinocytosis**, or "cell drinking," is the process by which liquids and dissolved substances are surrounded by small sacs of cell membrane. **Receptor-mediated endocytosis** is the process by which molecules enter cells through receptor molecules on the cell membrane.

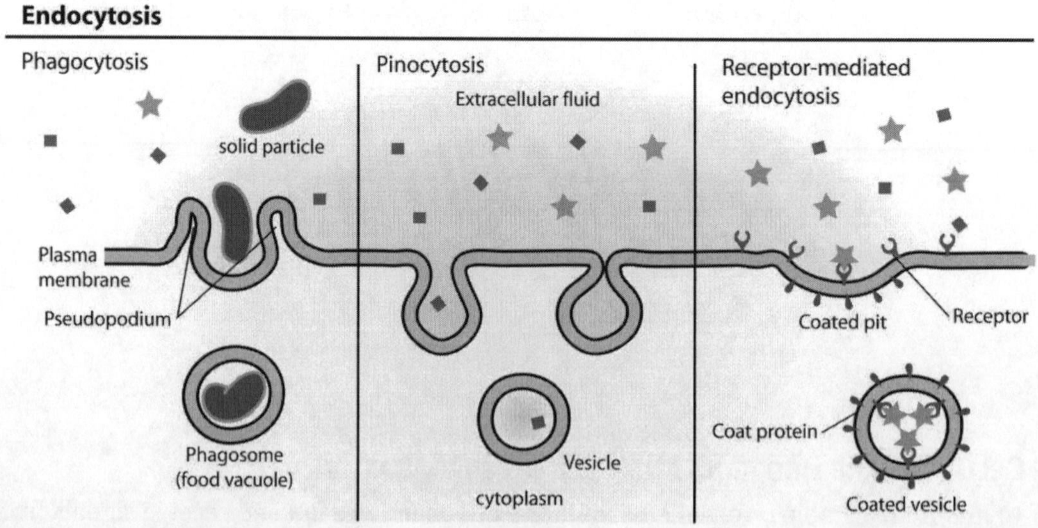

HORMONE ACTION AND FEEDBACK

In order to maintain homeostasis, the endocrine system often employs negative-feedback inhibition or positive-feedback regulation. In **negative-feedback inhibition**, an increase in an output of a reaction to a stimulus triggers a decrease in the stimulus, which in turn causes a decrease in the original output. In **positive-feedback regulation**, an increase in an output leads to further increase of the stimulus. An example of negative-feedback inhibition is the release of the hormones insulin and glucagon to maintain the level of glucose in the blood.

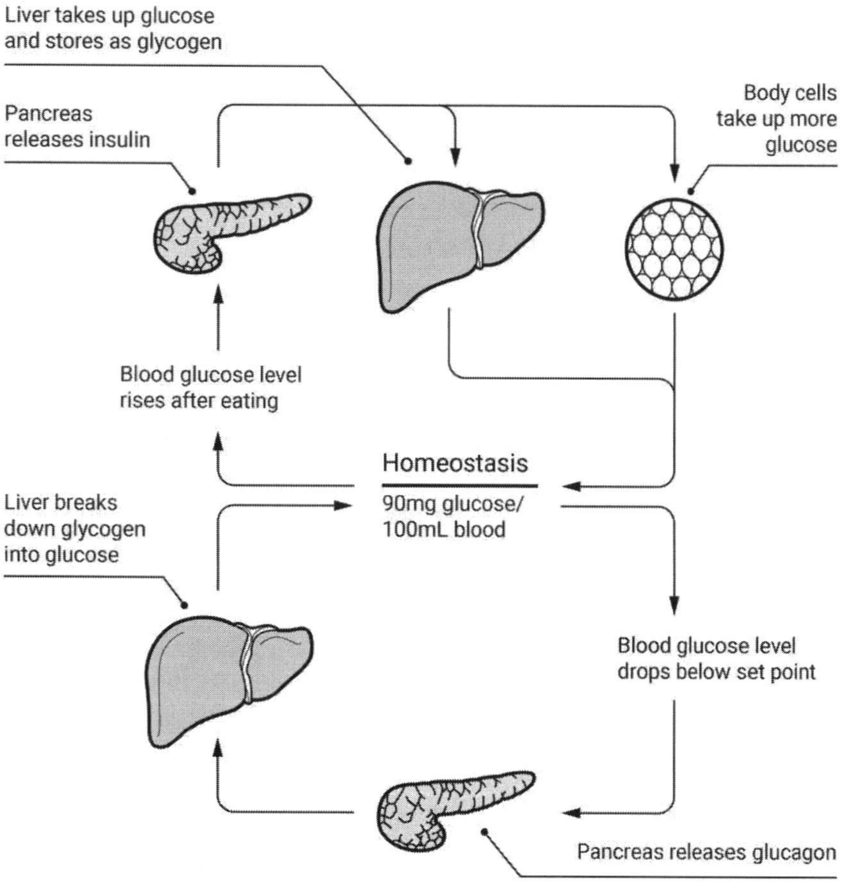

Cell Cycle and Cellular Division

Cell Cycle Stages

The cell cycle consists of three stages: interphase, mitosis, and cytokinesis. **Interphase** is the longest stage of the cell cycle and involves the cell growing and making a copy of its DNA. Cells typically spend more than 90% of the cell cycle in interphase. Interphase includes two growth phases called G_1 and G_2. The order of interphase is the first growth cycle, **GAP 1** (G_1 phase), followed by the **synthesis phase** (S), and ending with the second growth phase, **GAP 2** (G_2 phase). During the G_1 phase of interphase, the cell increases the number of organelles by forming diploid cells. During the S phase of interphase, the DNA is replicated, and the chromosomes are doubled.

During the G_2 phase of interphase, the cell synthesizes needed proteins and organelles, continues to increase in size, and prepares for mitosis. Once the G_2 phase ends, mitosis can begin.

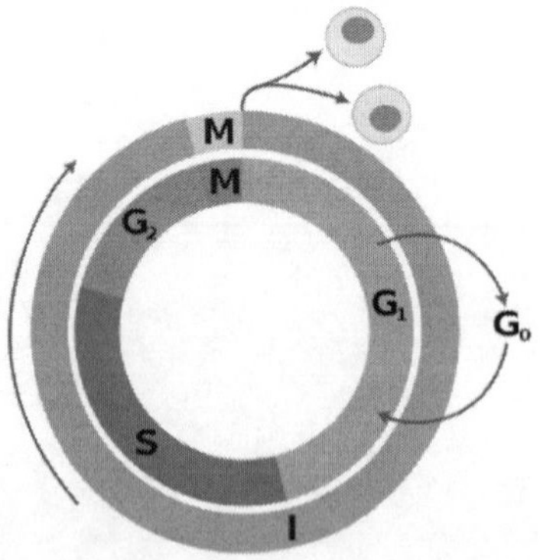

Mitosis

Mitosis is the asexual process of cell division. During mitosis, one parent cell divides into two identical daughter cells. Mitosis is used for growth, repair, and replacement of cells. Some unicellular organisms reproduce asexually by mitosis. Some multicellular organisms can reproduce by fragmentation or budding, which involves mitosis. Mitosis consists of four phases: prophase, metaphase, anaphase, and telophase. During **prophase**, the spindle fibers appear and the DNA is condensed and packaged as chromosomes that become visible. The nuclear membrane also breaks down, and the nucleolus disappears. During **metaphase**, the spindle apparatus is formed and the centromeres of the chromosomes line up on the equatorial plane. During **anaphase**, the centromeres divide and the two chromatids separate and are pulled toward the opposite poles of the cell. During **telophase**, the spindle fibers disappear, the nuclear membrane reforms, and the DNA in the chromatids is decondensed.

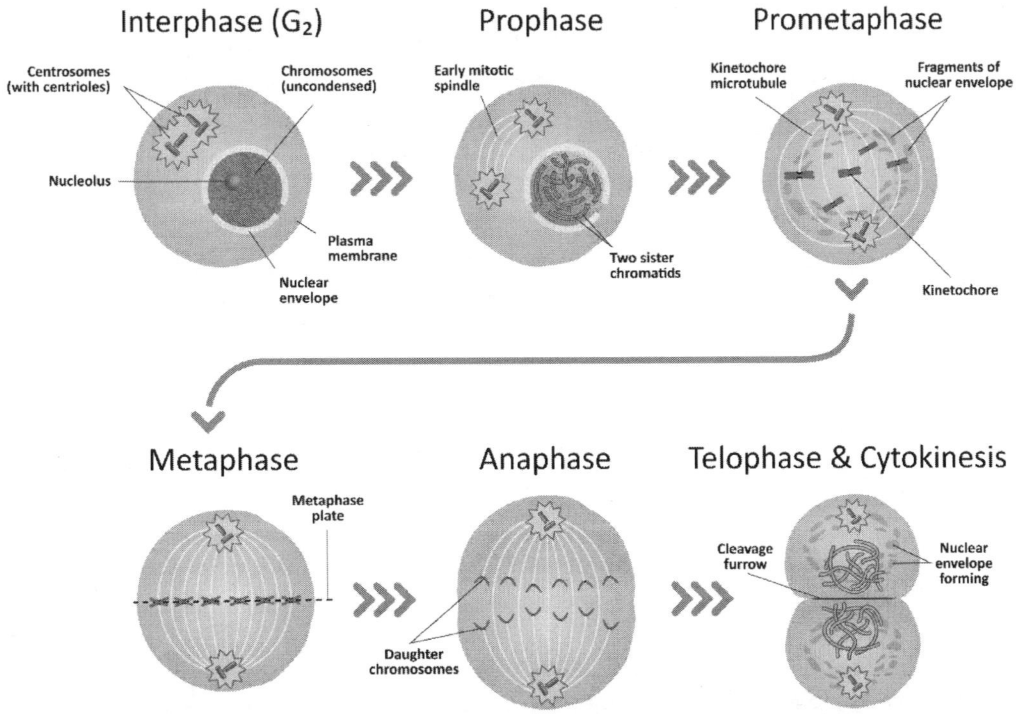

Review Video: Mitosis
Visit mometrix.com/academy and enter code: 849894

CYTOKINESIS

Cytokinesis is the dividing of the cytoplasm and cell membrane by the pinching of a cell into two new daughter cells at the end of mitosis. This occurs at the end of telophase when the actin filaments in the cytoskeleton form a contractile ring that narrows and divides the cell. In plant cells, a cell plate forms across the phragmoplast, which is the center of the spindle apparatus. In animal cells, as the contractile ring narrows, the cleavage furrow forms. Eventually, the contractile ring narrows down to the spindle apparatus joining the two cells and the cells eventually divide. Diagrams of the cleavage furrow of an animal cell and cell plate of a plant are shown below.

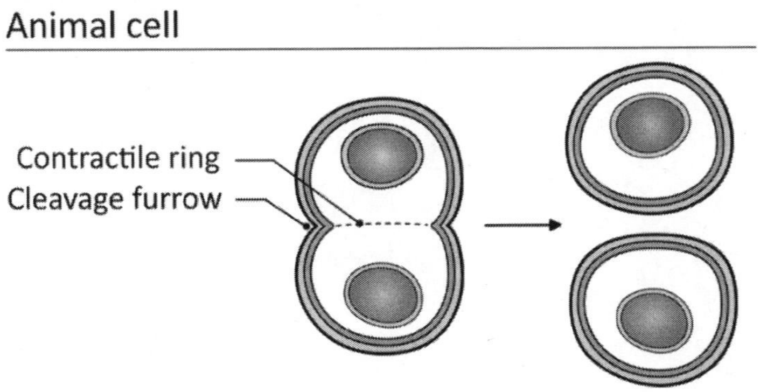

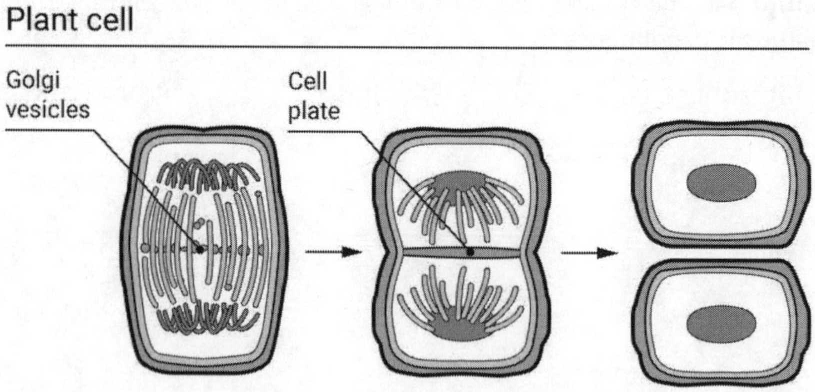

MEIOSIS

Meiosis is a type of cell division in which the number of chromosomes is reduced by half. Meiosis produces gametes, or egg and sperm cells. Meiosis occurs in two successive stages, which consist of a first mitotic division followed by a second mitotic division. During **meiosis I**, or the first meiotic division, the cell replicates its DNA in interphase and then continues through prophase I, metaphase I, anaphase I, and telophase I. At the end of meiosis I, there are two haploid daughter cells, each with half the number of chromosomes as the original diploid parent cell. Each chromosome consists of two sister chromatids, but these are considered a single chromosome. During **meiosis II**, the cell enters a brief interphase but does not replicate its DNA. Then, the cell continues through prophase II, metaphase II, anaphase II, and telophase II. During prophase II, the unduplicated chromosomes split. At the end of telophase II, there are four daughter cells that have half the number of chromosomes as the parent cell.

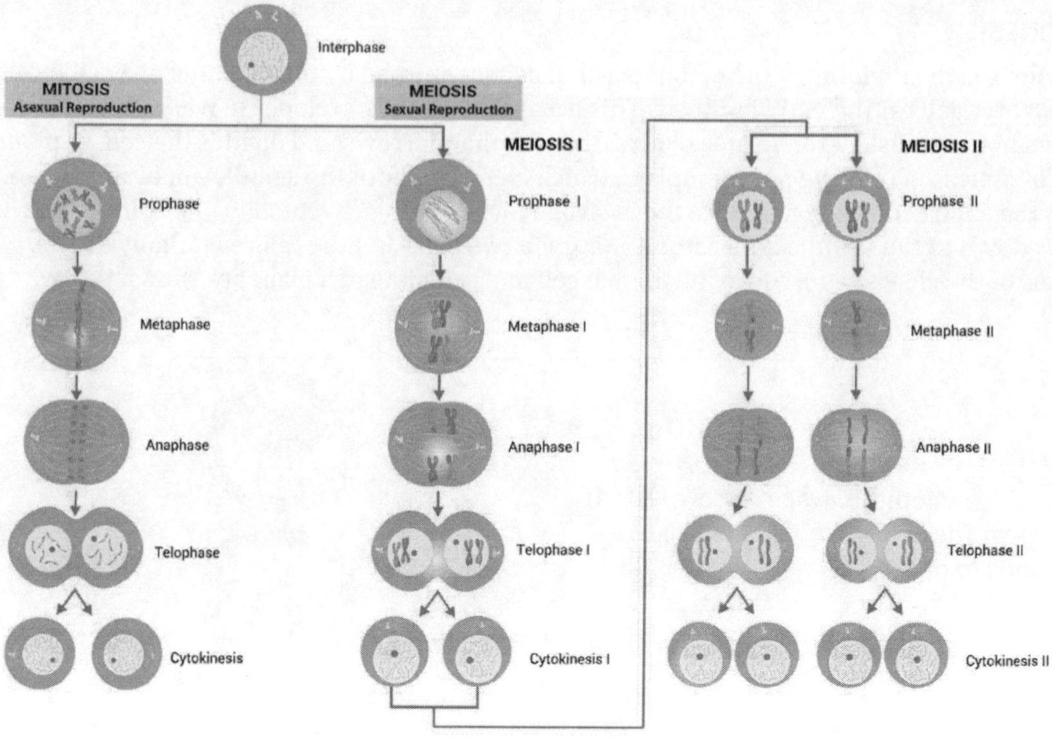

Cell Cycle Checkpoints

During the cell cycle, the cell goes through three checkpoints to ensure that the cell is dividing properly at each phase, that it is the appropriate time for division, and that the cell has not been damaged. The **first checkpoint** is at the end of the G_1 phase just before the cell undergoes the S phase, or synthesis. At this checkpoint, a cell may continue with cell division, delay the division, or rest. This **resting phase** is called G_0. In animal cells, the G_1 checkpoint is called **restriction**. Proteins called cyclin D and cyclin E, which are dependent on enzymes cyclin-dependent kinase 4 and cyclin-dependent kinase 2 (CDK4 and CDK2), respectively, largely control this first checkpoint. The **second checkpoint** is at the end of the G_2 phase just before the cell begins prophase during mitosis. The protein cyclin A, which is dependent on the enzyme CDK2, largely controls this checkpoint. During mitosis, the **third checkpoint** occurs at metaphase to check that the chromosomes are lined up along the equatorial plane. This checkpoint is largely controlled by cyclin B, which is dependent upon the enzyme CDK1.

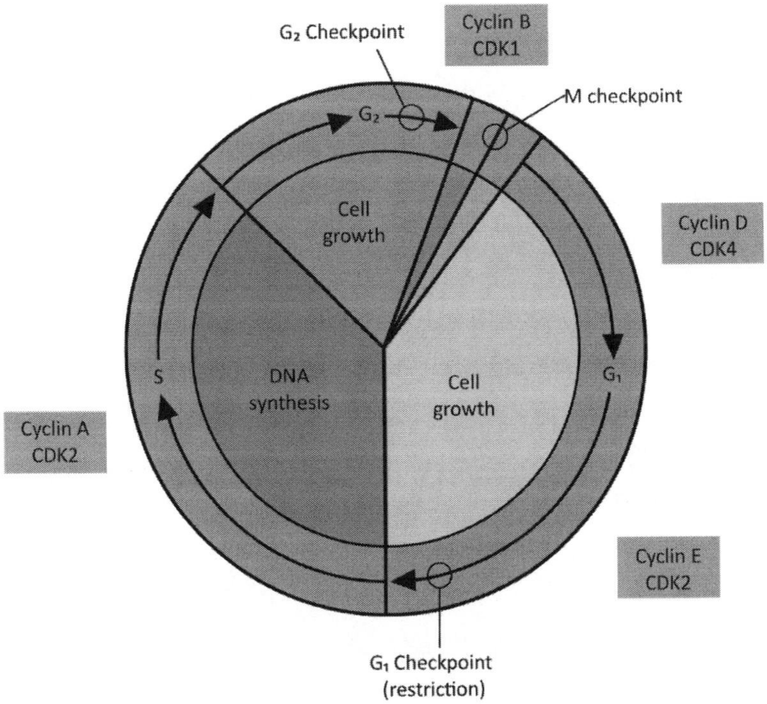

Nucleic Acids

Nucleotide Structure

A **nucleotide**, whether DNA or RNA, contains three components: a phosphate group, a ringed, five-carbon sugar (deoxyribose in DNA, ribose in RNA), and a nitrogen-containing base. The **phosphate group** binds to one side of the **ringed, five-carbon sugar**. The **nitrogen-containing base** binds to the opposite side of the ringed, five-carbon sugar. A nucleotide strand is formed by covalently linking the phosphate groups of the nucleotides into a linear sequence.

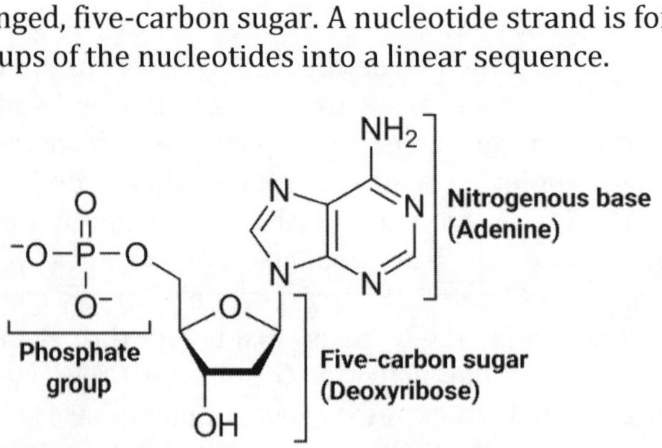

DNA and RNA

Structural Similarities

Structural similarities between DNA and RNA:

- DNA and RNA are both **nucleic acids** composed of nucleotides made up of a sugar, a base, and a phosphate molecule.
- DNA and RNA have three of their four bases in common: guanine, cytosine, and adenine.

Review Video: DNA Vs. RNA
Visit mometrix.com/academy and enter code: 184871

Structural, Locational, and Functional Differences

Structural differences between DNA and RNA:

- DNA contains the base thymine, but RNA replaces thymine with uracil.
- DNA contains the sugar deoxyribose, but RNA contains the sugar ribose.
- DNA is double stranded, but RNA is single stranded.

Locational: DNA is located in the nucleus and mitochondria. RNA is found in the nucleus, ribosomes, and cytoplasm.

Functional: DNA contains the genetic blueprint and instructions for the cell. RNA carries out those instructions and synthesizes proteins.

Types and Functions of RNA

Types of RNA include ribosomal RNA (rRNA), transfer RNA (tRNA), and messenger RNA (mRNA).

- **rRNA** forms the RNA component of the ribosome. It is evolutionarily conserved, which means it can be used to study relationships in organisms.
- **mRNA** is used by the ribosome to generate proteins (translation). The mRNA contains three-nucleotide "codons" that code for specific amino acids in a protein sequence.
- **tRNA** functions in translation by transferring an amino acid to the corresponding codon on the mRNA strand.

Review Video: DNA
Visit mometrix.com/academy and enter code: 639552

Complementary Base Pairing

According to **Chargaff's rule**, a DNA molecule always has a 1:1 ratio of purine to pyrimidine within it. The amount of adenine always equals the amount of thymine, and the amount of guanine always equals the amount of cytosine. (Note that the same rule holds for RNA, but the thymine is replaced with uracil.) In DNA, adenine always pairs with thymine, and guanine always pairs with cytosine. In RNA, adenine always pairs with uracil, and guanine always pairs with cytosine. The pairs are bonded together with hydrogen bonds.

Double Helix Structure of DNA

Double-stranded DNA consists of two complementary strands that adopt the shape of a double helix, which resembles a twisted ladder. The "sides" of the ladder are the sugar-phosphate backbones of the complementary strands. The "rungs" of the ladder are the nitrogenous bases, which are held together (base paired) by hydrogen bonds between the complementary nitrogenous bases in the opposite strand. In DNA, **adenine** (A) base pairs with **thymine** (T) and **guanine** (G) base pairs with **cytosine** (C). DNA also has an antiparallel structure, consisting of a 5' end and a 3' end, where the two strands of the DNA run in opposite directions for one another. The two ends of the DNA strand are coined 5' or 3' based on the specific carbon atom within the purine or pyrimidine ring that makes up the deoxyribose sugar. The 5' end of a DNA strand has a free phosphate group attached to the 5'-carbon atom of the deoxyribose sugar, while the 3' end of DNA has a free hydroxyl group at the 3'-carbon.

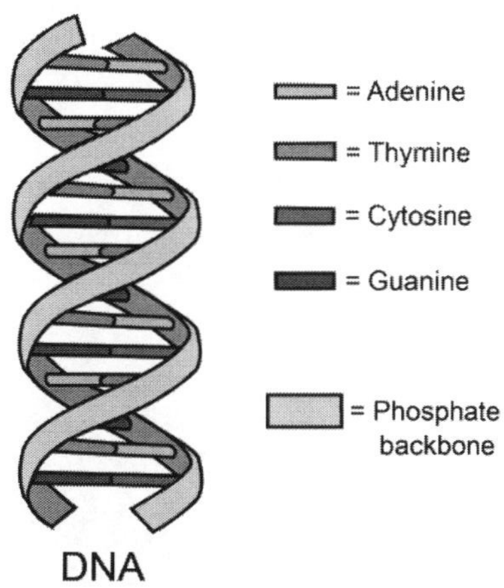

Organization of Prokaryotic DNA

Prokaryotes lack a nucleus and therefore prokaryotic DNA is organized primarily into a central loop contained in the cytoplasm. Prokaryotes may also contain smaller loops of DNA known as **plasmids** that contain other genes. Most prokaryotes lack histones, but Archaea are an example of prokaryotes that do contain histones.

Organization of Eukaryotic DNA

Eukaryotes have a nucleus with multiple chromosomes, each containing a tightly-compacted, double-helix DNA molecule. The structural sub-components of chromosomes include histones, nucleosomes, and chromatin.

- **Histones** are positively-charged, DNA-binding proteins.
- A **nucleosome** is composed of eight histone proteins around which approximately 146 base pairs of DNA are wrapped. The nucleosome is often called a "beads on a string" structure.

- **Chromatin** is made up of compacted nucleosomes.
- **Chromosomes** are made up of compacted chromatin.

RNA is also thought to play a role in chromatin structure.

TELOMERES

Eukaryotic chromosomes have **telomeres** located at their tips. Telomeres are repetitive sequences of DNA that maintain the ends of the linear chromosomes and keep those ends from deteriorating.

DNA REPLICATION

DNA replication begins when the double strands of the parent DNA molecule are unwound and unzipped. The enzyme **helicase** separates the two strands by breaking the hydrogen bonds between the base pairs that make up the rungs of the twisted ladder. These two single strands of DNA are called the **replication fork**. Each separate DNA strand provides a template for the complementary DNA bases, G with C and A with T. The opposite ends of DNA are called the 5' and 3' ends. After the DNA is separated, the enzyme **RNA primase** lays down an RNA primer that the enzyme **DNA polymerase** binds to initiate replication. DNA polymerase only synthesizes DNA from the 5' end towards the 3' end. Of the two strands open during replication, the strand with the 3' end will be replicated as a single, continuous strand, also known as the **leading strand**. The strand with the 5' end, which runs away from the fork, is known as the **lagging strand**, and will be replicated into shorter, unlinked segments known as Okazaki fragments. After bases are joined to the complementary base, the enzyme **exonuclease** removes the RNA primers used to initiate replication of the two strands. A separate DNA polymerase fills in gaps after the RNA primer is removed. The Okazaki fragments are joined by the enzyme DNA ligase.

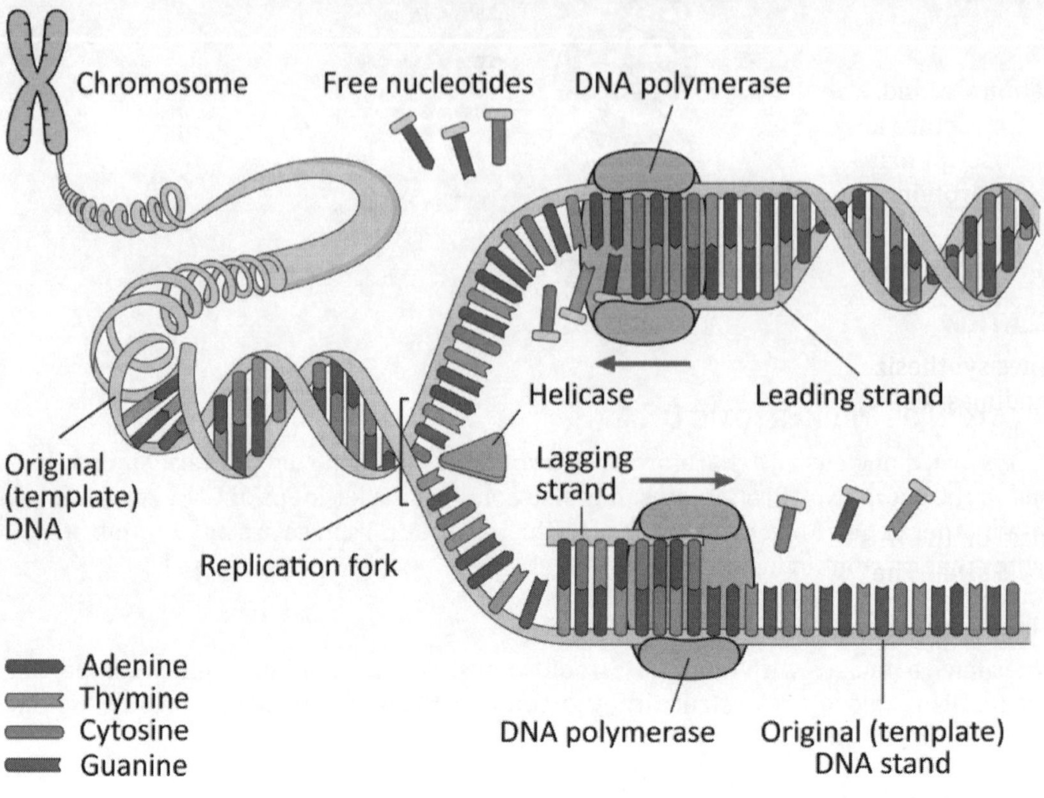

Protein Synthesis

Transcription

Transcription is the process by which a segment of DNA is copied onto a working blueprint called RNA. Each gene has a special region called a **promoter** that guides the beginning of the transcription process. **RNA polymerase** unwinds the DNA at the promoter region and makes an RNA copy of the DNA gene by adding the **complementary nucleotides**, G with C, C with G, T with A, and A with U. This forms a single strand of messenger RNA or mRNA.

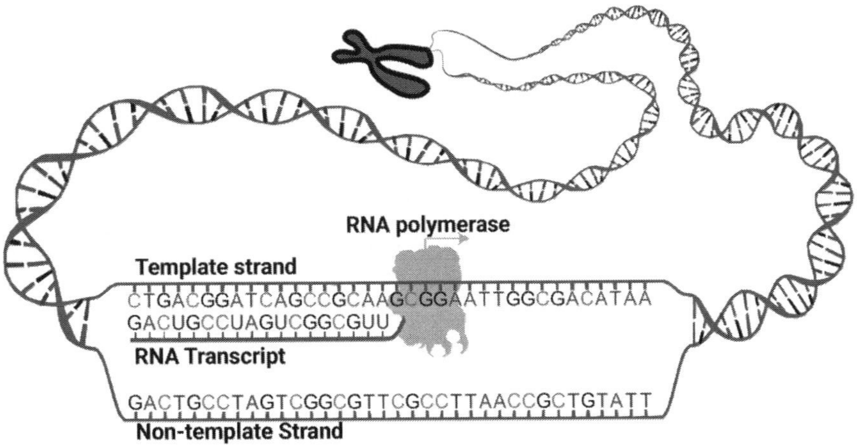

Processing mRNA

In addition to being transcribed, the mRNA must also be processed. First, a 5' cap (modified guanine nucleotide) is added, which helps promote ribosome recognition and preventing mRNA degradation. Second, a string of adenosine ribonucleotides are added to the 3' end of the mRNA, forming a structure known as a **poly(A) tail**. The poly(A) tail helps prevent mRNA degradation. The mRNA transcript may contain regions that do not code for protein, called **introns**. The regions that do code for protein are called **exons**. If introns are present, they will be removed in a process called splicing by a structure known as the **spliceosome**. After addition of the 5' cap, addition of the poly(A) tail, and splicing, the mRNA is ready for translation.

Translation

Ribosomes synthesize proteins from mRNA in a process called **translation**. The ribosome has three tRNA binding sites—A, P, and E. Translation initiates when the "**A site**" becomes occupied by the tRNA molecule corresponding to the mRNA start codon. The ribosome then moves the first tRNA from the "A site" to the "**P site**." The "A site" is then occupied by the tRNA molecule corresponding to the second mRNA codon. The ribosome then transfers the amino acid on the "P site" tRNA to the amino acid on the "A site" tRNA. The first tRNA, which now has no amino acid, is moved from the "P site" the "**E site**." The second tRNA, complexed to a chain of two amino acids, is moved from the "A site" to the "P site." The "A site" is then occupied by the tRNA corresponding to the third mRNA codon. The "P site" amino acid chain is transferred to the amino acid bound to the "A site" tRNA. The first tRNA then exits from the "E site" and the second and third tRNA molecules shift, opening the "A site" for the next tRNA. The growing amino acid chain continues to be transferred from the "P site" to the "A site" until translation is complete.

Review Video: Amino Acids
Visit mometrix.com/academy and enter code: 190385

Regulation of Gene Expression

Regulation of Gene Expression

Role of Promoters

Promoters are DNA sequences located upstream of the gene needed for transcription. Promoters signal the beginning of transcription. Special proteins called **transcription factors**, which bind to promoters, subsequently provide binding sites for the **RNA polymerase**, which is the enzyme that transcribes the RNA. Promoters in the Archaea and Eukaryota domains often contain a nucleotide sequence TATA, which is called a **TATA box**. The TATA box is usually 25 nucleotides upstream of the transcription start site, and it is the location at which the DNA is unwound.

Role of Enhancers

Enhancers are DNA sequences that regulate gene expression by providing a binding site for proteins that regulate RNA polymerase in transcribing proteins. Enhancers can greatly increase the expression of genes in their range. Enhancers are functional over large distances. Some enhancers are located within the gene they control while others can be hundreds or thousands of base pairs upstream or downstream from the genes they control. Most genes are controlled by two or three enhancers, but some may be controlled by more. Enhancers provide binding sites for regulatory proteins that either promote or inhibit RNA polymerase activity. Enhancers are more common in eukaryotes than prokaryotes.

Review Video: Regulation of Gene Expression
Visit mometrix.com/academy and enter code: 651793

Role of Transcription Factors

Transcription factors are DNA-binding proteins that help regulate gene expression in eukaryotes and prokaryotes. In eukaryotes that have promoter or enhancer regions, transcription factors bind near these regions and increase the ability of the RNA polymerase to start transcription. In eukaryotes, because genes are typically turned "off," transcription factors typically work to turn genes "on." The opposite is often true in bacteria, and transcription factors often work to turn genes off.

Role of Operons

Operons are segments of DNA or groups of genes that are controlled by one promoter. Operons consist of an operator, a promoter, and one or more structural genes. The **operator** provides a binding side for a repressor that inhibits the binding of RNA polymerase. The **promoter** provides the binding site for the RNA polymerase. The **structural genes** provide the sequence that codes for a protein. Operons are transcribed as single units and code for a single mRNA molecule, which produces proteins with related functions. Operons have been found in prokaryotes, eukaryotes, and viruses. For example, the lac (lactose) operon in certain bacteria controls the production of the enzymes needed to digest lactose. If lactose is already available in the cell, the lactose binds to the repressor protein to prevent the repressor protein from binding to the operator. The gene is transcribed, and the enzymes necessary for the digestion of the lactose are produced. If there is no lactose that needs to be digested, the repressor protein binds to the operator. The gene is not transcribed, and the enzyme is not produced. This allows the cell to only code for proteins as needed by the cell.

Role of Epigenetics

Epigenetics studies factors or mechanisms that determine if genes are active (switched on) or dormant (switched off). These mechanisms can alter gene function or gene expression without altering the sequences of the DNA itself. An example is the addition of a methyl group (**methylation**) to the histones. **Acetylation**, the addition of an acetyl group, and **phosphorylation**, the addition of a phosphoryl group, are also modifications to the proteins associated with DNA that can switch genes on or off or affect their activity level.

Differentiation and Specialization of Cells

Differential Gene Expression

Differential gene expression is the expression of different sets of gene by cells with identical DNA molecules. The unused genes in a differentiated cell remain in the cell but are not expressed. Actually, only a few genes are expressed in each cell. For example, during mammalian embryonic development, the undifferentiated zygote undergoes cell division through mitosis. As the number of cells increases, selected cells undergo differentiation to become specialized components in the developing tissues of the embryo.

Stem Cells

Stem cells are undifferentiated cells that can divide without limit and that can differentiate to produce the specialized cells that each organism needs. **Embryonic stem cells** are harvested from the embryo at the blastocyst stage or from the developing gonads of the embryo. Stem cells can be pluripotent or multipotent depending on their source. Early embryonic stem cells are **pluripotent**, which means they have not undergone any differentiation and have the ability to become any special type of cell. After embryonic stem cells begin to differentiate, they may be limited to specializing into a specific tissue type. These stem cells are considered to be **multipotent** because they can only develop into a few different types of cells. Adult stem cells, also called **somatic stem cells**, are harvested from organs and tissues and can differentiate into those types of cells in that particular organ or tissue. Umbilical cord blood stem cells can be harvested from the umbilical cord of a newborn baby. Adult stem cells and umbilical cord blood stem cells are multipotent. **Induced pluripotent cells** (iPS) are somatic cells that have been manipulated to act like pluripotent cells. Experiments have shown that iPS may be useful in treating diseases.

Mutations

Missense Mutations, Silent Mutations, and Nonsense Mutations

Mutations are changes in DNA sequences. **Point mutations** are changes in a single nucleotide in a DNA sequence. Three types of point mutations are missense, silent, and nonsense.

- **Missense mutations** result in a codon for a different amino acid. An example is mutating TGT (Cysteine codon) to TGG (Tryptophan codon).
- **Silent mutations** result in a codon for the same amino acid as the original sequence. An example is mutating TGT (Cysteine codon) to TGC (a different Cysteine codon).
- **Nonsense mutations** insert a premature stop codon, typically resulting in a non-functional protein. An example is mutating TGT (Cysteine codon) to TGA (STOP codon).

Review Video: Codons
Visit mometrix.com/academy and enter code: 978172

Frameshift Mutations and Inversion Mutations

Deletions and insertions can result in the addition of amino acids, the removal of amino acids, or cause a frameshift mutation. A **frameshift mutation** changes the reading frame of the mRNA (a new group of codons will be read), resulting in the formation of a new protein product. Mutations can also occur on the chromosomal level. For example, an **inversion** is when a piece of the chromosome inverts or flips its orientation.

Germline Mutations and Somatic Mutations

Mutations can occur in somatic (body) cells and germ cells (egg and sperm). **Somatic mutations** develop after conception and occur in an organism's body cells such as bone cells, liver cells, or brain cells. Somatic mutations cannot be passed on from parent to offspring. The mutation is limited to the specific descendent of the cell in which the mutation occurred. The mutation is not in the other body cells unless they are descendants of the originally mutated cell. Somatic mutations may cause cancer or diseases. Some somatic mutations are silent. **Germline mutations** are present at conception and occur in an organism's germ cells, which are only egg and sperms cells. Germline mutations may be passed on from parent to offspring. Germline mutations will be present in every cell of an offspring that inherits a germline mutation. Germline mutations may cause diseases. Some germline mutations are silent.

Mutagens

Mutagens are physical and chemical agents that cause changes or errors in DNA replication. Mutagens are external factors to an organism. Examples include ionizing radiation such as ultraviolet radiation, x-rays, and gamma radiation. Viruses and microorganisms that integrate their DNA into host chromosomes are also mutagens. Mutagens include environmental poisons such as asbestos, coal tars, tobacco, and benzene. Alcohol and diets high in fat have been shown to be mutagenic. Not all mutations are caused by mutagens. **Spontaneous mutations** can occur in DNA due to molecular decay.

Lab Techniques for Studying Biological Processes

Gel Electrophoresis

Gel electrophoresis is a technique used to separate macromolecules such as nucleic acids and proteins with regard to size. Fragments of DNA and RNA, as well as proteins, are separated according to length. Using different types of gel electrophoresis, proteins can also be separated according to electrical charge. The technique for gel electrophoresis is relatively simple. For example, to separate DNA strands, a solution containing the DNA strand is placed in a gel. When an electric current is passed through the gel, the DNA strands migrate from the negative end of the container to the positive end due to their negative charge because of their phosphate ions. Shorter DNA strands migrate faster than the longer DNA strands. This results in a series of bands. Each band contains DNA strands of a specific length. A DNA standard, commonly called a DNA ladder, is placed in the gel to provide a reference to determine the strand length. Lengths are measured in base pairs (bps).

Microscopy

Microscopy is used in many fields of biology, including microbiology. Bacteria, viruses, cell components, and molecules are too small to be seen by the naked eye. Several types of microscopes are available to examine these samples. There are **light microscopes**, which use visible light to study samples, and electron microscopes, which use beams of electrons. The light microscope (also called the compound microscope) uses two types of lenses (ocular and objective) to magnify objects. These are typically used when studying samples at the cellular level. Basic compound light microscopes are typically used in high school biology classes. Other compound light microscopes such as the dark-field microscope, phase-contrast microscope, and the fluorescent microscope are available for more specific uses. For tiny samples, such as viruses, cell components, or individual molecules, electron microscopes can be used. **Electron microscopes** use beams of electrons instead of light. Because beams of electrons have shorter wavelengths, electron microscopes have greater resolution than light microscopes. Resolution is the ability of a lens to reveal two points as being distinct. The two types of electron microscopy are transmission electron microscopy (TEM) and scanning electron microscopy (SEM). SEM is a newer technology than TEM and produces three-dimensional images.

SPECTROPHOTOMETRY

Spectrophotometry involves measuring the amount of visible light absorbed by a colored solution. There are **analog** and **digital spectrometers** that measure absorbance and transmittance. A **single beam spectrometer** measures relative light intensity. A **double beam spectrometer** compares light intensity between a reference sample and a test sample. Spectrometers measure the wavelength of light. Spectrometry not only involves working with visible light, but also near-ultraviolet and near-infrared light. A **spectrophotometer** includes an illumination source. An output wavelength is selected and beamed at the sample, the sample absorbs light, and the detector responds to the light and outputs an analog electronic current in a usable form. A spectrophotometer may require calibration. Some types can be used to identify unknown chemicals.

Review Video: Spectrophotometer
Visit mometrix.com/academy and enter code: 104413

DNA Technologies and Genetic Engineering

PCR

The **polymerase chain reaction (PCR)** is a laboratory technique used to rapidly copy selected segments of DNA. PCR can be performed on the DNA from a single cell. PCR is a hot-and-cold cycled reaction that uses a special heat-tolerant polymerase. The DNA sample is combined with this special DNA polymerase, primers, and free nucleotides. Primers are synthetic strands of DNA containing just a few bases. The first step is a high-temperature **denaturation step** (90–95°C) that causes the DNA strands to unwind. The second step is a low-temperature **annealing step** (~60°C) in which the primers anneal to the single-stranded DNA. The final step is an **activation step** that matches the activation temperature for the heat-resistant DNA polymerase (~70°C, depending on the enzyme). This final step results in the formation of newly-synthesized, double-stranded DNA. These steps will be repeated on the same sample for multiple cycles, typically about 30. The number of DNA copies generated is 2^N, where N is the number of cycles.

DNA SEQUENCING

DNA sequencing is a laboratory technique used to determine the order or linear sequence of nucleotides of DNA fragments. A PCR is used to isolate the needed DNA segment or DNA template. During PCR, some of each of the nucleotides containing the four bases (G, C, A, and T) are chemically altered and fluorescently tagged with different colors of dye. Also, the chemically altered nucleotides have the dideoxyribose sugar, which contains one less oxygen atom than the usual deoxyribose. When synthesis begins, the polymerase randomly adds either a regular nucleotide or an altered nucleotide. If the polymerase adds an altered nucleotide, synthesis stops. This way, each

DNA fragment of the same length is tagged with the same color. Then, electrophoresis is used to separate DNA fragments according to length. The DNA sequence can be read by reading the tags of the shortest fragments to the tags of the longest fragments.

Human Genome Project

In 1990, the **Human Genome Project (HGP)** was launched to map the human genome. The project involved scientists from 16 laboratories located in at least 6 different countries, and it was completed in 2003. The human genome consists of approximately 3.12 billion paired nucleotides. The genomes of several plants, animal, fungi, protists, bacteria, viruses, and even cell organelles have also been studied and mapped. Interesting comparisons can be made between these genomes. For example, the number of genes in an organism's genome does not indicate the complexity of that organism. Humans have approximately 21,000 genes, but the simpler roundworms have approximately 26,000 genes.

Gene Therapy

Gene therapy is an experimental but promising technique that introduces new genes into an organism to correct a specific disease caused by a defective gene. In gene therapy, the defective gene is replaced by a properly functioning gene. Gene therapy is most promising for diseases that are caused by a single defective gene. For example, gene therapy was first successfully used to treat severe combined immunodeficiency (SCID). One type of SCID is caused by a single defective gene on the X chromosome. Doctors removed some bone marrow from the test subjects, injected a retrovirus that was carrying the gene, and then re-implanted the bone marrow. The bone marrow cells then have the correct DNA sequence for the production of proteins for much-needed enzymes. Unfortunately, some of the first recipients developed leukemia, and the trials were halted. Later, researchers discovered that the leukemia was related to the location of the insertion of the retroviral vectors.

Cloning

Clones are exact biological copies of genes, cells, or multicellular organisms. There are natural clones and artificial clones. Many clones are produced in nature. For example, animals that can reproduce asexually by fragmentation or budding produce natural clones. Some plants such as strawberries can reproduce by stolons. Typically, in biology, cloning refers to gene cloning or the cloning of organisms. Gene cloning is the process of splicing genes that are needed to code for a specific protein and introducing them into a new cell with a DNA vector. Gene cloning has been used with bacteria in the production of human insulin and a human growth hormone replacement.

Cloning can also occur with an entire organism. This type of cloning is called a **somatic cell nuclear transfer**. The first mammal clone was Dolly the sheep. In this procedure, a nucleus of a somatic cell from the sheep to be cloned was transferred or injected into a denucleated egg cell of the surrogate mother sheep. The egg was stimulated to divide by electric shock, and then the embryo was implanted into the uterus of the surrogate mother. Dolly was born identical to the egg nucleus donor, not the surrogate mother. Dolly and other cloned mammals typically have serious health problems. Dolly aged prematurely possibly due to the shortened telomeres from the adult somatic cell nucleus.

Review Video: Genetic Cloning
Visit mometrix.com/academy and enter code: 289634

Genetic Engineering and Genetically Engineered Cells

Genetic engineering is the manipulation of DNA outside of normal reproduction. This modified DNA is called **recombinant DNA**. Genetic engineering is prevalent in gene cloning, which is used in the production of genetically modified (GM) organisms and the production of GM food. **Gene cloning** involves cloning a specific gene that is needed for a specific purpose. Genes can be inserted into cells of an entirely different species. Genetically engineered cells are also called transgenic cells. GM organisms such as plants or crops contain recombinant DNA. Many types of organisms such as plants, animals, fungi, and bacteria have been genetically modified. GM crops such as corn and soybeans can be engineered to be herbicide resistant to ensure that herbicides kill the weeds but not the crop plants. Crops can also be modified to be pest resistant in order to kill the insects that might damage the crops. In addition, several foods can be genetically modified to increase nutritional value.

Review Video: Genetic Engineering and Genetically Engineered Cells
Visit mometrix.com/academy and enter code: 548687

Characteristics of Living Versus Nonliving Things

Importance and Structural Organization of Cells

Cells are the basic structural units of all organisms. All organisms have a highly organized cellular structure. In single-celled organisms, that single cell contains all of the components necessary for life. In multicellular organisms, cells can become specialized. Different types of cells can have different functions. Life begins as a single cell whether by asexual or sexual reproduction. All cells contain DNA and RNA and can synthesize proteins. Each cell consists of nucleic acids, cytoplasm, and a cell membrane. Specialized organelles such as mitochondria and chloroplasts have specific functions within the cell.

Energy

All cells must obtain and use energy in order to grow, make repairs, and reproduce. Cells obtain the energy they need by the breaking of bonds of molecules. Cellular respiration is the process of converting nutrient molecules into energy. Cells also use energy to take in food, process that food, and eliminate waste. Organisms differ in how they obtain food. Plants and other autotrophs can produce their own energy through processes such as photosynthesis or chemosynthesis. Animals and other heterotrophs obtain their energy from consuming autotrophs or other heterotrophs.

Growth and Reproduction

All organisms must be capable of growth and reproduction. Growth is necessary for multicellular organisms to develop and mature. While all cells eventually die, growth allows cells to be replaced or repaired. Without growth from cell division, tissues could not be maintained or repaired. Through mitosis, most cells routinely replace themselves with identical daughter cells. Reproduction is necessary to increase the number of individuals in a population, since all organisms eventually die. Reproduction is either sexual by the joining of gametes or asexual by binary fission or some other related method.

Adaptation to Environment

Organisms must be able to adapt to their environment in order to thrive or survive. Individuals must be able to recognize stimuli in their surroundings and adapt quickly. For example, an individual euglena can sense light and respond by moving toward the light. Individual organisms must also be able to adapt to changes in the environment on a larger scale. For example, plants must be able to respond to the change in the length of the day to flower at the correct time. Populations must also be able to adapt to a changing environment. Evolution by **natural selection** is the process by which populations change over many generations to become better adapted to their environment, thus surviving longer and reproducing more successfully. For example, wooly mammoths were unable to adapt to a warming climate and are now extinct, but many species of deer did adapt and are abundant today.

Historical and Current Biological Classifications of Organisms

HISTORICAL AND CURRENT KINGDOM SYSTEMS

In 1735 Carolus Linnaeus devised a two-kingdom classification system. He placed all living things into either the *Animalia* kingdom or the *Plantae* kingdom. Fungi and algae were classified as plants. Also, Linnaeus developed the binomial nomenclature system that is still used today. In 1866, Ernst Haeckel introduced a three-kingdom classification system, adding the *Protista* kingdom to Linnaeus's animal and plant kingdoms. Bacteria were classified as protists and cyanobacteria were still classified as plants. In 1938, Herbert Copeland introduced a four-kingdom classification system in which bacteria and cyanobacteria were moved to the *Monera* kingdom. In 1969, Robert Whittaker introduced a five-kingdom system that moved fungi from the plant kingdom to the *Fungi* kingdom. Some algae were still classified as plants. In 1977, Carl Woese introduced a six-kingdom system in which in the *Monera* kingdom was replaced with the *Eubacteria* kingdom and the *Archaebacteria* kingdom.

How animals are classified

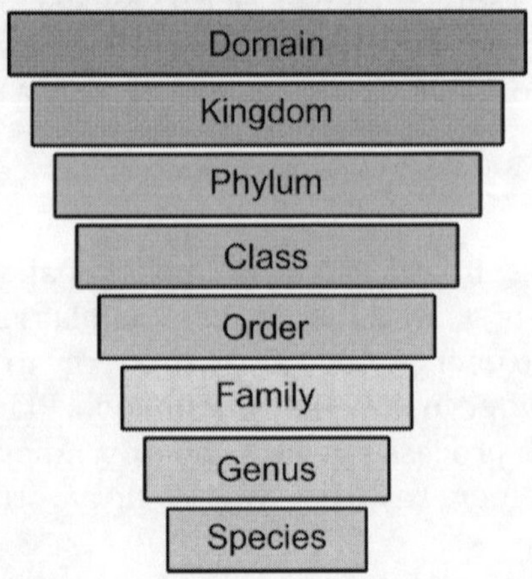

DOMAIN CLASSIFICATION SYSTEM

In 1990, Carl Woese introduced his domain classification system. **Domains** are broader groupings above the kingdom level. This system consists of three domains—*Archaea*, *Bacteria*, and *Eukarya*. All eukaryotes such as plants, animals, fungi, and protists are classified in the *Eukarya* domain. The *Bacteria* and *Archaea* domains consist of prokaryotes. Organisms previously classified in the *Monera* kingdom are now classified into either the *Bacteria* or *Archaea* domain based on their ribosomal RNA structure. Members of the *Archaea* domain often live in extremely harsh environments.

Review Video: Biological Classification Systems
Visit mometrix.com/academy and enter code: 736052

Viruses, Bacteria, Protists, Fungi, Plants, and Animals

VIRUSES

Viruses are nonliving, infectious particles that act as parasites in living organisms. Viruses are acellular, which means that they lack cell structure. Viruses cannot reproduce outside of living cells. The structure of a virus is a nucleic acid genome, which may be either DNA or RNA, surrounded by a protective protein coat or **capsid**. In some viruses, the capsid may be surrounded by a lipid membrane or envelope. Viruses can contain up to 500 genes and have various shapes. They usually are too small to be seen without the aid of an electron microscope. Viruses can infect plants, animals, fungi, protists, and bacteria. Viruses can attack only specific types of cells that have specific receptors on their surfaces. Viruses do not divide or reproduce like living cells. Instead, they use the host cell they infect by "reprogramming" it, using the nucleic acid genome, to make more copies of the virus. The host cell usually bursts to release these copies.

> **Review Video: Viruses and Antiviral Drugs**
> Visit mometrix.com/academy and enter code: 984455

BACTERIA

Bacteria are small, prokaryotic, single-celled organisms. Bacteria have a circular loop of DNA (plasmid) that is not contained within a nuclear membrane. Bacterial ribosomes are not bound to the endoplasmic reticulum, as in eukaryotes. A cell wall containing peptidoglycan surrounds the bacterial plasma membrane. Some bacteria such as pathogens are further encased in a gel-like, sticky layer called the **capsule**, which enhances their ability to cause disease. Bacteria can be autotrophs or heterotrophs. Some bacterial heterotrophs are saprophytes that function as decomposers in ecosystems. Many types of bacteria share commensal or mutualistic relationships with other organisms. Most bacteria reproduce asexually by binary fission. Two identical daughter cells are produced from one parent cell. Some bacteria can transfer genetic material to other bacteria through a process called conjugation, while some bacteria can incorporate DNA from the environment in a process called transformation.

PROTISTS

Protists are small, eukaryotic, single-celled organisms. Although protists are small, they are much larger than prokaryotic bacteria. Protists have three general forms, which include plantlike protists, animal-like protists, and fungus-like protists. **Plantlike protists** are algae that contain chlorophyll and perform photosynthesis. Animal-like protists are **protozoa** with no cell walls that typically lack chlorophyll and are grouped by their method of locomotion, which may use flagella, cilia, or a different structure. **Fungus-like protists**, which do not have chitin in their cell walls, are generally grouped as either slime molds or water molds. Protists may be autotrophic or heterotrophic. Autotrophic protists include many species of algae, while heterotrophic protists include parasitic, commensal, and mutualistic protozoa. Slime molds are heterotrophic fungus-like protists, which consume microorganisms. Some protists reproduce sexually, but most reproduce asexually by binary fission. Some reproduce asexually by spores while others reproduce by alternation of generations and require two hosts in their life cycle.

FUNGI

Fungi are nonmotile organisms with eukaryotic cells and contain chitin in their cell walls. Most fungi are multicellular, but a few including yeast are unicellular. Fungi have multicellular filaments called **hyphae** that are grouped together into the mycelium. Fungi do not perform photosynthesis and are considered heterotrophs. Fungi can be parasitic, mutualistic or free living. Free-living fungi include mushrooms and toadstools. Parasitic fungi include fungi responsible for ringworm and athlete's foot. Mycorrhizae are mutualistic fungi that live in or near plant roots increasing the roots' surface area of absorption. Almost all fungi reproduce asexually by spores, but most fungi also have a sexual phase in the production of spores. Some fungi reproduce by budding or fragmentation.

Review Video: Feeding Among Heterotrophs
Visit mometrix.com/academy and enter code: 836017

PLANTS

Plants are multicellular organisms with eukaryotic cells containing cellulose in their cell walls. Plant cells have chlorophyll and perform photosynthesis. Plants can be vascular or nonvascular. **Vascular plants** have true leaves, stems, and roots that contain xylem and phloem. **Nonvascular plants** lack true leaves, stems and roots and do not have any true vascular tissue but instead rely on diffusion and osmosis to transport most of materials or resources needed to survive. Almost all plants are autotrophic, relying on photosynthesis for food. A small number do not have chlorophyll and are parasitic, but these are extremely rare. Plants can reproduce sexually or asexually. Many plants reproduce by seeds produced in the fruits of the plants, while some plants reproduce by seeds on cones. One type of plant, ferns, reproduce by a different system that utilizes spores. Some plants can even reproduce asexually by vegetative reproduction.

Review Video: Kingdom Plantae
Visit mometrix.com/academy and enter code: 710084

STRUCTURE, ORGANIZATION, MODES OF NUTRITION, AND REPRODUCTION OF ANIMALS

Animals are multicellular organism with eukaryotic cells that do not have cell walls surrounding their plasma membranes. Animals have several possible structural body forms. Animals can be relatively simple in structure such as sponges, which do not have a nervous system. Other animals are more complex with cells organized into tissues, and tissues organized into organs, and organs even further organized into systems. Invertebrates such as arthropods, nematodes, and annelids have complex body systems. Vertebrates including fish, amphibians, reptiles, birds, and mammals are the most complex with detailed systems such as those with gills, air sacs, or lungs designed to exchange respiratory gases. All animals are heterotrophs and obtain their nutrition by consuming autotrophs or other heterotrophs. Most animals are motile, but some animals move their environment to bring food to them. All animals reproduce sexually at some point in their life cycle. Typically, this involves the union of a sperm and egg to produce a zygote.

Characteristics of the Major Animal Phyla

CHARACTERISTICS OF THE MAJOR ANIMAL PHYLA

BODY PLANES

Animals can exhibit bilateral symmetry, radial symmetry, or asymmetry. With **bilateral symmetry**, the organism can be cut in half along only one plane to produce two identical halves. Most animals, including all vertebrates such as mammals, birds, reptiles, amphibians, and fish, exhibit bilateral symmetry. Many invertebrates including arthropods and crustaceans also exhibit bilateral symmetry. With **radial symmetry**, the organism can be cut in half along several planes to produce two identical halves. Starfish, sea urchins, and jellyfish exhibit radial symmetry. With **asymmetry**, the organism exhibits no symmetry. Very few organisms in the animal phyla exhibit asymmetry, but a few species of sponges are asymmetrical.

Body Cavities

Animals can be grouped based on their types of body cavities. A **coelom** is a fluid-filled body cavity between the alimentary canal and the body wall. The three body plans based on the formation of the coelom are coelomates, pseudocoelomates, and acoelomates. **Coelomates** have a true coelom located within the mesoderm. Most animals including arthropods, mollusks, annelids, echinoderms, and chordates are coelomates. **Pseudocoelomates** have a body cavity called a pseudocoelom. **Pseudocoeloms** are not considered true coeloms. Pseudocoeloms are located between mesoderm and endoderm instead of actually in the mesoderm as in a true coelom. Pseudocoelomates include roundworms and rotifers. **Acoelomates** do not have body cavities. Simple or primitive animals such as sponges, jellyfish, sea anemones, hydras, flatworms, and ribbon worms are acoelomates.

Modes of Reproduction

Animals can reproduce sexually or asexually. Most animals reproduce sexually. In **sexual reproduction**, males and females have different reproductive organs that produce **gametes**. Males have testes that produce sperm, and females have ovaries that produce eggs. During fertilization, a sperm cell unites with an egg cell, forming a **zygote**. Fertilization can occur internally such as in most mammals and birds or externally such as aquatic animals such as fish and frogs. The zygote undergoes cell division, which develops into an embryo and eventually develops into an adult organism. Some embryos develop in eggs such as in fish, amphibians, reptiles, and birds. Some mammals are **oviparous** meaning that they lay eggs, but most are **viviparous** meaning they have a uterus in which the embryo develops. One particular type of mammal called **marsupials** give birth to an immature fetus that finishes development in a pouch. However, there are some animals reproduce **asexually**. For example, hydras reproduce by budding, and starfish and planarians can reproduce by fragmentation and regeneration. Some fish, frogs, and insects can even reproduce by parthenogenesis, which is a type of self-reproduction without fertilization.

Modes of Temperature Regulation

Animals can be classified as either homeotherms or poikilotherms. **Homeotherms**, also called warm-blooded animals or **endotherms**, maintain a constant body temperature regardless of the temperature of the environment. Homeotherms such as mammals and birds have a high metabolic rate because a lot of energy is needed to maintain the constant temperature. **Poikilotherms**, also called cold-blooded animals or **ectotherms**, do not maintain a constant body temperature. Their body temperature fluctuates with the temperature of the environment. Poikilotherms such as arthropods, fish, amphibians, and reptiles have metabolic rates that fluctuate with their body temperature.

Hierarchy of Multicellular Organisms

Organizational Hierarchy within Multicellular Organisms

Cells are the smallest living units of organisms. Tissues are groups of cells that work together to perform a specific function. Organs are groups of tissues that work together to perform a specific function. Organ systems are groups of organs that work together to perform a specific function. An organism is an individual that contains several body systems.

Cells

Cells are the basic structural units of all living things. Cells are composed of various molecules including proteins, carbohydrates, lipids, and nucleic acids. All animal cells are eukaryotic and have a nucleus, cytoplasm, and a cell membrane. Organelles include mitochondria, ribosomes, endoplasmic reticulum, Golgi apparatuses, and vacuoles. Specialized cells are numerous, including but not limited to, muscle cells, nerve cells, epithelial cells, bone cells, blood cells, and cartilage cells. Cells can be grouped together in tissues to perform specific functions.

Tissues

Tissues are groups of cells that work together to perform a specific function. Tissues can be grouped into four broad categories: muscle tissue, connective tissue, nerve tissue, and epithelial tissue. Muscle tissue is involved in body movement. **Muscle tissues** can be composed of skeletal muscle cells, cardiac muscle cells, or smooth muscle cells. Skeletal muscles include the muscles commonly called biceps, triceps, hamstrings, and quadriceps. Cardiac muscle tissue is found only in the heart. Smooth muscle tissue provides tension in the blood vessels, controls pupil dilation, and aids in peristalsis. **Connective tissues** include bone tissue, cartilage, tendons, ligaments, fat, blood, and lymph. **Nerve tissue** is located in the brain, spinal cord, and nerves. **Epithelial tissue** makes up the layers of the skin and various membranes. Tissues are grouped together as organs to perform specific functions.

Organs and Organ Systems

Organs are groups of tissues that work together to perform specific functions. **Organ systems** are groups of organs that work together to perform specific functions. Complex animals have several organs that are grouped together in multiple systems. In mammals, there are 11 major organ systems: integumentary system, respiratory system, cardiovascular system, endocrine system, nervous system, immune system, digestive system, excretory system, muscular system, skeletal system, and reproductive system.

Human Anatomy and Physiology

Body Systems

Functions of the human body can be divided into the following body systems.

- **Cardiovascular**: Pumps blood throughout the body via the heart and blood vessels
- **Respiratory**: Regulates gas exchange (oxygen intake and carbon dioxide expulsion)
- **Digestive**: Transforms food into energy and eliminates solid waste
- **Urinary**: Removes waste and toxins from the blood and expels them from the body through urine
- **Endocrine**: Releases hormones into the bloodstream to control metabolism, growth, and reproduction
- **Immune and Lymphatic Systems**: Defends against all foreign substances
- **Integumentary**: Skin prevents moisture loss, regulates temperature, protects from sunburn, and senses pain, pressure, touch, hot and cold
- **Musculoskeletal**: Skeletal muscles move the body, smooth muscles control the physical functioning of internal organs, and cardiac muscle pumps blood. The skeleton supports and shapes, protects internal organs, stores minerals, and produces blood cells
- **Nervous**: Controls movement, memory, and senses and communicates with the outside world
- **Reproductive**: Allows continuation of the human species through reproduction and childbearing and differentiates the sexes

Note that different models may have overlapping approaches to the body systems. For instance, the excretory system is not listed above, but the functions of the excretory systems overlap and are covered by the urinary and digestive systems.

THE THREE PRIMARY BODY PLANES

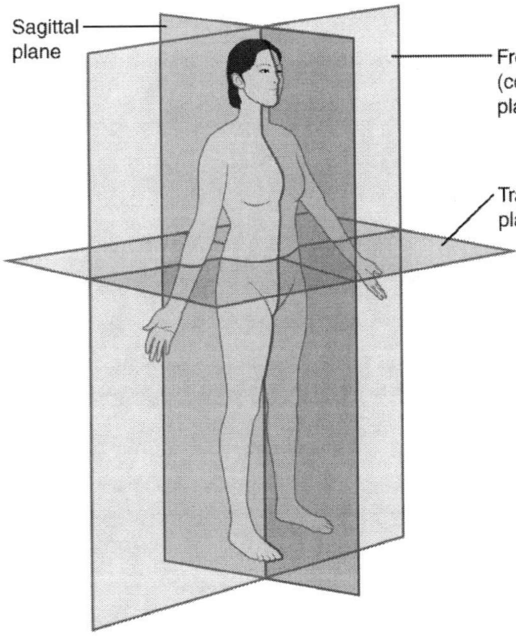

- The **transverse (or horizontal) plane** divides the patient's body into imaginary upper (*superior*) and lower (*inferior or caudal*) halves.
- The **sagittal plane** divides the body, or any body part, vertically into right and left sections. The sagittal plane runs parallel to the midline of the body.
- The **coronal (or frontal) plane** divides the body, or any body structure, vertically into front and back (*anterior* and *posterior*) sections. The coronal plane runs vertically through the body at right angles to the midline.

TERMS OF DIRECTION

- **Medial** means *nearer to the midline* of the body. In anatomical position, the little finger is medial to the thumb.
- **Lateral** is the opposite of medial. It refers to structures *further away from the body's midline*, at the sides. In anatomical position, the thumb is lateral to the little finger.
- **Proximal** refers to structures *closer to the center* of the body. The hip is proximal to the knee.
- **Distal** refers to structures *further away from the center* of the body. The knee is distal to the hip.
- **Anterior** refers to structures in *front.*
- **Posterior** refers to structures *behind.*
- **Cephalad** and **cephalic** are adverbs meaning towards the *head.* **Cranial** is the adjective, meaning of the *skull.*
- **Caudad** is an adverb meaning towards the *tail* or posterior. **Caudal** is the adjective, meaning of the *hindquarters.*
- **Superior** means *above*, or closer to the head.
- **Inferior** means *below*, or closer to the feet.

CARDIOVASCULAR SYSTEM

The main functions of the **cardiovascular system** are gas exchange, the delivery of nutrients and hormones, and waste removal. The cardiovascular system consists primarily of the heart, blood, and blood vessels. The **heart** is a pump that pushes blood through the arteries. **Arteries** are blood vessels that carry blood away from the heart, and **veins** are blood vessels that carry blood back to the heart. The exchange of materials between blood and cells occur in the **capillaries**, which are the smallest of the blood vessels.

Review Video: Functions of the Circulatory System
Visit mometrix.com/academy and enter code: 376581

Review Video: Mnemonics for Heart Anatomy and Physiology
Visit mometrix.com/academy and enter code: 849489

Review Video: Electrical Conduction System of the Heart
Visit mometrix.com/academy and enter code: 624557

Review Video: How the Heart Functions
Visit mometrix.com/academy and enter code: 569724

HEART CHAMBERS AND VALVES

There are four chambers of the heart that have valves separating them and regulating a one-way flow of blood between the chambers.

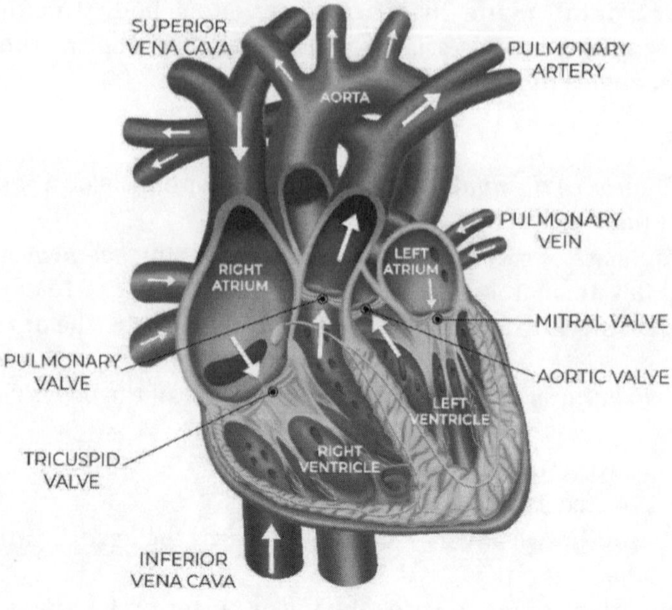

Respiratory System

The primary function of the **respiratory system** is to move air in and out of the body in order to facilitate the exchange of oxygen and carbon dioxide. The respiratory system consists of the nasal passages, pharynx, larynx, trachea, bronchial tubes, lungs, and diaphragm. **Bronchial tubes** branch into **bronchioles**, which end in clusters of alveoli. The **alveoli** are tiny sacs inside the lungs where gas exchange takes place. When the **diaphragm** contracts, the volume of the chest increases, which reduces the pressure in the **lungs**. Then, air is inhaled through the nose or mouth and passes through the pharynx, larynx, trachea, and bronchial tubes into the lungs. When the diaphragm relaxes, the volume in the chest cavity decreases, forcing the air out of the lungs. The respiratory system works jointly with the **cardiovascular system** by taking **oxygenated blood** (red blood cells) and distributing them through arteries and capillaries. **Deoxygenated blood** (carbon dioxide) is transported via the venous system back to the lungs to exhaled. The respiratory system also functions to enhance speech and smell.

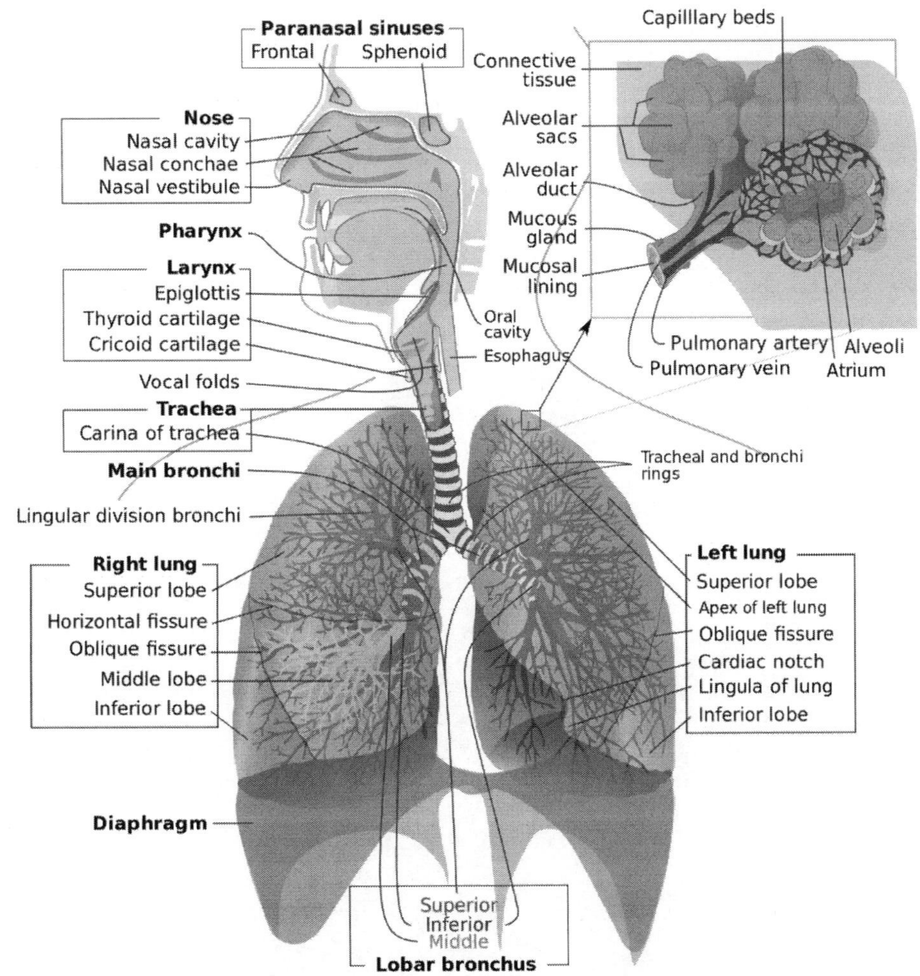

Review Video: Respiratory System
Visit mometrix.com/academy and enter code: 783075

Review Video: Pulmonary Circuit
Visit mometrix.com/academy and enter code: 955608

DIGESTIVE SYSTEM

The main function of the **digestive system** is to process the food that is consumed by an organism. This includes mechanical and chemical processing. Depending on the organism, **mechanical processes**, or the physical process of breaking food into smaller pieces, can happen in various ways. Mammals have teeth to chew their food, while many animals such as birds, earthworms, crocodilians, and crustaceans have a gizzard or gizzard-like organ that grinds their food. **Chemical digestion** includes breaking food into simpler nutrients that the body can use for specific processes. While chewing, saliva (which contains special enzymes) is secreted to begin the breakdown of starches. Many animals such as mammals, birds, reptiles, amphibians, and fish have a stomach that stores and absorbs food. Gastric juice containing enzymes and hydrochloric acid is mixed with the food. The intestine or intestines absorb nutrients and reabsorb water from the undigested material. Additionally, many animals have a liver, gallbladder, and pancreas, which aid in digestion of proteins and fats. Undigested wasted are eliminated from the body through an anus or cloaca.

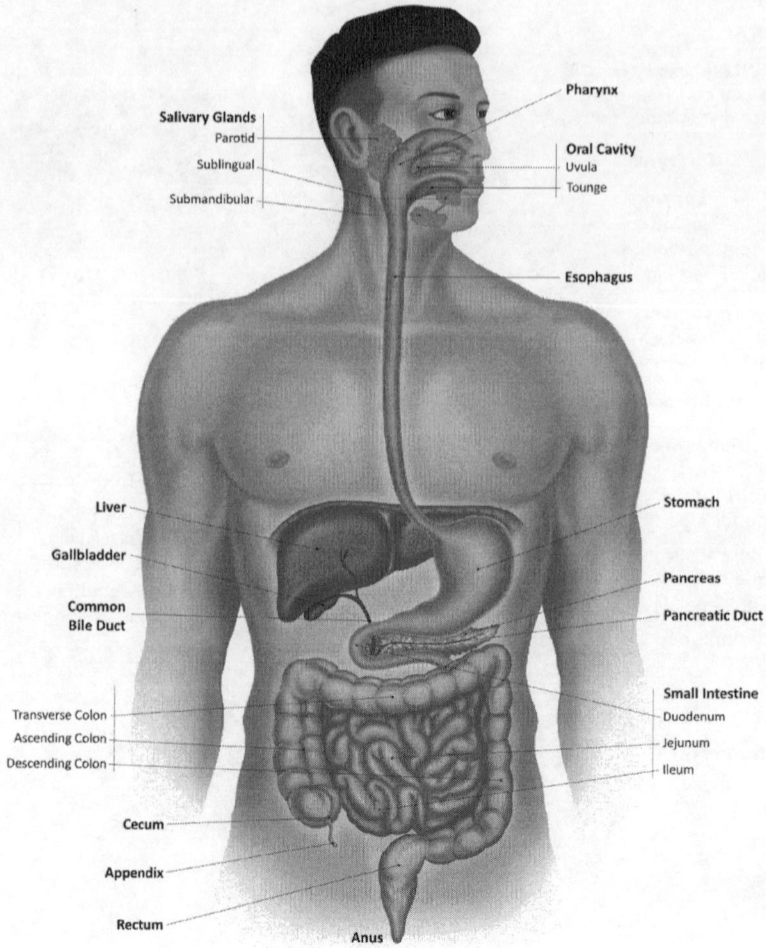

Review Video: Gastrointestinal System
Visit mometrix.com/academy and enter code: 378740

Urinary System

The **urinary system** consists of the bladder, kidneys, ureter, and urethra. Their main function is to eliminate waste products by expelling urine. This system also maintains homeostatic balance of water by excreting excess urine, maintaining electrolytes in the blood stream, and regulating blood Ph levels. This balance of water is crucial to body functioning as dehydration can lead to low blood pressure, which in turn can result in metabolic shock. **Metabolic shock** is characterized by low blood pressure that affects the kidneys, liver, and brain. **Dehydration** can also affect the muscular, system resulting in cramps from poor thermal regulation and altered fluid movement across tissue membranes.

Kidneys

The **kidneys** are involved in blood filtration, pH balance, and the reabsorption of nutrients to maintain proper blood volume and ion balance. The **nephron** is the working unit of the kidney. The parts of the nephron include the glomerulus, Bowman's capsule, and loop of Henle. Filtration takes place in the nephron's **glomerulus.** Water and dissolved materials such as glucose and amino acids pass on into the Bowman's capsule. Depending on concentration gradients, water and dissolved materials can pass back into the blood primarily through the proximal convoluted tubule. Reabsorption and water removal occurs in the **loop of Henle** and the conducting duct. Urine and other nitrogenous wastes pass from the kidneys to the bladders and are expelled.

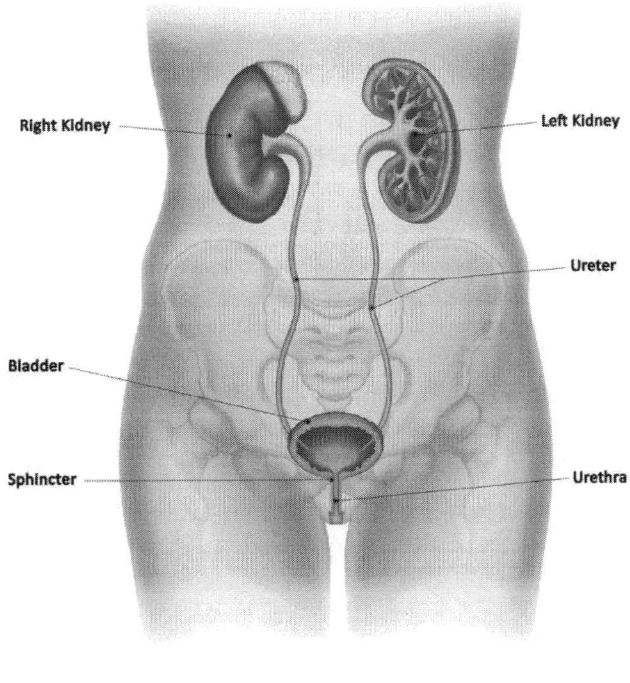

Review Video: Urinary System
Visit mometrix.com/academy and enter code: 601053

Endocrine System

The **endocrine system** consists of several ductless glands, which secrete hormones directly into the bloodstream. The **pituitary gland** controls the functions of the other glands in the system, regulates skeletal growth, and initiates the development of reproductive organs. The **pineal gland** regulates sleep cycles. The **thyroid gland** regulates metabolism and work with the **parathyroid glands** to help regulate the calcium level in the blood. The **adrenal glands** secrete the emergency hormone epinephrine, stimulate body repairs, and regulate sodium and potassium levels in the blood. The **islets of Langerhans**, located in the pancreas, secrete insulin and glucagon to regulate the level of blood sugar. In females, **ovaries** produce estrogen, which stimulates sexual development, and progesterone, which functions during pregnancy. In males, the **testes** secrete testosterone, which stimulates sexual development and sperm production.

Gland	Hormones	Disease
Adrenal Cortex	Aldosterone Cortisol Androgens	Addison's Disease Cushing's Disease
Adrenal Medulla	Epinephrine Norepinephrine	Anxiety Attacks Depression
Anterior Pituitary	Adrenocorticotropic hormone (ACTH) Follicle-stimulating hormone (FSH) Gonadotropic hormones Growth hormone (GH) Luteinizing hormone (LH) Prolactin Thyroid Stimulating Hormone (TSH)	Dwarfism Gigantism
Hypothalamus/ Posterior Pituitary	Inhibiting hormones (stop the release of other hormones) Antidiuretic hormone (ADH) Oxytocin Releasing hormones (trigger the release of other hormones)	Diabetes Insipidus
Kidneys	Calcitriol Erythropoietin	Hypertension
Ovaries	Estrogen Progesterone	Endometriosis Menometrorrhagia
Pancreas	Insulin Glucagon	Diabetes Mellitus
Parathyroid	Parathyroid hormone	Tetany Renal calculi
Pineal	Melatonin	Alzheimer's Disease
Testes	Testosterone	Gynecomastia Klinefelter Syndrome
Thymus	Thymic factor (TF) Thymosin Thymic humoral factor (THF) Thymopoietin	DiGeorge Syndrome

Gland	Hormones	Disease
Thyroid	Calcitonin Thyroxine (T4) Triiodothyronine (T3)	Cretinism Hypo/Hyperthyroidism Goiter Myxedema
Digestive tract	Gastrin Cholecystokinin Secretin Ghrelin Motilin	Gastritis Gastroesophageal reflux

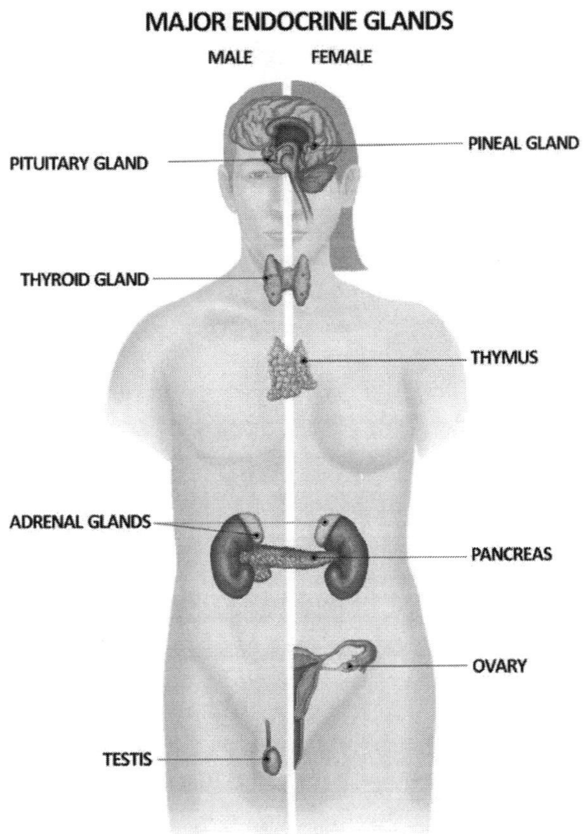

Review Video: Endocrine System
Visit mometrix.com/academy and enter code: 678939

Immune and Lymphatic Systems

Immune System

The **immune system** in animals defends the body against infection and disease. The immune system can be divided into two broad categories: innate immunity and adaptive immunity. **Innate immunity** includes the skin and mucous membranes, which provide a physical barrier to prevent pathogens from entering the body. Special chemicals including enzymes and proteins in mucus, tears, sweat, and stomach juices destroy pathogens. Numerous white blood cells such as neutrophils and macrophages protect the body from invading pathogens. **Adaptive immunity** involves the body responding to a specific antigen. Typically, B-lymphocytes or B cells produce antibodies against a specific antigen, and T-lymphocytes or T-cells take special roles as helpers, regulators, or killers. Some T-cells function as memory cells.

Review Video: Immune System
Visit mometrix.com/academy and enter code: 622899

Lymphatic System

The **lymphatic system** is connected to the cardiovascular system through a network of capillaries. The lymphatic system filters out organisms that cause disease, controls the production of disease-fighting antibodies, and produces white blood cells. The lymphatic system also prevents body tissues from swelling by draining fluids from them. Two of the most important areas in this system are the right lymphatic duct and the thoracic duct. The **right lymphatic duct** moves the immunity-bolstering lymph fluid through the top half of the body, while the **thoracic duct** moves lymph throughout the lower half. The spleen, thymus, and lymph nodes all generate and store the chemicals which form lymph and which are essential to protecting the body from disease.

The **lymphatic system** consists of the **thymus**, **lymph nodes**, **bone marrow**, and **spleen**. They primarily serve to distribute filtered fluids throughout the body and to remove excess fluid and debris. **White blood cells** are a key element of the lymphatic system which serve to prevent disease and repair the body after infection to prevent further illness.

Integumentary System

The integumentary system includes skin, hair, nails, sense receptors, sweat glands, and oil glands. The **skin** acts as a sensory organ, provides an exterior barrier against disease, regulates body temperature through perspiration, manufactures chemicals and hormones, and provides a place for nerves from the nervous system and parts of the circulation system to travel through. Skin has three layers: epidermis, dermis, and subcutaneous. The **epidermis** is the thin, outermost, waterproof layer. The **dermis** has the sweat glands, oil glands, and hair follicles. The **subcutaneous layer** has connective tissue. Also, this layer has **adipose** (i.e., fat) tissue, nerves, arteries, and veins.

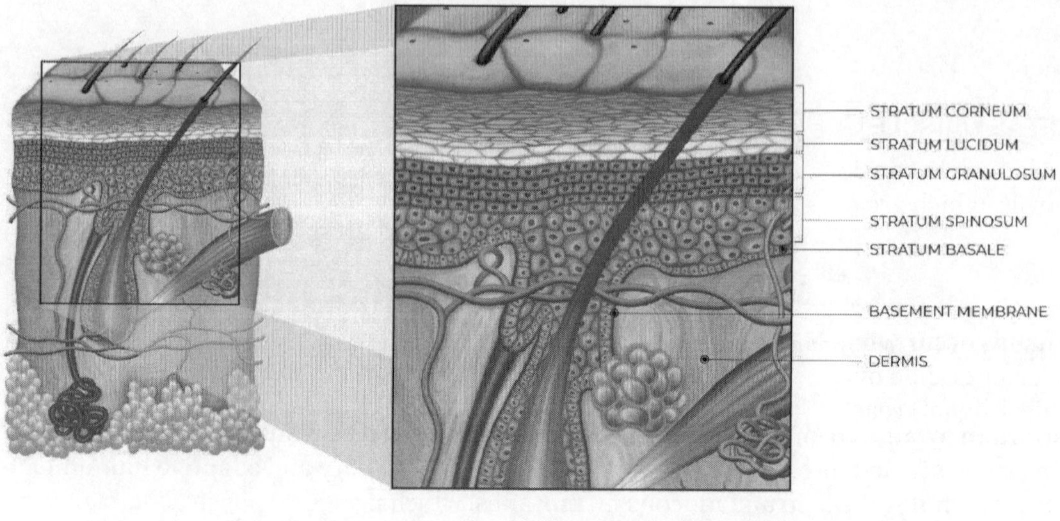

Review Video: Integumentary System
Visit mometrix.com/academy and enter code: 655980

Muscular System

The **muscular system** works in concert with the **skeletal system** to move the body and perform such core functions as cardiac activity. Key elements include:

- **Smooth muscle tissues** are involuntary muscles that are found in the walls of internal organs such as the stomach, intestines, and blood vessels. Smooth muscle tissues, or **visceral tissue,** is nonstriated. Smooth muscle cells are shorter and wider than skeletal muscle fibers. Smooth muscle tissue is also found in sphincters or valves that control the movement of material through openings throughout the body.
- **Cardiac muscle** tissue is involuntary muscle that is found only in the heart. Like skeletal muscle cells, cardiac muscle cells are also striated.
- **Skeletal muscles** are voluntary muscles that work in pairs to move parts of the skeleton. Skeletal muscles are composed of **muscle fibers** (cells) that are bound together in parallel bundles. Skeletal muscles are also known as **striated muscle** due to their striped histological appearance under a microscope.

Only skeletal muscle interacts with the skeleton to move the body. When they contract, the muscles transmit force to the attached bones. Working together, the muscles and bones act as a system of levers that move around the joints.

Review Video: Muscular System
Visit mometrix.com/academy and enter code: 967216

Major Muscles

The human body has more than 650 skeletal muscles than account for approximately half of a person's weight. Starting with the head and face, the temporalis and masseter move the mandible (lower jaw bone). The orbicularis oculi closes the eye. The orbicularis oris draws the lips together. The sternocleidomastoids move the head. The trapezius moves the shoulder, and the pectoralis major, deltoid, and latissimus dorsi move the upper arm. The biceps brachii and the triceps brachii move the lower arm. The rectus abdominis, external oblique, and erector spine move the trunk. The external and internal obliques elevate and depress the ribs. The gluteus maximus moves the upper leg. The quadriceps femoris, hamstrings, and sartorius move the lower leg. The gastrocnemius and the soleus extend the foot.

Skeletal Muscle Contraction

Skeletal muscles consist of numerous muscle fibers. Each muscle fiber contains a bundle of myofibrils, which are composed of multiple repeating contractile units called sarcomeres. **Myofibrils** contain two protein microfilaments: a thick filament and a thin filament. The **thick filament** is composed of the protein myosin. The **thin filament** is composed of the protein actin. The dark bands (striations) in skeletal muscles are formed when thick and thin filaments overlap. Light bands occur where the thin filament is overlapped. Skeletal muscle attraction occurs when the thin filaments slide over the thick filaments shortening the sarcomere. When an action potential (electrical signal) reaches a muscle fiber, calcium ions are released. According to the sliding filament model of muscle contraction, these calcium ions bind to the myosin and actin, which assists in the binding of the myosin heads of the thick filaments to the actin molecules of the thin filaments. Adenosine triphosphate released from glucose provides the energy necessary for the contraction.

Review Video: Muscular System
Visit mometrix.com/academy and enter code: 967216

SKELETAL SYSTEM

The skeletal system serves many functions including providing structural support, movement, and protection; producing blood cells; and storing substances such as fat and minerals. The **axial skeleton** transfers the weight from the upper body to the lower appendages. Bones provide attachment points for muscles. The cranium protects the brain. The vertebrae protect the spinal cord. The rib cage protects the heart and lungs. The pelvis protects the reproductive organs. **Joints** including hinge joints, ball-and-socket joints, pivot joints, ellipsoid joints, gliding joints, and saddle joints. The **red marrow** manufactures red and white blood cells. All bone marrow is red at birth, but adults have approximately one-half red bone marrow and one-half yellow bone marrow. Yellow bone marrow stores fat.

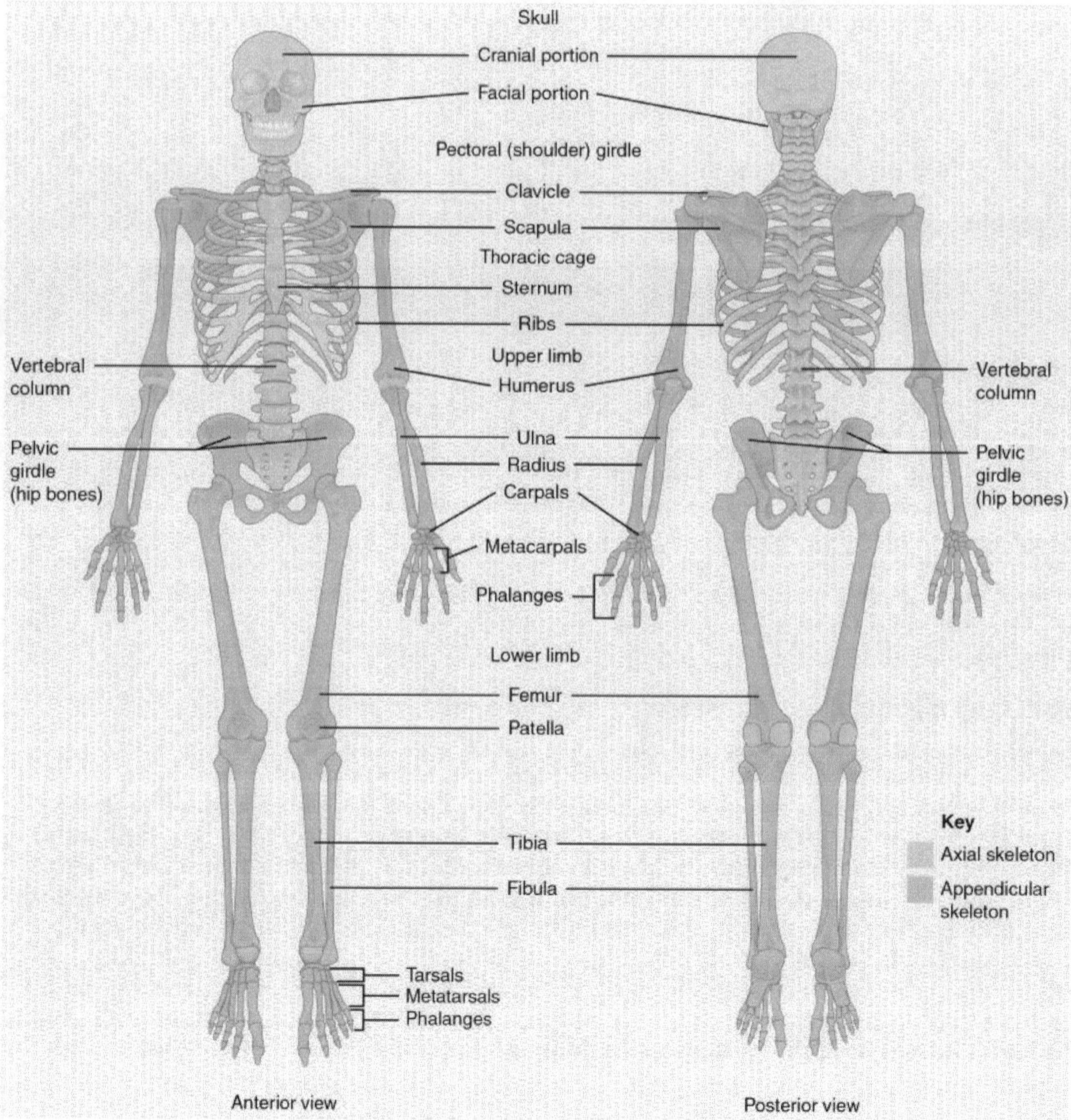

Structure of Axial Skeleton and Appendicular Skeleton

The **human skeletal system**, which consists of 206 bones along with numerous tendons, ligaments, and cartilage, is divided into the axial skeleton and the appendicular skeleton.

The **axial skeleton** consists of 80 bones and includes the vertebral column, rib cage, sternum, skull, and hyoid bone. The **vertebral column** consists of 33 vertebrae classified as cervical vertebrae, thoracic vertebrae, lumbar vertebrae, and sacral vertebrae. The **rib cage** includes 12 paired ribs, 10 pairs of true ribs and two pairs of floating ribs, and the **sternum**, which consists of the manubrium, corpus sterni, and xiphoid process. The **skull** includes the cranium and facial bones. The **ossicles** are bones in the middle ear. The **hyoid bone** provides an attachment point for the tongue muscles. The axial skeleton protects vital organs including the brain, heart, and lungs.

The **appendicular skeleton** consists of 126 bones including the pectoral girdle, pelvic girdle, and appendages. The **pectoral girdle** consists of the scapulae (shoulder blades) and clavicles (collarbones). The **pelvic girdle** attaches to the sacrum at the sacroiliac joint. The upper appendages (arms) include the humerus, radius, ulna, carpals, metacarpals, and phalanges. The lower appendages (legs) include the femur, patella, fibula, tibia, tarsals, metatarsals, and phalanges.

The axial skeleton and the appendicular skeleton:

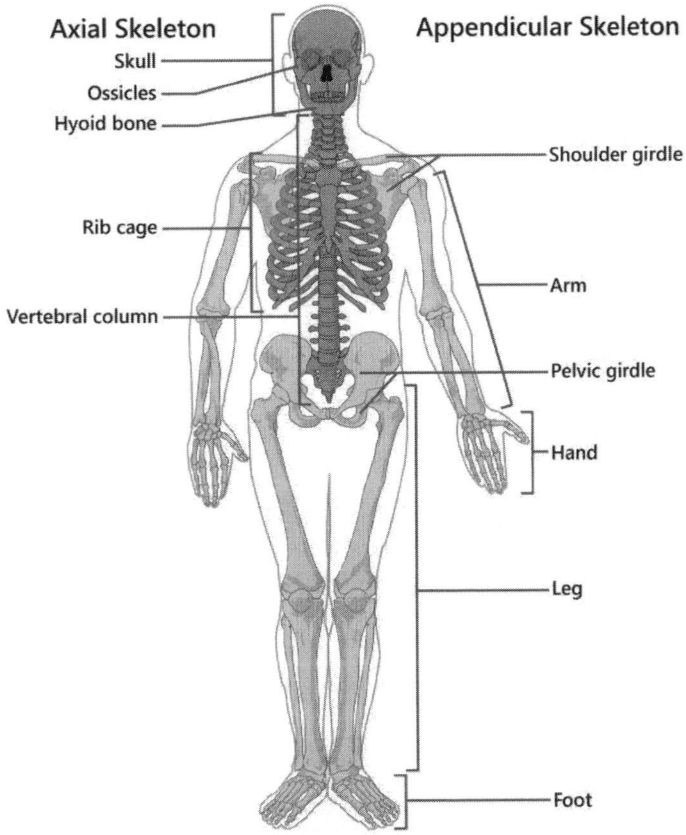

Review Video: Skeletal System
Visit mometrix.com/academy and enter code: 256447

Nervous System

The human **nervous system** consists of the **central nervous system** (i.e., brain and spinal cord) and the **peripheral nervous system** (i.e., nerves). They deliver voluntary and involuntary messages throughout the body. Core functions, such as digestion and respiration, are controlled by the brain via messages sent through the peripheral nervous system. The brain also receives external cues to regulate temperature and activate certain muscle groups.

> **Review Video: Function of the Nervous System**
> Visit mometrix.com/academy and enter code: 708428

The human nervous system senses, interprets, and issues commands as a response to conditions in the body's environment. This process is made possible by a complex communication system of cells called **neurons**.

Messages are sent across the plasma membrane of neurons through a process called **action potential**. These messages occur when a neuron is stimulated past a necessary threshold. These stimulations occur in a sequence from the stimulation point of one neuron to its contact with another neuron. At the point of contact, called a **chemical synapse**, a substance is released that stimulates or inhibits the action of the adjoining cell. A network of nerves composed of neurons fans out across the body and forms the framework for the nervous system. The direction the information flows depends on the specific organizations of nerve circuits and pathways.

> **Review Video: What is the Function of the Nervous System**
> Visit mometrix.com/academy and enter code: 708428

The Somatic Nervous system and the Reflex Arc

The somatic nervous system (**SNS**) controls the five senses and the voluntary movement of skeletal muscle. So, this system has all of the neurons that are connected to sense organs. Efferent (motor) and afferent (sensory) nerves help the somatic nervous system operate the senses and the movement of skeletal muscle. **Efferent nerves** bring signals from the central nervous system to the sensory organs and the muscles. **Afferent nerves** bring signals from the sensory organs and the muscles to the central nervous system. The somatic nervous system also performs involuntary movements which are known as reflex arcs.

A **reflex**, the simplest act of the nervous system, is an automatic response without any conscious thought to a stimulus via the reflex arc. The **reflex arc** is the simplest nerve pathway, which bypasses the brain and is controlled by the spinal cord. For example, in the classic knee-jerk response (patellar tendon reflex), the stimulus is the reflex hammer hitting the tendon, and the response is the muscle contracting, which jerks the foot upward. The stimulus is detected by sensory receptors, and a message is sent along a **sensory** (afferent) neuron to one or more

interneurons in the spinal cord. The interneuron(s) transmit this message to a **motor** (efferent) neuron, which carries the message to the correct **effector** (muscle).

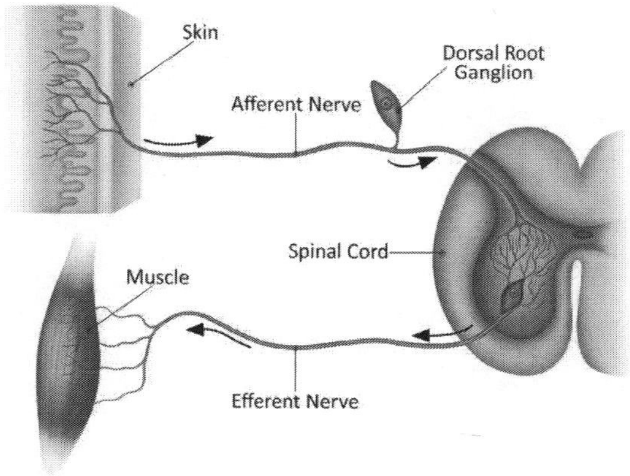

THE EYES

The eyes are a sensory organ, and therefore, belong to the nervous system. The main **parts of the eye** and their functions are as follows:

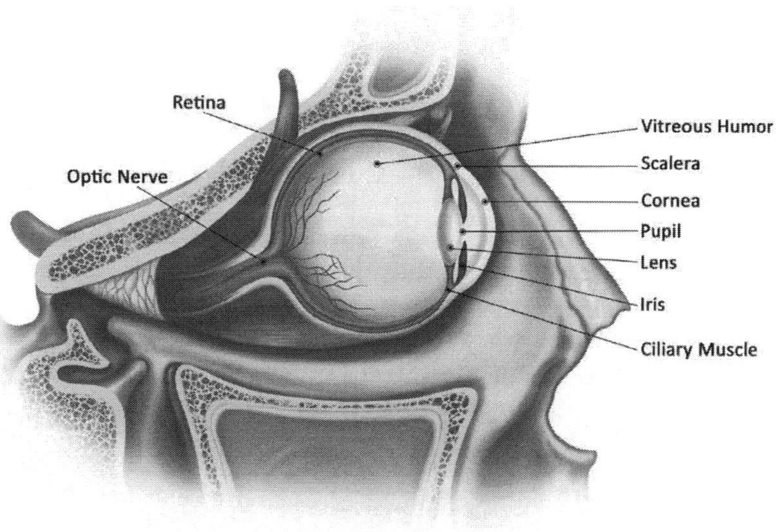

- **Aqueous humor** is watery fluid that maintains eye pressure.
- The **bony orbit** is the socket protecting the eye.
- **Cranial nerves** that help with the function of the eye such as movement or vision include:
    - the optic nerve (cranial nerve II)
    - oculomotor (III)
    - trochlear (IV)
    - trigeminal (V)
    - abducens (VI)
    - vagus (X) nerves
- **Eyelashes and lids** protect the eye and sweep out particles.
- **Extrinsic muscles** focus the eye.
- The **lacrimal glands** are tear ducts to moisten the eye.
- The **lens** refracts light.
- The **optic disc** is the blind spot.
- The **pupil** regulates light entry.
- The **retina** has rods for black and white imaging and cones for color imaging, and helps trigger the optic nerve to send impulses to the brain.
- The **macula** is at the retinal center that is very sensitive to light. The black spot in the center is called the fovea which provides the sharpest vision.
- The **choroid** is a black layer behind the retina that absorbs light and nourishes the retina.
- The **cornea** is the window at the front of the eye that helps with focus.
- The **iris** regulates light entry.
- The **sclera** is tough, white fibrous connective tissue holding nerves and vessels that acts as protection for the eye.
- The **suspensory ligament** connects the lens to the ciliary muscles of the iris.
- The **vitreous humor** is jelly that maintains the eye's shape and refracts images.

Reproductive System

The **reproductive system** consists of the prostate, testicle, penis, and scrotum in males and ovaries, uterus, vagina, fallopian tubes, and mammary glands in females. The primary function is the creation of human life. **Sperm** is produced by the testes and is delivered to the ovary-produced **eggs** in the fallopian tubes for fertilization. The uterus then serves as the home for the developing fetus. **Mammary glands** secrete nutrients for the newborn child.

Male Reproductive System

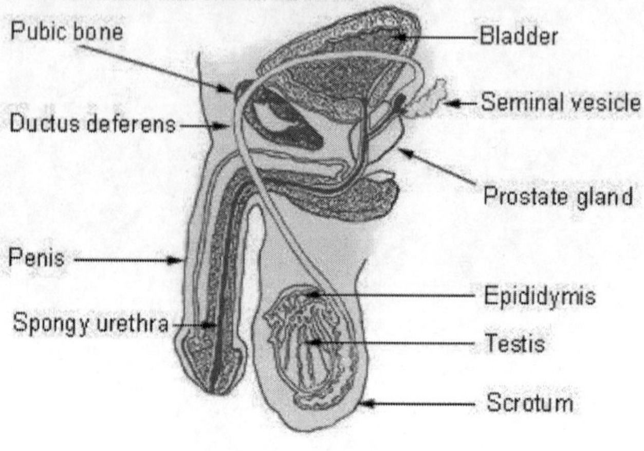

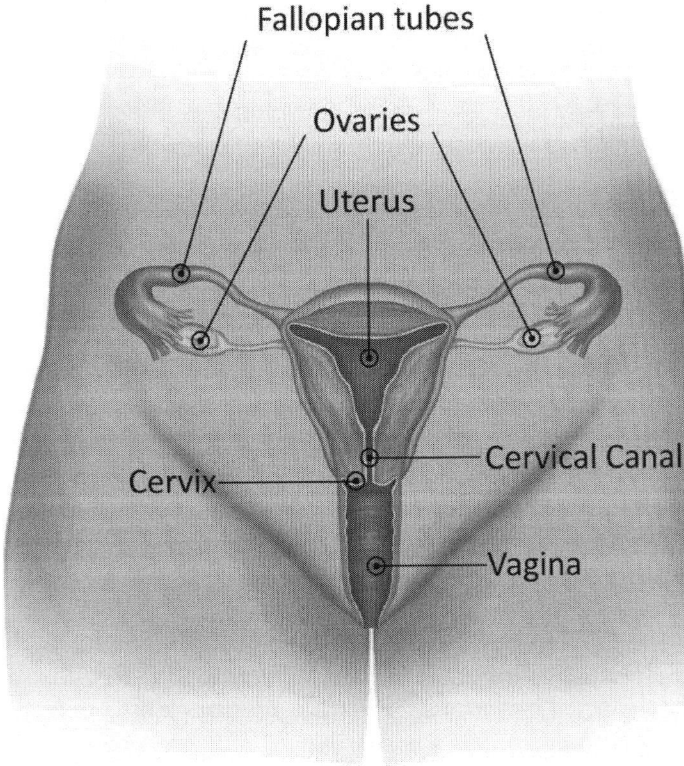

Review Video: Reproductive Systems
Visit mometrix.com/academy and enter code: 505450

Interconnectedness of Body Systems

Respiratory and Circulatory Systems Working Together

Body systems work in concert with each other to respond to increasing and decreasing demands on the body and regulate **homeostasis**, the manner in which the human body regulates itself based on internal and external conditions in order to maintain a physiological balance. For example, the heart pumps blood through the **circulatory system** to distribute oxygenated blood throughout the body to meet physiological demands at any given time. Blood becomes oxygenated in the lungs (**respiratory system**) after excess **carbon dioxide** is released from the body through respiration. Inspiration of **oxygen** into the lungs allows the blood to become oxygen-rich so as to be distributed throughout the body. When physiological demands of the body increase (i.e., quickly climbing stairs), inspiration of oxygen increases and the heart pumps faster in order to more efficiently increase the delivery of oxygenated blood throughout the body. When the intense physical activity subsides, breathing slows and the heart returns to a normal resting heart rate.

Impact of Diet and Exercise on the Circulatory System

The delivery of **oxygenated blood** throughout the body can be accomplished more efficiently with a pattern of consistent exercise and good dietary habits. **Aerobic** activity strengthens the heart by increasing the oxygen carrying capacity of the red blood cells (**hemoglobin**) while also lowering resting blood pressure. In addition, aerobic exercise helps increase high density lipoproteins (HDL) (i.e., "good cholesterol") and decreasing low density lipoproteins (i.e., "bad cholesterol") which helps keep the arteries (**circulatory system**) clear. Consistent and adequate physical activity also helps regulate blood sugars, which can reduce the likelihood of developing Type II diabetes. A high fiber, low fat diet also directly contributes to lower blood sugar levels, cholesterol management, and helps maintain healthy bowels (**digestive system**). Combining regular aerobic physical activity with a high fiber, low fat diet is one of the most effective methods to improve one's cardiovascular health, maintain a healthy weight, and increase personal longevity.

Homeostasis

Maintenance of Homeostasis in Organisms

Role of Feedback Mechanisms

Homeostasis is the regulation of internal chemistry to maintain a constant internal environment. This state is controlled through various feedback mechanisms that consist of receptors, an integrator, and effectors. **Receptors** such as mechanoreceptors or thermoreceptors in the skin detect the stimuli. Then, an **integrator**, such as the brain or spinal cord, receives the information concerning the stimuli and sends out signals to other parts of the body. Finally, **effectors**, such as muscles or glands, respond to the stimulus. Basically, the receptors receive the stimuli and notify an integrator, which signals the effectors to respond.

Feedback mechanisms can be negative or positive. **Negative-feedback** mechanisms are mechanisms that provide a decrease in response with an increase in stimulus that inhibits the stimulus, which in turn decreases the response. **Positive-feedback** mechanisms are mechanisms that provide an increase in response with an increase in stimulus, which actually increases the stimulus, which in turn increases the response.

Role of Hypothalamus

The hypothalamus plays a major role in the homoeostasis of vertebrates. The **hypothalamus** is the central portion of the brain just above the brainstem and is linked to the endocrine system through the pituitary gland. The hypothalamus releases special hormones that influence the secretion of pituitary hormones. The hypothalamus regulates the fundamental physiological state by controlling body temperature, hunger, thirst, sleep, behaviors related to attachment, sexual development, fight-or-flight stress response, and circadian rhythms.

Role of Endocrine System and Hormones

All vertebrates have an **endocrine system** that consists of numerous ductless glands that produce hormones to help coordinate many functions of the body. **Hormones** are signaling molecules that are received by receptors. Many hormones are secreted in response to signals from the pituitary gland and hypothalamus gland. Other hormones are secreted in response to signals from inside the body. Hormones can consist of amino acids, proteins, or lipid molecules such as steroid hormones. Hormones can affect target cells, which have the correct receptor that is able to bind to that particular hormone. Most cells have receptors for more than one type of hormone. Hormones are distributed to the target cells in the blood by the cardiovascular system. Hormones incorporate feedback mechanisms to help the body maintain homeostasis.

Role of Antidiuretic Hormone

Antidiuretic hormone (ADH) helps maintain homeostasis in vertebrates. ADH is produced by the posterior pituitary gland, and it regulates the reabsorption of water in the kidneys and concentrates the urine. The stimulus in this feedback mechanism is a drop in blood volume due to water loss. This signal is picked up by the hypothalamus, which signals the pituitary gland to secrete ADH. ADH is carried by the cardiovascular system to the nephrons in the kidneys signaling them to reabsorb more water and send less out as waste. As more water is reabsorbed, the blood volume increases, which is monitored by the hypothalamus. As the blood volume reaches the set point, the hypothalamus signals for a decrease in the secretion of ADH, and the cycle continues.

Role of Insulin and Glucagon

Insulin and glucagon are hormones that help maintain the glucose concentration in the blood. Insulin and glucagon are secreted by the clumps of endocrine cells called the **pancreatic islets** that are located in the pancreas. Insulin and glucagon work together to maintain the blood glucose level. **Insulin** stimulates cells to remove glucose from the blood. **Glucagon** stimulates the liver to convert glycogen to glucose. After eating, glucose levels increase in the blood. This stimulus signals the pancreas to stop the secretion of glucagon and to start secreting insulin. Cells respond to the insulin and remove glucose from the blood, lowering the level of glucose in the blood. Later, after eating, the level of glucose in the blood decreases further. This stimulus signals the pancreas to secrete glucagon and decrease the secretion of insulin. In response to the stimulus, the liver converts glycogen to glucose, and the level of glucose in the blood rises. When the individual eats, the cycle begins again.

Thermoregulation

Animals exhibit many adaptations that help them achieve homeostasis, or a stable internal environment. Some of these adaptions are behavioral. Most organisms exhibit some type of behavioral thermoregulation. **Thermoregulation** is the ability to keep the body temperature within certain boundaries. The type of behavioral thermoregulation depends on whether the animal is an ectotherm or an endotherm. **Ectotherms** are "cold-blooded," and their body temperature changes with their external environment. **Endotherms** are "warm-blooded" and maintain a stable body temperature by internal means.

To regulate their temperature, ectotherms often move to an appropriate location. For example, fish move to warmer waters while animals will climb to higher grounds. **Diurnal ectotherms** such as reptiles often bask in the sun to increase their body temperatures. Butterflies are special ectotherms classified as **heliotherms** since they get nearly all of their heat from basking in the sun.

While they have internal systems that regulate temperature, many endotherms that live in hot environments have adapted to the nocturnal lifestyle. Desert animals are often nocturnal to escape high daytime temperatures. Other nocturnal animals sleep during the day in underground burrows or dens.

Reproduction, Development, and Growth in Animals

Gamete Formation

Gametogenesis is the formation of gametes, or reproductive cells. Gametes are produced by meiosis. **Meiosis** is a special type of cell division that consists of two consecutive mitotic divisions referred to as meiosis I and meiosis II. **Meiosis I** is a reduction division in which a diploid cell is reduced to two haploid daughter cells that contain only one of each pair of homologous chromosomes. During **meiosis II**, those haploid cells are further divided to form four haploid cells. **Spermatogenesis** in males produces four viable sperm cells from each complete cycle of meiosis. **Oogenesis** produces four daughter cells, but only one is a viable egg and the other three are polar bodies.

Fertilization

Fertilization is the union of a sperm cell and an egg cell to produce a zygote. Many sperm may bind to an egg, but only one joins with the egg and injects its nuclei into the egg. Fertilization can be external or internal. **External fertilization** takes place outside of the female's body. For example, many fish, amphibians, crustaceans, mollusks, and corals reproduce externally by **spawning** or releasing gametes into the water simultaneously or right after each other. Reptiles and birds reproduce by **internal fertilization**. All mammals except monotremes (e.g. platypus) reproduce by internal fertilization.

Embryonic Development

Embryonic development in animals is typically divided into four stages: cleavage, patterning, differentiation, and growth. **Cleavage** occurs immediately after fertilization when the large single-celled zygote immediately begins to divide into smaller and smaller cells without an increase in mass. A hollow ball of cells forms a blastula. Next, during patterning, gastrulation occurs. During gastrulation, the cells are organized into three primary germ layers: ectoderm, mesoderm, and endoderm. Then, the cells in these layers differentiate into special tissues and organs. For example, the nervous system develops from the ectoderm. The muscular system develops from the mesoderm. Much of the digestive system develops from the endoderm. The final stage of embryonic development is growth and further tissue specialization. The embryo continues to grow until ready for hatching or birth.

Postnatal Growth

Postnatal growth occurs from hatching or birth until death. The length of the postnatal growth depends on the species. Elephants can live 70 years, but mice only about 4 years. Right after animals are hatched or born, they go through a period of rapid growth and development. In vertebrates, bones lengthen, muscles grow in bulk, and fat is deposited. At maturity, bones stop growing in length, but bones can grow in width and repair themselves throughout the animal's lifetime, and muscle deposition slows down. Fat cells continue to increase and decrease in size throughout the animal's life. Growth is controlled by genetics but is also influenced by nutrition and disease. Most animals are sexually mature in less than two years and can produce offspring.

Characteristics of Major Plant Divisions

Vascular and Nonvascular Plants

Vascular plants, also referred to as **tracheophytes**, have dermal tissue, meristematic tissue, ground tissues, and vascular tissues. Nonvascular plants, also referred to as **bryophytes**, do not have the vascular tissue xylem and phloem. Vascular plants can grow very tall, whereas nonvascular plants are short and close to the ground. Vascular plants can be found in dry regions, but nonvascular plants typically grow near or in moist areas. Vascular plants have leaves, roots, and stems, but nonvascular plants have leaf-like, root-like, and stem-like structures that do not have true vascular tissue. Nonvascular plants have hair-like **rhizoids**, that act like roots by anchoring them to the ground and absorbing water. Vascular plants include angiosperms, gymnosperms, and ferns. Nonvascular plants include mosses and liverworts.

Flowering Versus Nonflowering Plants

Angiosperms and gymnosperms are both vascular plants. **Angiosperms** are flowering plants, and **gymnosperms** are non-flowering plants. Angiosperms reproduce by seeds that are enclosed in an ovary, usually in a fruit, while gymnosperms reproduce by unenclosed or "naked" seeds on scales, leaves, or cones. Angiosperms can be further classified as either monocots or dicots, depending on if they have one or two cotyledons, respectively. Angiosperms include grasses, garden flowers, vegetables, and broadleaf trees such as maples, birches, elms, and oaks. Gymnosperms include conifers such as pines, spruces, cedars, and redwoods.

Review Video: Kingdom Plantae Characteristics
Visit mometrix.com/academy and enter code: 710084

Monocots and Dicots

Angiosperms can be classified as either monocots or dicots. The seeds of **monocots** have one cotyledon, and the seeds of **dicots** have two cotyledons. The flowers of monocots have petals in multiples of three, and the flowers of dicots have petals in multiples of four or five. The leaves of monocots are slender with parallel veins, while the leaves of dicots are broad and flat with branching veins. The vascular bundles in monocots are distributed throughout the stem, whereas the vascular bundles in dicots are arranged in rings. Monocots have a **fibrous root system**, and dicots have a **taproot system**.

Major Plant Tissues and Organs

Plant Dermal Tissue

Plant dermal tissue is called the epidermis, and is usually a single layer of closely-packed cells that covers leaves and young stems. The epidermis protects the plant by secreting the cuticle, which is a waxy substance that helps prevent water loss and infections. The epidermis in leaves has tiny pores called **stomata**. Guard cells in the epidermis control the opening and closing of the stomata. The epidermis usually does not have chloroplasts. The epidermis may be replaced by periderm in older plants. The **periderm** is also referred to as bark. The layers of the periderm are cork cells or phellem, phelloderm, and cork cambium or phellogen. Cork is the outer layer of the periderm and consists of nonliving cells. The periderm protects the plant and provides insulation.

Plant Vascular Tissue

The two major types of plant vascular tissue are xylem and phloem. Xylem and phloem are bound together in vascular bundles. A meristem called vascular cambium is located between the xylem and phloem and produces new xylem and phloem. **Xylem** is made up of tracheids and vessel elements. All vascular plants contain tracheids, but only angiosperms contain vessel elements. Xylem provides support and transports water and dissolved minerals unidirectionally from the roots upward using processes like transpiration pull and root pressure. Phloem is made up of companion cells and sieve-tube cells. **Phloem** transports dissolved sugars produced during photosynthesis and other nutrients bidirectionally to non-photosynthetic areas of the plant. By active transport, the companion vessels move glucose in and out of the sieve-tube cells.

Plant Ground Tissue

The three major types of ground tissue are parenchyma tissue, collenchyma tissue, and sclerenchyma tissue. Most ground tissue is made up of parenchyma. **Parenchyma** is formed by parenchyma cells, and it function in photosynthesis, food storage, and tissue repair. The inner tissue of a leaf, mesophyll, is an example of parenchyma tissue. **Collenchyma** is made of collenchyma cells and provides support in roots, stems, and petioles. **Sclerenchyma** tissue is made of sclereid cells, which are more rigid than the collenchyma cells, and provides rigid support and protection. Plant sclerenchyma tissue may contain cellulose or lignin. Fabrics such as jute, hemp, and flax are made of sclerenchyma tissue.

PLANT MERISTEMATIC TISSUE

Meristems or meristematic tissues are regions of plant growth. The cells in meristems are undifferentiated and always remain **totipotent**, which means they can always develop into any type of special tissue. Meristem cells can divide and produce new cells, which can aid in the process of regenerating damaged parts. Cells of meristems reproduce asexually through mitosis or cell division that is regulated by hormones. The two types of meristems are lateral meristems and apical meristems. **Primary growth** occurs at **apical meristems**, located at the tip of roots and shoots, and increases the length of the plant. Primary meristems include the protoderm, which produces epidermis; the procambium, which produces cambium, or lateral meristems; xylem and phloem; and the ground meristem, which produces ground tissue including parenchyma. **Secondary growth** occurs at the lateral or secondary meristems and causes an increase in diameter or thickness.

FLOWERS

The primary function of flowers is to produce seeds for reproduction of the plant. Flowers have a **pedicel**, a stalk with a receptacle or enlarged upper portion, which holds the developing seeds. Flowers also can have sepals and petals. **Sepals** are leaflike structures that protect the bud. **Petals**, which are collectively called the corolla, help to attract pollinators. Plants can have stamens, pistils, or both depending on the type of plant. The **stamen** consists of the anther and filament. The end of the stamen is called the **anther** and is where pollen is produced. Pollen also contains sperm, which is needed in order for a proper plant zygot to form. The **pistil** consists of the stigma, style, and ovary. The ovary contains the ovules, which house the egg cells.

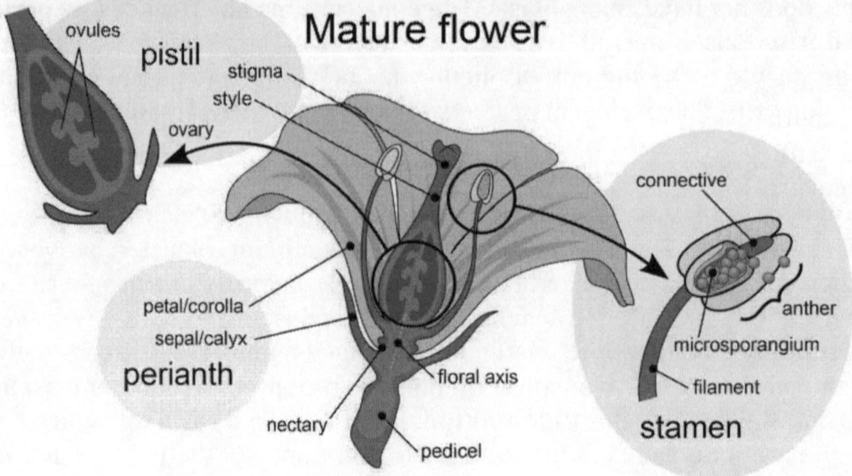

STEMS

Plants can have either woody or nonwoody (herbaceous) stems. **Woody** stems consist of wood, or bark, as a structural tissue, while **herbaceous** stems are very flexible. The stem is divided into nodes and internodes. Buds are located at the nodes and may develop into leaves, roots, flowers, cones, or more stems. Stems consist of dermal tissue, ground tissue, and vascular tissue. **Monocot stems have vascular bundles distributed through the stem. Dicots have rings of vascular bundles**. Stems have four main functions: (1) they provide support to leaves, flowers, and fruits;

(2) they transport materials in the xylem and phloem; (3) they store food; and (4) they have meristems, which provide all of the new cells for the plant.

MONOCOT	DICOT
Single Cotyledon 	Two Cotyledon 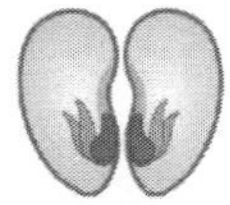
Long Narrow Leaf Parallel Veins 	Broad Leaf Network of Veins 
Vascular Bundles Scattered 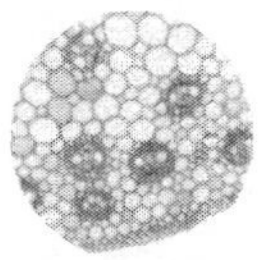	Vascular Bundles in a Ring 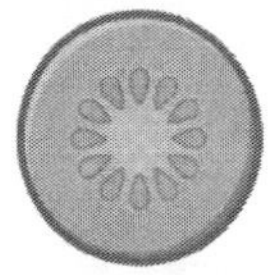
Floral Parts in Multiples of 3 	Floral Parts in Multiples of 4 or 5 

LEAVES

The primary function of a **leaf** is to manufacture food through photosynthesis. The leaf consists of a flat portion called the **blade** and a stalk called the **petiole**. The edge of the leaf is called the margin and can be entire, toothed, or lobed. Veins transport food and water and make up the skeleton of the leaf. The large central vein is called the **midrib**. The blade has an upper and lower epidermis. The epidermis is covered by a protective cuticle. The lower epidermis contains many stomata, which are pores that allow air to enter and leave the leaf. Stomata also regulate transpiration. The middle portion of the leaf is called the **mesophyll**. The mesophyll consists of the palisade mesophyll and the spongy mesophyll. Most photosynthesis occurs in chloroplasts located in the palisade mesophyll.

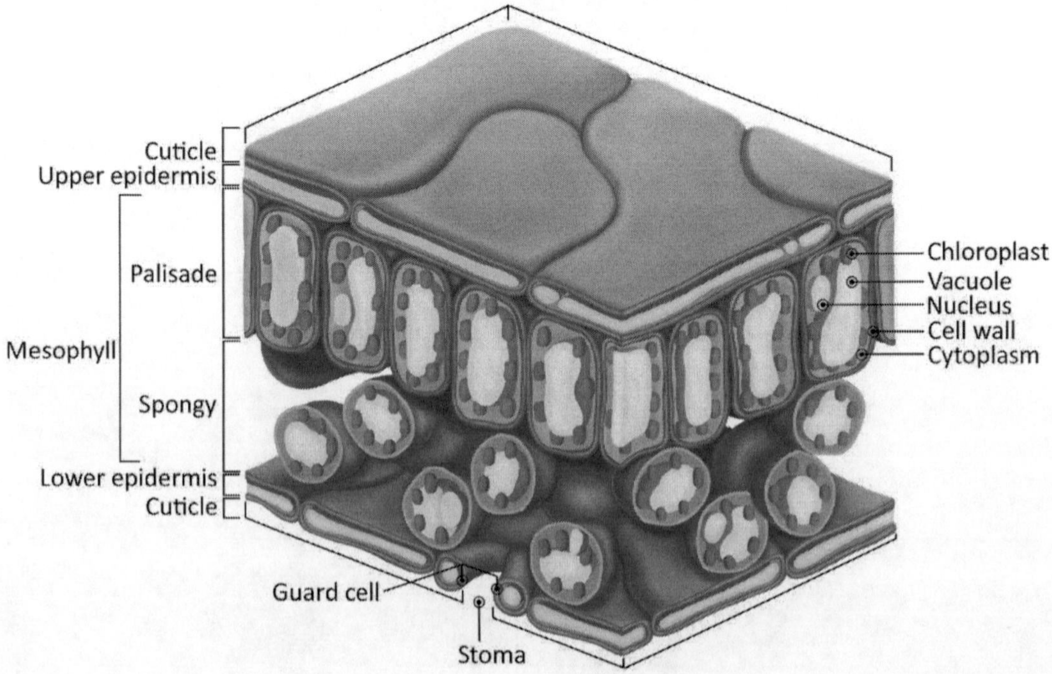

Roots

The primary functions of roots are to anchor the plant, absorb materials, and store food. The two basic types of root systems are taproot systems and fibrous root systems. **Taproot systems** have a primary root with many smaller secondary roots. **Fibrous root systems**, which lack a primary root, consist of a mass of many small secondary roots. The root has three main regions: the area of maturation, the area of elongation, and the area of cell division or the meristematic region. The root is covered by an epidermal cell, some of which develops into root hairs. **Root hairs** absorb water and minerals by osmosis, and capillary action helps move the water upward through the roots to the rest of the plant. The center of the root is the **vascular cylinder**, which contains the xylem and phloem. The vascular cylinder is surrounded by the cortex where the food is stored. Primary growth occurs at the root tip. Secondary growth occurs at the vascular cambium located between the xylem and phloem.

Plant Life Cycles and Reproductive Strategies

Pollination Strategies

Pollination is the transfer of pollen from the anther of the stamen to the stigma of the pistil on the same plant or on a different plant. Pollinators can be either **abiotic** (not derived from a living organism) or **biotic** (derived from a living organism). Abiotic pollinators include wind and water. Approximately 20% of pollination occurs by abiotic pollinators. For example, grasses are typically pollinated by wind, and aquatic plants are typically pollinated by water. Biotic pollinators include insects, birds, mammals, and occasionally reptiles. Most biotic pollinators are insects. Many plants have colored petals and strong scents, which attract insects. Pollen rubs off on the insects and is transferred as they move from plant to plant.

Seed Dispersal Methods

Methods of **seed dispersal** can be abiotic or biotic. Methods of seed dispersal include gravity, wind, water, and animals. Some plants produce seeds in fruits that get eaten by animals and then are distributed to new locations in the animals' waste. Some seeds (e.g. dandelions) have structures to aid in dispersal by wind. Some seeds have barbs that get caught in animal hair or bird feathers and are then carried to new locations by the animals. Interestingly, some animals bury seeds for food storage but do not return for the seeds. The seeds of aquatic plants can be dispersed by water, while the seeds of plants near rivers, streams, lakes, and beaches (e.g. coconuts) are also often dispersed by water. Some plants, in a method called **mechanical dispersal**, can propel or shoot their seeds away from them even up to several feet. For example, touch-me-nots and violets utilize mechanical dispersal.

Alternation of Generations

Alternation of generations, also referred to as **metagenesis**, contains both a sexual phase and an asexual phase in the life cycle of the plant. Mosses and ferns reproduce by alternation of generations: the sexual phase is called the **gametophyte**, and the asexual phase is called the **sporophyte**. During the sexual phase, a sperm fertilizes an egg to form a zygote. By mitosis, the zygote develops into the sporophyte. The sporangia in the sori of the sporophyte produce the spores through meiosis. The spores germinate and by mitosis produce the gametophyte.

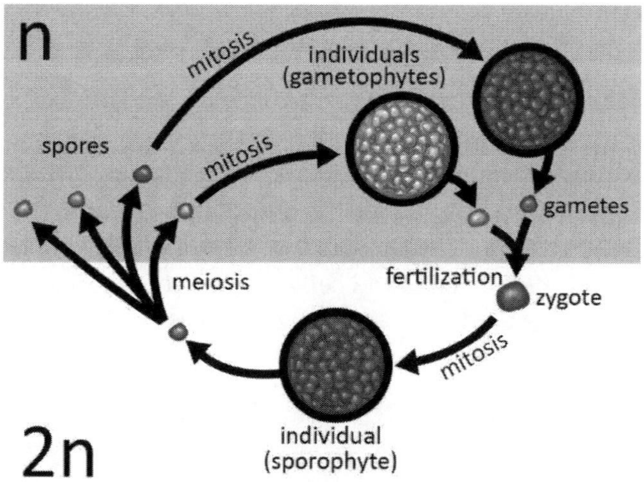

Plant Transportation of Water and Nutrients

Obtaining and Transporting Water and Inorganic Nutrients

Inorganic nutrients and water enter plants through the root hair and travel to the xylem. Once the water, minerals, and salts have crossed the endodermis, they must be moved upward through the xylem by water uptake. Most of a plant's water is lost through the stomata by transpiration. This loss is necessary to provide the tension needed to pull the water and nutrients up through the xylem. In order to maintain the remaining water that is necessary for the functioning of the plant, guard cells control the stomata. Whether an individual stoma is closed or open is controlled by two guard cells. When the guard cells lose water and become flaccid, they collapse together, closing the stoma. When the guard cells swell with water and become turgid, they move apart, opening the stoma.

Use of Roots

Plant roots have numerous root hairs that absorb water and inorganic nutrients such as minerals and salts. Root hairs are thin, hair-like outgrowths of the root's epidermal cells that exponentially increase the root's surface area. Water molecules cross the cell membranes of the root hairs by **osmosis** and then travel on to the vascular cylinder. Inorganic nutrients are transported across the cell membranes of the root endodermis by **active transport**. The endodermis is a single layer of cells that the water and nutrients must pass through by osmosis or active transport. To control mineral uptake by the roots, Casparian strips act as an extracellular diffusion barrier, and forces nutrients to be pulled into the plant. While water passes through by osmosis, mineral uptake is controlled by transport proteins.

Use of Xylem

The xylem contains dead, water-conducting cells called tracheids and vessels. The movement of water upward through the tracheids and vessels is explained by the **cohesion-tension theory**. First, water is lost through evaporation of the plant's surface through transpiration. This can occur at any surface exposed to air but is mainly through the stomata in the epidermis. This transpiration puts the water inside the xylem in a state of tension. Because water is cohesive due to the strong hydrogen bonds between molecules, the water is pulled up the xylem as long as the water is transpiring.

Products of Photosynthesis

Glucose Produced During Photosynthesis

Plants produce glucose, a simple carbohydrate or monosaccharide, during photosynthesis. Plants do not transport glucose molecules directly, but instead glucose undergoes reactions to form sucrose, starch, and cellulose which are then used in different ways. Glucose is joined to a fructose molecule to form **sucrose**, a disaccharide, which is transported in sap. Like glucose, sucrose is also considered a simple carbohydrate. Starches and cellulose are complex carbohydrates consisting of long chains of glucose molecules called polysaccharides. Plants use **starch** to store glucose, and **cellulose** for rigidity in cell walls.

Use of Phloem to Transport Products of Photosynthesis

The movement of sugars and other materials from the leaves to other tissues throughout the plants is called **translocation**. Nutrients are translocated from **sources**, or areas with excess sugars such as mature leaves, to **sinks**, areas where sugars are needed (i.e. roots or developing seeds). Phloem vessels are found in the vascular bundles along with the xylem. Phloem contains conducting cells called sieve elements, which are connected end to end in sieve tubes. **Sieve tubes** carry sap from sugar sources to sugar sinks. Phloem sap contains mostly sucrose dissolved in water. The sap can also contain proteins, amino acids, and hormones. Some plants transport sugar alcohols. Loading the sugar into the sieve tubes causes water to enter the tubes by osmosis, creating a higher hydrostatic pressure at the source end of the tube. This pressure is what causes nutrients to move upward towards the sink areas. Sugar is removed from the sieve tube at the sink end and the solute potential is increased, thus causing water to leave the phloem. This process is referred to as the **pressure-flow mechanism**.

Chapter Quiz

Ready to see how well you retained what you just read? Scan the QR code to go directly to the chapter quiz interface for this study guide. If you're using a computer, simply visit the online resources page at **mometrix.com/resources719/csetbiolifesci** and click the Chapter Quizzes link.

Ecosystems: Interactions, Energy, and Dynamics

Transform passive reading into active learning! After immersing yourself in this chapter, put your comprehension to the test by taking a quiz. The insights you gained will stay with you longer this way. Scan the QR code to go directly to the chapter quiz interface for this study guide. If you're using a computer, simply visit the online resources page at **mometrix.com/resources719/csetbiolifesci** and click the Chapter Quizzes link.

Hierarchical Structure of the Biosphere

Biosphere

Components

The **biosphere** is the region of the earth inhabited by living things. The components of the biosphere from smallest to largest are organisms, populations, communities, ecosystems, and biomes. Organisms of the same species make up a **population**. All of the populations in an area make up the **community**. The community combined with the physical environment for a region forms an **ecosystem**. Several ecosystems are grouped together to form large geographic regions called **biomes**.

Population

A **population** is a group of all the individuals of one species in a specific area or region at a certain time. A **species** is a group of organisms that can breed and produce fertile offspring. There may be many populations of a specific species in a large geographic region. **Ecologists** study the size, density, and growth rate of populations to determine their stability. Population size continuously changes with births, deaths, and migrations. The population density is the number of individuals per unit of area. Growth rates for a population may be exponential or logistic. Ecologists also study how the individuals are dispersed within a population. Some species form clusters, while others are evenly or randomly spaced. However, every population has limiting factors. Changes in the environment or geography can reduce or limit population size. The individuals of a population interact with each other and with other organisms in the community in various ways, including competition and predation, which have direct impacts population size.

Community Interactions

A **community** is all of the populations of different species that live in an area and interact with each other. Community interaction can be intraspecific or interspecific. **Intraspecific interactions** occur between members of the same species. **Interspecific interactions** occur between members of different species. Different types of interactions include competition, predation, and symbiosis. Communities with high diversity are more complex and more stable than communities with low diversity. The level of diversity can be seen in a food web of the community, which shows all the feeding relationships within the community.

Ecosystems

An **ecosystem** is the basic unit of ecology. An ecosystem is the sum of all the biotic and abiotic factors in an area. **Biotic factors** are all living things such as plants, animals, fungi, and microorganisms. **Abiotic factors** include the light, water, air, temperature, and soil in an area. Ecosystems obtain the energy they need from sunlight. Ecosystems also contain biogeochemical cycles such as the hydrologic cycle and the nitrogen cycle. Ecosystems are generally classified as either terrestrial or aquatic. All of the living things within an ecosystem are called its community. The number and variety of living things within a community describes the ecosystem's **biodiversity**. However, each ecosystem can only support a limited number of organisms known as the **carrying capacity**.

Influences on Population Size

Biotic and Abiotic Factors in an Ecosystem

Every ecosystem consists of multiple abiotic and biotic factors. **Abiotic factors** are the nonbiological physical and chemical factors that affect the ecosystem. Abiotic factors include soil type, atmospheric conditions, sunlight, water, wind, chemical elements, and natural disturbances. In aquatic ecosystems, abiotic factors include salinity, turbidity, water depth, current, temperature, and light. **Biotic factors** are all of the living organisms in the ecosystem. Biotic factors include plants, algae, fungi, bacteria, archaea, animals, and protozoa.

Influence of Resource Availability and Abiotic Factors on Population Size

Population size is affected by resource availability and abiotic factors. As the population density increases, intraspecific competition for available resources intensifies. If the availability of resources decreases, death rates may increase and birth rates may decrease. For example, territoriality for mating or nesting may limit available resources for individuals in a population and limit the population size. Abiotic factors such as temperature, rainfall, wind, and light intensity all influence the population size. For example, temperatures near a species' tolerance limit may decrease the population. Natural disasters such as fire or flood can destroy resources and greatly decrease a population's size. In general, any abiotic factor that reduces or limits resources will also reduce or limit population size.

Significance of Habitat and Niche to Populations

The **habitat** of an organism is the type of place where that organism usually lives. A habitat is a piece of an environmental area, which may be a geographic area or even the body of another organism. The habitat describes an organism's natural living environment. A habitat includes biotic and abiotic factors such as temperature, light, food resources, and predators. Whereas a habitat describes an organism's "home," a niche can be thought of as an organism's "occupation." A **niche** describes an organism's functional role in the community and how the organism uses its habitat. A niche can be quite complex because it should include the impacts that the organism has on the biotic and abiotic surroundings. Niches can be broad or narrow.

Influence of Competition and Predation on Population Size

Feeding relationships between organisms can affect population size. Competition and predation both tend to limit population size. **Competition** occurs when two individuals need the same resource. This competition can be **intraspecific**, which is between members of the same species, or **interspecific**, which is between members of different species. Intraspecific competition reduces resources as that species' own population increases, which limits population growth. Interspecific competition reduces resources as a different species uses those same resources. **Predation** occurs when one individual is a food resource for another individual. Predator and prey populations can cycle over a range of years. If prey resources increase, predator numbers increase. An example of the predator-prey population cycle is the Canadian lynx and snowshoe hare.

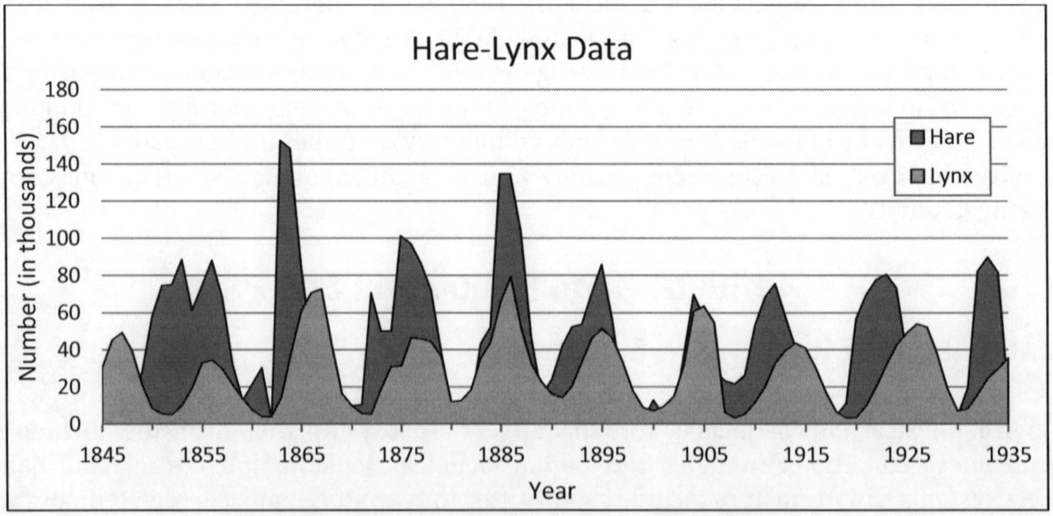

Models of Population Growth

Logistic Population Growth Model

Populations vary over time due to deaths, births, immigration, and emigration. In most situations, resources such as food, water, and shelter are limited. Each environment or habitat can only support a limited number of individuals, which is known as the **carrying capacity**. Population growth models that factor in the carrying capacity are called **logistic growth models**. With logistic population growth models, the rate of population growth decreases as the population size increases. Logistic growth graphs as an S-shaped curve. Comparing logistic growth and exponential growth shows that the graph for exponential growth continues to become steeper, but the graph for logistics growth levels off once the population reaches the carrying capacity. As the population increases, fewer resources are available per individual. This limits the number of individuals that can occupy that environment or habitat.

Exponential Population Growth Model

While populations change over time due to births, deaths, and migrations, sometimes conditions are near ideal and populations can increase at their maximum rate, exhibiting exponential growth. **Exponential growth** is growth in which the rate of change is proportional to the increasing size in an exponential progression. Exponential growth graphs as a J-shaped curve. Exponential growth is often observed in single-celled organisms such as bacteria or protozoa in which the population or number of cells increases by a factor of two per unit of time. One cell divides into two cells, which divide into four cells, and so forth. The exponential growth model describes population growth under ideal conditions and does not take limiting factors or carrying capacity into account. Realistically, exponential growth cannot occur indefinitely, but it may occur for a period of time. It does show a species' capacity for increase and may be helpful when studying a particular species or ecosystem. For example, if a species with no natural predator is introduced into a new habitat, that species may experience exponential growth. If this growth is allowed to go unchecked, the population may overshoot the carrying capacity and then starve. Efforts may need to be taken to reduce the population before this occurs.

Reproduction and Mortality in Populations

Advantages and Disadvantages of Asexual Reproduction in Animals

Very few species of animals reproduce by asexual reproduction, and nearly all of those species also have the ability to reproduce sexually. While not common, asexual reproduction is useful for animals that tend to stay in one place and may not find mates. Asexual reproduction takes considerably less effort and energy than sexual reproduction. In asexual reproduction, all of the offspring are genetically identical to the parent. This can be a disadvantage because of the lack of genetic variation. Although asexual reproduction is advantageous in a stable environment, if the environment changes, the organisms may lack the genetic variability to survive or selectively adapt.

Review Video: Asexual Reproduction
Visit mometrix.com/academy and enter code: 565616

Life Histories

The **life history** of a species describes the typical organism's life cycle from birth through reproduction to death. Life histories can typically be classified as opportunistic life histories or equilibrial life histories. Species exhibiting **opportunistic life histories** are typically small, short-lived organisms that have a high reproductive capacity but invest little time and care into their offspring. Their population sizes tend to oscillate significantly over periods of several years. Species exhibiting **equilibrial life histories** are typically large, long-lived organisms that have a low reproductive capacity but invest much time and care into their offspring. Their populations tend to fluctuate within a smaller range. A general observation is that species that tend to produce numerous offspring typically tend to invest little care into that offspring, resulting in a high mortality rate of that offspring. Organisms of species that tend to produce few offspring typically invest much more care into that offspring, resulting in a lower mortality rate.

Relationships between Species

Symbiosis

Many species share a special nutritional relationship with another species, called **symbiosis**. The term symbiosis means "living together." In symbiosis, two organisms share a close physical relationship that can be helpful, harmful, or neutral for each organism. Three forms of symbiotic relationships are parasitism, commensalism, and mutualism. **Parasitism** is a relationship between two organisms in which one organism is the parasite, and the other organism is the host. The parasite benefits from the relationship because the parasite obtains its nutrition from the host. The host is harmed from the relationship because the parasite is using the host's energy and giving nothing in return. For example, a tick and a dog share a parasitic relationship in which the tick is the parasite, and the dog is the host. **Commensalism** is a relationship between two organisms in which one benefits, and the other is not affected. For example, a small fish called a remora can attach to the belly of a shark and ride along. The remora is safe under the shark, and the shark is not affected. **Mutualism** is a relationship between two organisms in which both organisms benefit. For example, a rhinoceros usually can be seen with a few tick birds perched on its back. The tick birds are helped by the easy food source of ticks, and the rhino benefits from the tick removal.

Predation

Predation is a special nutritional relationship in which one organism is the predator, and the other organism is the prey. The predator benefits from the relationship, but the prey is harmed. The predator hunts and kills the prey for food. The predator is specially adapted to hunt its prey, and the prey is specially adapted to escape its predator. While predators harm (kill) their individual prey, predation usually helps the prey species. Predation keeps the population of the prey species under control and prevents them from overshooting the carrying capacity, which often leads to starvation. Also, predation usually helps to remove weak or slow members of the prey species leaving the healthier, stronger, and better adapted individuals to reproduce. Examples of predator-prey relationships include lions and zebras, snakes and rats, and hawks and rabbits.

Competition and Territoriality

Competition is a relationship between two organisms in which the organisms compete for the same vital resource that is in short supply. Typically, both organisms are harmed, but one is usually harmed more than the other, which provides an avenue for natural selection. Organisms compete for resources such as food, water, mates, and space. **Interspecific competition** is between members of different species, while **intraspecific competition** is between members of the same species. **Territoriality** can be considered to be a type of interspecific competition for space. Many animals including mammals, birds, reptiles, fish, spiders, and insects have exhibited territorial behavior. Once territories are established, there are fewer conflicts between organisms. For example, a male redwing blackbird can establish a large territory. By singing and flashing his red patches, he is able to warn other males to avoid his territory, and they can avoid fighting.

Altruistic Behaviors Between Animals

Altruism is a self-sacrificing behavior in which an individual animal may serve or protect another animal. For example, in a honey bee colony there is one queen with many workers (females). There are also drones (males), but only during the mating seasons. Adult workers do all the work of the hive and will die defending it. Another example of altruism is seen in a naked mole rat colony. Each colony has one queen that mates with a few males, and the rest of the colony is nonbreeding and lives to service the queen, her mates, and her offspring.

Review Video: Mutualism, Commensalism, and Parasitism
Visit mometrix.com/academy and enter code: 757249

Ecological Succession

Changes During Primary and Secondary Succession

Ecological succession is the process by which a community changes over time. The final stage of this succession is a climax community, which remains relatively unchanged unless a major event causes it to change or become destroyed. The two types of ecological succession are primary succession and secondary succession. **Primary succession** occurs in a region where there is no soil and also has never been populated, such as a new volcanic island or a region where a glacier has retreated. During the pioneer stage, the progression of species is typically lichen and algae, followed by small annual plants, then perennial herbs and grasses. During the intermediate stage, shrubs, grasses, and shade-intolerant trees are dominant. Finally, after hundreds of years, a climax community is reached with shade-tolerant trees. **Secondary succession** occurs when a climax community is destroyed or nearly destroyed, such as after a forest fire or in an abandoned field. With secondary succession, the area starts with soil and seeds from the original climax community. Typically, weeds and annuals are dominant in the first two years. This is followed by grasses and biennials. In a few years, shrubs and perennials are dominant, followed by pine trees, which are eventually replaced by deciduous trees. Secondary succession takes place in less than 100 years.

Review Video: Ecological Succession
Visit mometrix.com/academy and enter code: 466994

Types of Biomes

Biomes

The biosphere consists of numerous biomes. A **biome** is a large region that supports a specific community. Each biome has a characteristic climate and geography. Differences in latitude, altitude, and worldwide patterns affect temperature, precipitation, and humidity. Biomes can be classified as terrestrial or aquatic biomes. **Terrestrial biomes** include ecosystems with land environments, such as tundra, coniferous forest, temperate broadleaf forest, temperate grassland, chaparral, desert, savannas, and tropical forests. Terrestrial biomes tend to grade into each other in regions called ecotones. **Aquatic biomes** are water-dwelling ecosystems. Aquatic biomes include areas such as lakes, rivers, estuaries, coral reefs, oceanic pelagic zone, intertidal zone, and the abyssal zone.

Aquatic Biomes

Aquatic biomes are characterized by multiple factors including the temperature of the water, the amount of dissolved solids in the water, the availability of light, the depth of the water, and the material at the bottom of the biome. Aquatic biomes are classified as marine or freshwater biomes based on the amount of dissolved salt in the water. **Marine biomes** include the intertidal zone, the pelagic zone, the benthic zone, the abyssal zone, coral reefs, and estuaries. Marine biomes have a salinity of at least 35 parts per thousand. **Freshwater biomes** include lakes, ponds, rivers, and streams. Freshwater biomes have a salinity that is less than 0.5 parts per thousand. Lakes and ponds, which are relatively stationary, consist of two zones: the littoral zone and the limnetic zone. The **littoral zone** is closest to the shore and is home to many plants (floating and rooted), invertebrates, crustaceans, amphibians, and fish. The **limnetic zone** is further from the shore and has no rooted plants. Rivers and streams typically originate in the mountains and make their way to the oceans. Because this water is running and colder, it contains different plants and animals than lakes and ponds. For example, salmon, trout, crayfish, plants, and algae are found in rivers and streams.

MARINE REGIONS

Marine regions are located in three broad areas: the ocean, estuaries, and coral reefs. The ocean consists of two general regions: the pelagic zone and the benthic zone. The **pelagic zone** is in the open ocean. Organisms in the pelagic zone include phytoplankton such as algae and bacteria; zooplankton such as protozoa and crustaceans; and larger animals such as squid, sharks, and whales. The **benthic zone** consists of the ocean floor. Organisms in the benthic zone can include sponges, clams, oysters, starfish, sea anemones, sea urchins, worms, and fish. The deepest part of the benthic zone is called the **abyssal plain** and is usually very cold and dark. This is the deep ocean floor, which is home to numerous scavengers, many of which have light-generating capability. **Estuaries** are somewhat-enclosed coastal regions where water from rivers and streams is mixed with seawater. **Coral reefs** are located in warm, shallow water. Corals are small colonial animals that share a mutualistic relationship with algae.

TERRESTRIAL BIOMES

Terrestrial biomes are classified predominantly by their vegetation, which is primarily determined by precipitation and temperature. **Tropical rainforests** experience the highest annual precipitation and relatively high temperatures. The dominant vegetation in tropical forests is tall evergreen trees. **Temperate deciduous forests** experience moderate precipitation and temperatures. The dominant vegetation is deciduous trees. **Boreal forests** experience moderate precipitation and lower temperatures. The dominant vegetation is coniferous trees. The **tundra** experiences lower precipitation and cold temperatures. The dominant vegetation is shrubs. The **savanna** experiences lower precipitation and high temperatures. The dominant vegetation is grasses. **Deserts** experience the lowest precipitation and the hottest temperatures. The dominant vegetation is scattered thorny plants.

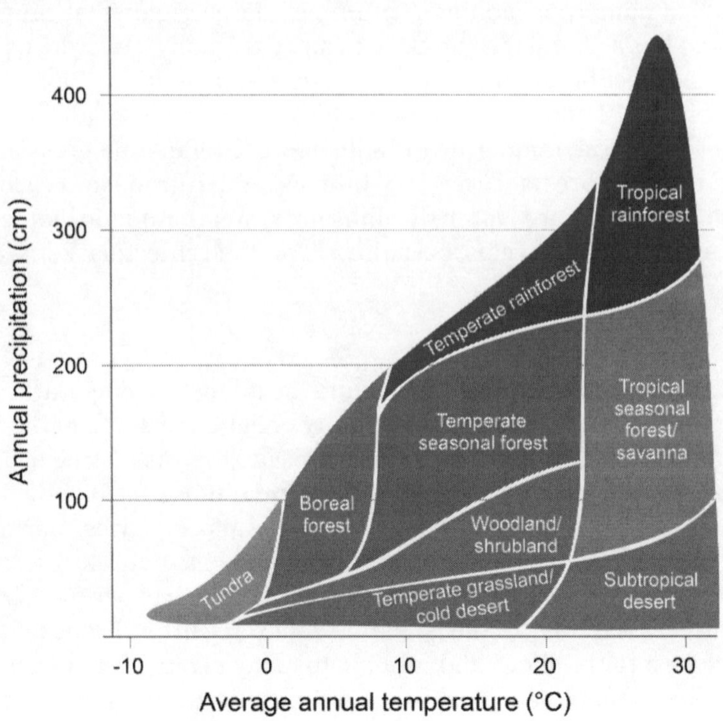

Energy Flow in the Environment

Using Trophic Levels with an Energy Pyramid

Energy flow through an ecosystem can be tracked through an energy pyramid. An **energy pyramid** shows how energy is transferred from one trophic level to another. **Producers** always form the base of an energy pyramid, and the consumers form successive levels above the producers. Producers only store about 1% of the solar energy they receive. Then, each successive level only uses about 10% of the energy of the previous level. That means that **primary consumers** use about 10% of the energy used by primary producers, such as grasses and trees. Next, **secondary consumers** use 10% of primary consumers' 10%, or 1% overall. This continues up for as many trophic levels as exist in a particular ecosystem.

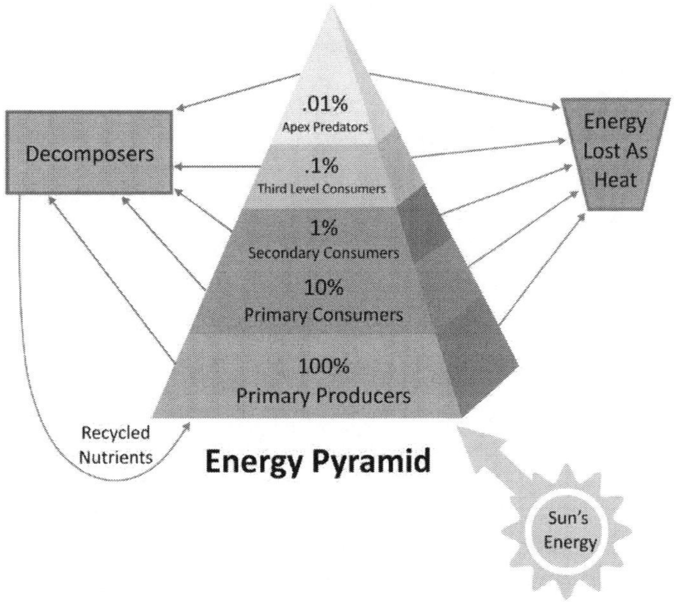

Food Web

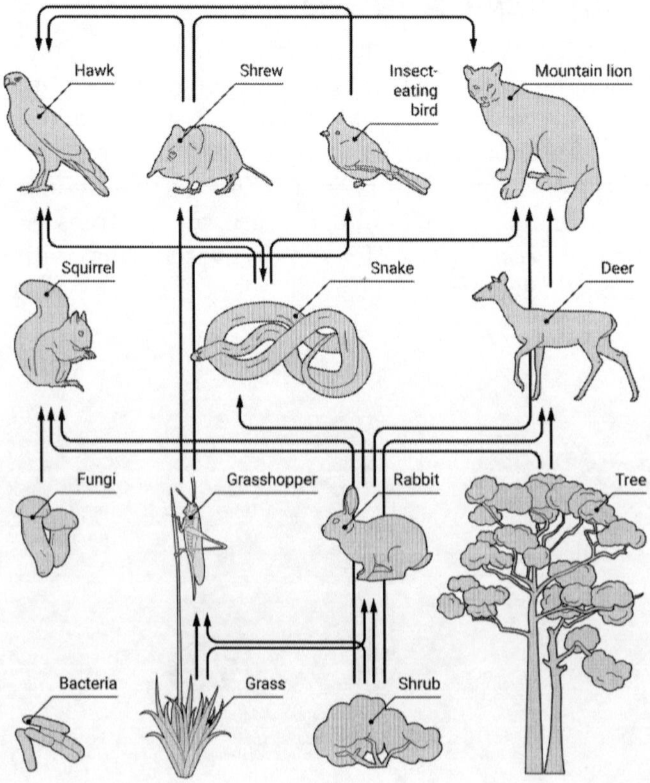

Energy flow through an ecosystem can be illustrated by a **food web**. Energy moves through the food web in the direction of the arrows. In the food web, producers such as grass, trees, and shrubs use energy from the sun to produce food through photosynthesis. Herbivores or primary consumers such as squirrels, grasshoppers, and rabbits obtain energy by eating the producers. Secondary consumers, which are carnivores such as snakes and shrews, obtain energy by eating the primary consumers. Tertiary consumers, which are carnivores such as hawks and mountain lions, obtain energy by eating the secondary consumers. Note that the hawk and the mountain lion can also be considered quaternary consumers in this food web if a different food chain within the web is followed.

Review Video: Food Webs
Visit mometrix.com/academy and enter code: 853254

Biogeochemical Cycles

Water Cycle

The water cycle, also referred to as the **hydrologic cycle**, is a biogeochemical cycle that describes the continuous movement of the Earth's water. Water in the form of **precipitation** such as rain or snow moves from the atmosphere to the ground. The water is collected in oceans, lakes, rivers, and other bodies of water. Heat from the sun then causes water to **evaporate** from those oceans, lakes, rivers, and other bodies of water. As plants transpire, this water also undergoes evaporation. This water vapor collects in the sky and forms clouds. As the water vapor in the clouds cools, the water vapor **condenses** or sublimes depending on the conditions. Then, water moves back to the ground in the form of precipitation.

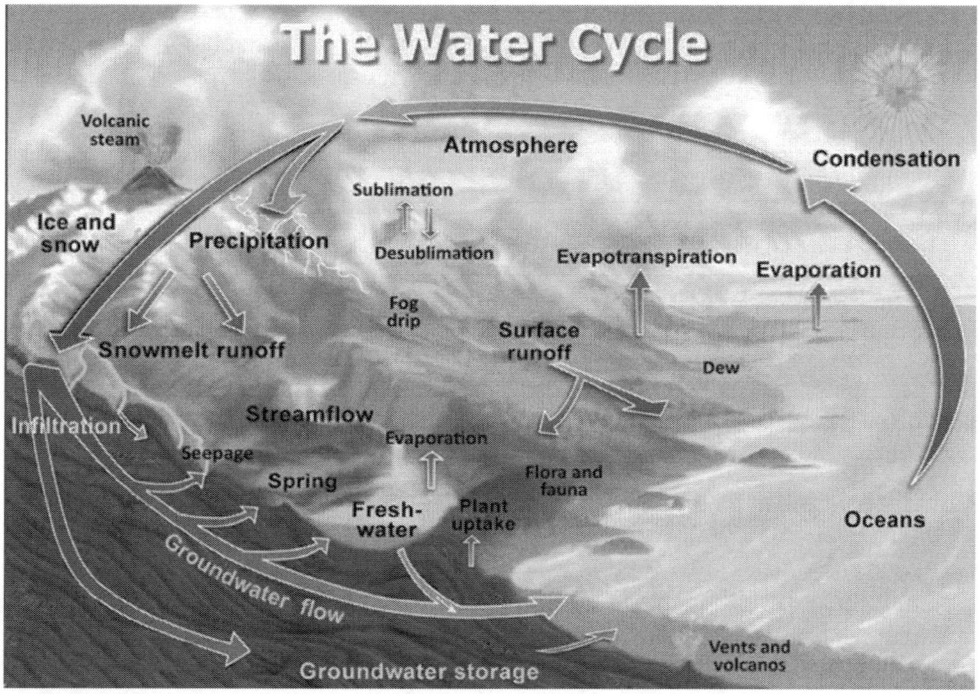

Carbon Cycle

The **carbon cycle** is a biogeochemical cycle that describes the continuous movement of the Earth's carbon. Carbon is in the atmosphere, the soil, living organisms, fossil fuels, oceans, and freshwater systems. These areas are referred to as **carbon reservoirs**. Carbon flows between these reservoirs in an exchange called the carbon cycle. In the atmosphere, carbon is in the form of carbon dioxide. Carbon moves from the atmosphere to plants through the process of photosynthesis. Carbon moves from plants to animals through food chains, and then moves from living organisms to the soil when these organisms die. Carbon moves from living organisms to the atmosphere through cellular respiration. Carbon moves from fossil fuels to the atmosphere when fossil fuels are burned. Carbon moves from the atmosphere to the oceans and freshwater systems through absorption.

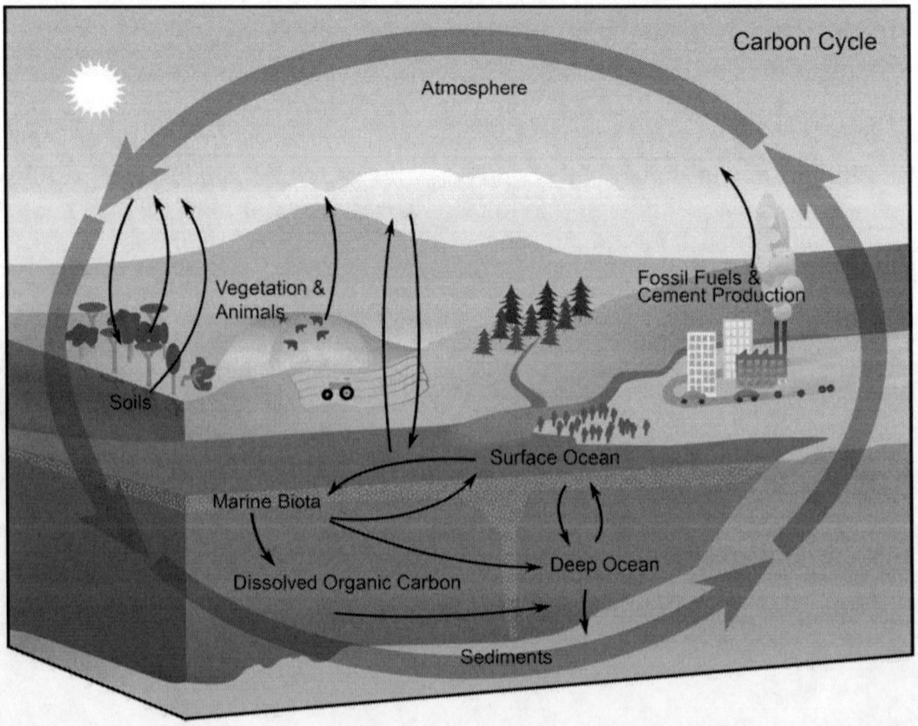

Nitrogen Cycle

The **nitrogen cycle** is a biogeochemical cycle that describes the continuous movement of the Earth's nitrogen. Approximately 78% of the Earth's atmosphere consists of nitrogen in its elemental form N_2. Nitrogen is essential to the formation of proteins, but most organisms cannot use nitrogen in this form and require the nitrogen to be converted into some form of **nitrates**. Lightning can cause nitrates to form in the atmosphere, which can be carried to the soil by rain to be used by plants. Legumes have nitrogen-fixing bacteria in their roots, which can convert the N_2 to ammonia (NH_3). Nitrifying bacteria in the soil can also convert ammonia into nitrates. Plants absorb nitrates from the soil, and animals can consume the plants and other animals for protein. Denitrifying bacteria can convert unused nitrates back to nitrogen to be returned to the atmosphere.

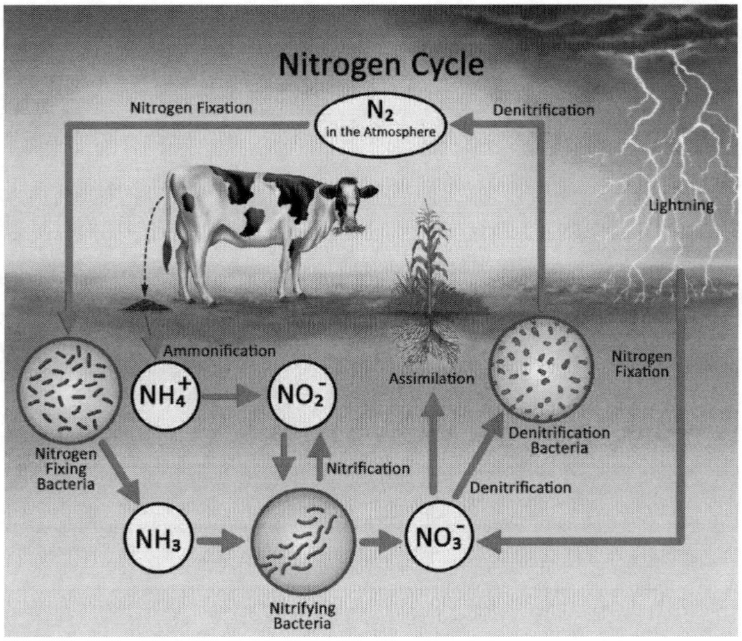

Phosphorus Cycle

The **phosphorus cycle** is a biogeochemical cycle that describes the continuous movement of the Earth's phosphorus. Phosphorus is found in rocks. When these rocks weather and erode, the phosphorus moves into the soil. The phosphorus found in the soil and rocks is in the form of phosphates or compounds with the PO_4^{3-} ion. When it rains, phosphates can be dissolved into the water. Plants are able to use phosphates from the soil. Plants need phosphorus for growth and development. Phosphorus is also a component of DNA, RNA, ATP, cell membranes, and bones. Plants and algae can absorb phosphate ions from the water and convert them into many organic compounds. Animals can get phosphorus by eating food or drinking water. When organisms die, the phosphorus is returned to the soil. This is the slowest of all biogeochemical cycles.

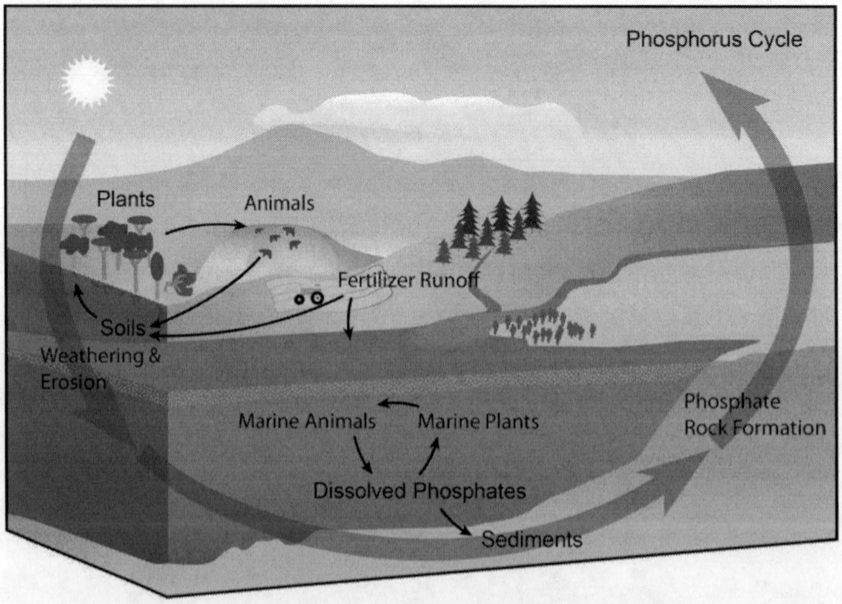

Effects of Natural Disturbances

Natural Disturbances That Affect Ecosystems

A **natural disturbance** is an event caused by nature, not human activity. Natural disturbances can be brought on by weather such as droughts, storms, wind, freezing, and fires from lightning. Other natural disturbances include earthquakes, volcanic eruptions, and diseases. Natural disturbances can disrupt or disturb the ecosystem in many ways, such as altering resources or removing individuals from the community. Natural disturbances can cover small regions, or they can affect an entire ecosystem. The effect may be long lasting and take several years to recover, or the effect may be minor and take only a few months to recover.

Effect of Fragmentation of Ecosystems on Biodiversity

Habitats can become fragmented due to natural disturbances such as fire, volcanic activity, and climate change. Some of the original habitat is destroyed during **fragmentation**, reducing the total area of the habitat. As a result, there may be insufficient food or other resources to support a species. The resulting habitats may also be reproductively isolated from each other, thus limiting genetic variation and biodiversity. Small fluctuations in resources or climate can be catastrophic in small populations. Larger populations may be able to overcome these fluctuations in variation.

Human Effect on Ecological Systems

Effects of Human Population on Ecological Systems and Biodiversity

Human population has been increasing at a near-exponential rate for the past 50 years. As the human population increases, the demand for resources such as food, water, land, and energy also increases. As the human population increases, the number of other species decreases due to habitat destruction, introduced species, and overhunting. The increased greenhouse gases and resulting climate changes have also significantly affected many ecosystems as temperatures rise and habitats are slowly changed or even destroyed. Increasing human population means increasing pollution, which harms habitats. Many animals have become extinct due to the effects of an exponentially increasing human population. High rates of extinction greatly reduce biodiversity.

Habitat Destruction by Humans on Ecological Systems and Biodiversity

Many habitats have been altered or destroyed by humans. In fact, habitat destruction brought about by human endeavors has been the most significant cause of species extinctions, which has resulted in the decrease in biodiversity throughout the world. As the human population has increased exponentially, the extinction rate has also increased exponentially. This is largely due to habitat destruction by humans. Humans use many resources in their agriculture, industry, mining, logging, and recreation. For example, humans have cleared much land for agriculture and urban development. As habitats are destroyed, species are either destroyed or displaced. Often, habitats are fragmented into smaller areas, which only allow for small populations that are under threat by predators, diseases, weather, and limited resources. Areas near the coastline are especially affected, including estuaries, coral reefs, wetlands, and mangrove forests. Nearly half of all mangrove ecosystems have been destroyed by human activity. Coral reefs have nearly been decimated from pollution such as oil spills and exploitation from the aquarium fish market and coral market.

Effects of Introduced Species on Ecological Systems and Biodiversity

Introduced species are species that are moved into new geographic regions by humans. They are also called invasive or nonnative species. Introduction can be intentional, such as the introduction of livestock, or unintentional, such as the introduction of Dutch elm disease. Introduced species can disrupt their new communities by using the limited resources and preying on other members of the community. Introduced species are often free from predators and can reproduce exponentially. This typically causes a decrease in biodiversity. Introduced species are contributors or even responsible for numerous extinctions. For example, zebra mussels, which are native to the Black Sea and the Caspian Sea, were accidentally introduced to the Great Lakes. The zebra mussels greatly reduced the amount of plankton available for the native mussel species, many of which are now endangered.

Impact of Nonpoint Sources of Pollution on the Environment

Nonpoint-source pollution is the leading cause of water pollution in the United States. Nonpoint-source pollution is pollution that does not flow through a pipe, channel, or container. Most nonpoint-source pollution is due to agricultural runoff. Urban runoff from lawns, streets, and parking lots is also treated as nonpoint-source pollution because much of that storm water does not go into a storm drain before entering streams, rivers, lakes, or other bodies of water. Urban runoff contains chemicals such as lawn fertilizers, motor oils, grease, pesticides, soaps, and detergents, each of which is harmful to the environment.

Effects of Remediation on Ecological Systems and Biodiversity

In **remediation**, or land rehabilitation, environmental damages are reversed or stopped by attempting to restore land to its prior condition. Examples of remediation are reforestation and mine reclamation. Mining reclamation includes the backfilling of open-pit mines and covering ores containing sulfides to prevent rain from mixing with them to produce sulfuric acid. **Reforestation** is the restocking of forests and wetlands. This can at least partially offset the damaging effects brought about by the deforestation. Reforestation can help reduce global warming due to an increase in the absorption of light by the trees. Restoration can also help to restore the carbon cycle and counter erosion. Reforestation can help maintain or preserve the biodiversity of the region and possibly increase biodiversity if new organisms immigrate into the region.

Pollution Mitigation and the Clean Air Act

Pollution mitigation has greatly reduced pollution and its effects during the past 40 years. The **Clean Air Act** has reduced pollution by requiring that new industrial sites contain pollution-control technology. These technologies avoid or minimize the negative effects on the environment. For example, new coal-fired power plants are fitted with pollution-control devices that greatly reduce and nearly eliminate sulfur dioxide and nitrogen oxide emissions. This greatly reduces acid rain, improves water quality, and improves the overall health of ecosystems. Reducing acid rain improves soil quality, which in turn improves the health of producers, which consequently improves the health of consumers, essentially strengthening the entire ecosystem. Reduced greenhouse gas emissions have lessened the impact of global warming such as rising sea levels due to melting glaciers and the resulting loss of habitats and biodiversity. Reduced smog and haze improves the intensity of sunlight required for photosynthesis.

Resource Management

Resource management such as waste management and recycling greatly impacts the environment. **Waste management** is the monitoring, collection, transportation, and recycling of waste products. Well-managed landfills include using clay or another lining material to prevent liquid leachate and layers of soil on top to reduce odors and vermin. Wastes, including hazardous biomedical waste, can also be incinerated to reduce waste volume. However, incineration does emit pollutants and greenhouse gases. Proper waste management always includes recycling. **Recycling** is a method to recover resources. Recycled materials can be reprocessed into new products. Metals such as aluminum, copper, and steel are recycled. Plastics, glass, and paper products can also be recycled. In addition, organic materials such as plant materials and food scraps can be composted. The current trend is to shift from waste management to resource recovery. Wastes should be minimized and reduced to minimize the need for disposal. Unavoidable nonrecyclable wastes should be converted to energy by combustion if at all possible.

Impact of Global Warming, Rising Sea Levels, and Flooding on Society

Global warming caused largely by greenhouse gas emission will greatly affect society in the next several years. The increase in global temperature leads to more extreme levels of otherwise normal weather events such hurricanes, tornadoes, floods, and droughts. Rising temperatures cause weather patterns to shift, leading to even more floods and droughts. Rising temperatures mean a decrease in glaciers, sea ice, ice sheets, and snow cover, which contributes to rising sea levels. Rising sea levels lead to habitat change or loss, which greatly affects numerous species, but could also mean higher storm surges and related issues. Some motile species are already moving north to cooler climates. Earlier annual snowmelt and runoff may overwhelm water management systems.

Endangered Species Act

The **Endangered Species Act** (ESA) of 1973 has had a positive impact on many species. The law was designed to protect "imperiled species" from extinction due to factors such as loss of habitat, overhunting, and lack of conservation. The ESA also protects the species' ecosystems and removes threats to those ecosystems. If an animal is placed on the endangered or threatened list, it is prohibited to "harass, harm, pursue, hunt, shoot, wound, kill, trap, capture, or collect, or to attempt to engage in any such conduct" with the endangered animal. The populations of many imperiled species have increased significantly, including the whooping crane, the gray wolf, the red wolf, and the Hawaiian goose. Some species have even been removed from the endangered species list, including the bald eagle, the peregrine falcon, the gray whale, and the grizzly bear. The ESA has protected numerous species while balancing human economic needs and rights to private property.

National Park System

The purpose of the **National Park System** is to "conserve the scenery and the natural and historic objects and the wildlife therein and to provide for the enjoyment of the same in such manner and by such means as will leave them unimpaired for the enjoyment of future generations." The National Park System protects complete ecosystems and houses great biodiversity. National parks are an integral part of the survival of many species. National parks provide a home to hundreds of endangered or threatened species. Studies show that preserved habitats near national parks help many species better survive with the resources they need. This will prevent fragmentation and further habitat loss. Nevertheless, National parks may be threatened by invasion species or pressure for use of land along park boundaries. Biodiversity is threatened even within national parks. Even though many are vast, they are often not large enough to support a species population on their own.

Effects of Extraction of Minerals and Oil Drilling

The extraction of mineral and energy resources by mining and drilling has harmful effects on the environment including pollution and alterations to ecosystems. **Mining** often requires large amounts of deforestation, which harms habitats and affects biodiversity. Mining also causes water pollution. Toxic chemicals such as mercury and sulfuric acid are used in the mining process and are released into bodies of water, harming the aquatic life. If these toxic chemicals are leaked, the ground water is polluted. Rainwater mixes with the heavy metals in mines and produces an acid runoff that harms aquatic life, birds, and mammals. The pollution is especially bad in countries without proper mining regulations. Open-pit mines and mountaintop removal techniques are especially harsh to the environment, and reclamation is often not regulated in developing countries. Oil drilling is controversial due to habitat disruption or loss as well as the potential of an oil spill occurring. Oil spills are toxic to wildlife and difficult to clean up. Offshore drilling uses seismic waves to locate oil, which disturbs whales and dolphins and has been tied to hundreds of beached whales.

Sustainable Agriculture

The management of natural resources and the renewability or **sustainability** of those natural resources greatly impact society. Sustainable agriculture involves growing foods in economical ways that do not harm resources. If left unchecked, farming can deplete the soil of valuable nutrients. Crops grown in these depleted soils are less healthy and more susceptible to disease. Sustainable agriculture uses more effective pest control such as insect-resistant corn, which reduces runoff and water pollution in the surrounding area. Sustainable forestry involves replenishing trees as trees are being harvested, which maintains the environment.

Renewable and Nonrenewable Energy Resources

Energy sources such as wind, solar power, and biomass energy are all **renewable**. Wind power is clean with no pollution and no greenhouse gas emissions. Disadvantages of wind power include the use of land for wind farms, threats to birds, and the expense to build. Solar power has no greenhouse gas emissions, but some toxic metal wastes result in the production of photovoltaic cells, and solar power requires large areas of land. Biomass energy is sustainable, but its combustion produces greenhouse emissions. Farming biomass requires large areas of land. Fossil fuels, which are **nonrenewable**, cause substantially more air pollution and greenhouse gas emissions, contributing to habitat loss and global warming.

> **Review Video: Renewable and Nonrenewable Resources**
> Visit mometrix.com/academy and enter code: 840194

Global and Local Ecology

Flow of Biotic Material Between Ecosystems

Various events can cause the **flow of materials and energy** from one ecosystem to another. In this sense, the local ecosystem is related to the global ecosystem. Both biotic and abiotic elements of an ecosystem can flow into another environment. **Abiotic factors** move through natural processes, such as erosion and deposition of sediment and transportation of those materials by rivers and weather systems. Harvesting of materials such as water, natural gas, and trees also plays a large role, as many materials used for building and survival and may be transported from one ecosystem to another. Plants are often moved through similar processes, whether by harvesting and planting by humans, or by passive systems of seed dispersal through rivers and animals. Animal movement is usually referred to as **migration**, and it is primarily driven by the pursuit of food, safety from predators and harsh environmental conditions, and reproductive opportunity. Ecosystems function through the interaction and balance of biotic and abiotic factors, such as competition and predation and reliance on water supply. As biotic and abiotic factors constantly flow from one local ecosystem to another, the balance has to shift constantly to accommodate ecological change on a global scale.

Chapter Quiz

Ready to see how well you retained what you just read? Scan the QR code to go directly to the chapter quiz interface for this study guide. If you're using a computer, simply visit the online resources page at **mometrix.com/resources719/csetbiolifesci** and click the Chapter Quizzes link.

Heredity: Inheritance and Variation of Traits

Transform passive reading into active learning! After immersing yourself in this chapter, put your comprehension to the test by taking a quiz. The insights you gained will stay with you longer this way. Scan the QR code to go directly to the chapter quiz interface for this study guide. If you're using a computer, simply visit the online resources page at **mometrix.com/resources719/csetbiolifesci** and click the Chapter Quizzes link.

Mendel's Laws

Law of Segregation

The **law of segregation** states that the alleles for a trait separate when gametes are formed, which means that only one of the pair of alleles for a given trait is passed to the gamete. This can be shown in monohybrid crosses, which can be used to show which allele is **dominant** for a single trait. A **monohybrid cross** is a genetic cross between two organisms with a different variation for a single trait. The first monohybrid cross typically occurs between two **homozygous** parents. Each parent is homozygous for a separate allele (gg or GG) for a particular trait. For example, in pea plants, green seeds (G) are dominant over yellow seeds (g). Therefore, in a genetic cross of two pea plants that are homozygous for seed color, the F_1 generation will be 100% **heterozygous** green seeds.

	g	g
G	Gg	Gg
G	Gg	Gg

Review Video: Punnett Square
Visit mometrix.com/academy and enter code: 853855

Monohybrid Cross for a Cross Between Two Gg Parents

If the plants with the heterozygous green seeds are crossed, the F_1 generation should be 50% heterozygous green (Gg), 25% homozygous green (GG), and 25% homozygous yellow (gg).

	G	g
G	GG	Gg
g	Gg	gg

Law of Independent Assortment

Mendel's law of independent assortment states that alleles of one characteristic or trait separate independently of the alleles of another characteristic. Therefore, the allele a gamete receives for one gene does not influence the allele received for another gene due to the allele pairs separating independently during gamete formation. This means that traits are transmitted independently of each other. This can be shown in dihybrid crosses.

Gene, Genotype, Phenotype, and Allele

A **gene** is a portion of DNA that identifies how traits are expressed and passed on in an organism. A gene is part of the genetic code. Collectively, all genes form the **genotype** of an individual. The genotype includes genes that may not be expressed, such as recessive genes. The **phenotype** is the physical, visual manifestation of genes. It is determined by the basic genetic information and how genes have been affected by their environment.

An **allele** is a variation of a gene. Also known as a trait, it determines the manifestation of a gene. This manifestation results in a specific physical appearance of some facet of an organism, such as eye color or height. The genetic information for eye color is a gene. The gene variations responsible for blue, green, brown, or black eyes are called alleles. **Locus** (plural, *loci*) refers to the location of a gene or alleles.

Review Video: Genotype vs Phenotype
Visit mometrix.com/academy and enter code: 922853

Dominant and Recessive Genes

Gene traits are represented in pairs with an uppercase letter for the **dominant trait** (A) and a lowercase letter for the **recessive trait** (a). Genes occur in pairs (AA, Aa, or aa). There is one gene on each chromosome half supplied by each parent organism. Since half the genetic material is from each parent, the offspring's traits are represented as a combination of these. A dominant trait only requires one gene of a gene pair for it to be expressed in a phenotype, whereas a recessive requires both genes in order to be manifested. For example, if the mother's genotype is Dd and the father's is dd, the possible combinations are Dd and dd. The dominant trait will be manifested if the genotype is DD or Dd. The recessive trait will be manifested if the genotype is dd. Both DD and dd are **homozygous** pairs. Dd is **heterozygous**.

Dihybrid Cross for the F_2 Generation of a Cross between GGRR and ggrr Parents

A **dihybrid cross** is a genetic cross for two traits that each have two alleles. For example, in pea plants, green seeds (G) are dominant over yellow seeds (g), and round seeds (R) are dominant over wrinkled seeds (r). In a genetic cross of two pea plants that are homozygous for seed color and seed shape (GGRR or ggRR), the F_1 generation will be 100% heterozygous green and round seeds (GgRr). If these F_1 plants (GgRr) are crossed, the resulting F_2 generation is shown below. Out of the 16 total genotypes for the cross of green, round seeds, there are only four possible phenotypes, or physical traits of the seed: green and round seed (GGRR, GGRr, GgRR, or GgRr), green and wrinkled seed (GGrr or Ggrr), yellow and round seed (ggRR or ggRr) , or yellow and wrinkled seed (ggrr).

There are nine green and round seed plants, three green and wrinkled seed plants, three yellow and round seed plants, and only one yellow and wrinkled seed plant. This cross has a **9:3:3:1 ratio**.

	GR	gR	Gr	gr
GR	GGRR	GgRR	GGRr	GgRr
gR	GgRR	ggRR	GgRr	ggRr
Gr	GGRr	GgRr	GGrr	Ggrr
gr	GgRr	ggRr	Ggrr	ggrr

PEDIGREE

Pedigree analysis is a type of genetic analysis in which an inherited trait is studied and traced through several generations of a family to determine how that trait is inherited. A **pedigree** is a chart arranged as a type of family tree using symbols for people and lines to represent the relationships between those people. Squares usually represent males, and circles represent females. Horizontal lines represent a male and female mating, and the vertical lines beneath them represent their children. Usually, family members who possess the trait are fully shaded and those who only carry the trait are half-shaded. Genotypes and phenotypes are determined for each individual if possible. The pedigree below shows the family tree of a family in which the first male who was red-green color blind mated with the first female who was unaffected. They had five children. The three sons were unaffected, and the two daughters were carriers.

Inheritance of Red-Green Color Blindness: an X-linked Recessive Trait

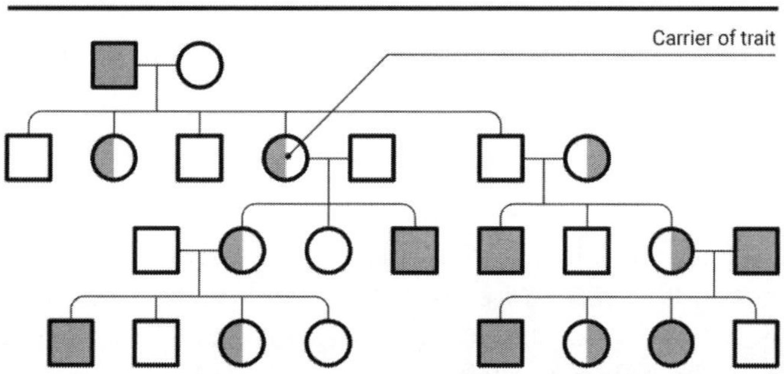

Non-Mendelian Inheritance

NON-MENDELIAN INHERITANCE CONCEPTS

LINKAGE

Linkage is an exception to Mendel's law of independent assortment. Linkage can occur when two genes are located on the same chromosome. Each chromosome has several genes, and those genes tend to be inherited together. Genes that are located on the same chromosome and tend to be inherited together are called **linkage groups**. Because the genes are on the same chromosome, they do not separate during meiosis. During meiosis, the genes in a linkage group always go into the same gamete together. Due to linkage, genes with different characteristics are inherited together more frequently than is predicted using the laws of probability. An example of a linkage group is found on chromosome number 4. This linkage group includes genes for Parkinson's disease, narcolepsy, and Huntington's disease.

Review Video: Mendelian and Non-Mendelian Genetics
Visit mometrix.com/academy and enter code: 113159

SEX-LINKED INHERITANCE

Sex-linked inheritance is an exception to Mendel's law of independent assortment. In human genetics, females have two X chromosomes, and males have one X and one Y chromosome. **Sex-linked traits** are carried on the X chromosome. Because females have two X chromosomes, they have two copies of genes found on the X chromosome. Females may possess a recessive allele for various disorders on one X chromosome, but as long as they possess the dominant allele for normal functioning on the other X chromosome, they will not have the disorder. Females who are heterozygous for a trait such as color blindness or hemophilia are only carriers. Because males have only one X chromosome, if they possess the recessive allele for a disorder, it will be expressed. Examples of traits that are a result of sex linkage are color blindness, hemophilia, a form of muscular dystrophy, and some forms of anemia.

MULTIPLE ALLELES

Multiple alleles result in a type of non-Mendelian inheritance. In Mendelian inheritance, only two alleles for each gene exist. For example, Mendel's pea plants were either tall or short, and the plants had either yellow or green pods. Often, there are more than two possibilities for a particular trait. For example, in human genetics, blood type has many variations. Multiple allele inheritance occurs where there are more than two different alleles of a gene for a particular trait. Even though there may be several alleles for a particular trait, each individual can still only possess two of those possible alleles. For example, the three human blood alleles are I^A (blood contains type A antigens), I^B (blood contains type B antigens), and *i* (blood contains neither type A nor type B antigens).

Blood types and their possible genotypes are shown below.

Blood Type (Phenotype)	Genotype
A	I^AI^A, I^AI^O
B	I^BI^B, I^BI^O
AB	I^AI^B
O	*ii*

INCOMPLETE DOMINANCE

Incomplete dominance is an exception to Mendel's law of dominance. In these situations, there is no dominant or recessive allele. Instead, both alleles of a heterozygote are expressed, and when they are, they blend or mix. For example, there are two alleles for petal color for snapdragons: red (C^R) and white (C^W). Crossing a red snapdragon with a white snapdragon yields an F_1 generation that is 100% heterozygous pink. Crossing two pink snapdragons yields an F_2 generation that is 50% heterozygous pink (C^RC^W), 25% homozygous white (C^WC^W), and 25% homozygous red (C^RC^R).

LAWS OF DOMINANCE AND CODOMINANCE

The **law of dominance** states that a dominant trait is always expressed. **Codominance** is an exception to the law of dominance. In codominance, a heterozygote simultaneously expresses both genes for a trait without blending. For example, in certain horses, the hair colors red (D^R) and white (D^W) are codominant. Horses with the genotype D^RD^W have coats composed of both red hairs and white hairs, which—when mixed together—causes their coats to have a golden color.

POLYGENIC INHERITANCE

Polygenic inheritance occurs when a trait is determined by the interaction of many different genes. In Mendelian genetics, traits are determined by just one pair of genes with two alleles. For example, Mendel's pea plants had either red or white flowers, and his plants were either tall or short. An example of polygenic genetic inheritance in human genetics is skin color and height. Each is controlled by at least four pairs of genes. Skin color has many variations between very light and very dark. Height has many variations between very short and very tall. Eye color and intelligence are also polygenic.

EPISTASIS

Epistasis occurs when a gene at one locus inhibits the expression of a gene at another locus. For example, in mice, black hair (B) is dominant over brown hair (b). But a different gene at a different locus determines whether or not pigment is deposited (C for deposited and c for not deposited) on the mouse hair. A black mouse with genotypes BB or Bb will only have that color deposited if the pigment genotype is CC or Cc. A black mouse with genotype BBcc will be white. A brown mouse can have genotypes bbCC or bbCc, but a mouse with genotype bbcc will also be white.

PLEIOTROPY

In Mendelian inheritance, each gene can influence only one trait. Most genes can affect many traits or have multiple phenotypes. **Pleiotropy** is the situation in which one gene influences several seemingly unrelated traits. A gene that affects multiple traits is **pleiotropic**. Pleiotropy can be due to normal or mutated genes. Genes code for proteins. Because proteins are often used in more than one tissue or more than one area of the body, a missing protein can cause many complications. For example, the hormone insulin is a protein. If the insulin receptors are faulty, then the cells cannot recognize and use the insulin. Other examples of pleiotropy include inherited diseases such as cystic fibrosis, sickle-cell anemia, phenylketonuria (PKU), and albinism.

MITOCHONDRIAL INHERITANCE

Mitochondria are cellular organelles that produce energy for the cell. Mitochondria contain their own DNA consisting of 37 genes arranged in a circular structure. Mitochondrial DNA is transmitted maternally, which means that these mitochondrial genes are only inherited from the mother. The offspring's mitochondria only come from the oocyte (egg cell), not from the sperm. Sperm cells only contain mitochondria in their tails, which does not enter the egg during fertilization. Mitochondrial inheritance is not consistent with Mendelian inheritance in which the zygote derives half of the genetic material from the mother and half from the father. Most of these genes code for proteins related to muscular disorders.

Common Human Genetic Disorders

Chromosomal Changes that Lead to Down Syndrome

Down syndrome is a type of **aneuploidy** (abnormal number of chromosomes) in which an individual has three copies of chromosome 21, as shown in the karyotype below. When a gamete with an extra 21st chromosome unites with a normal gamete, the result is a group of three chromosomes instead of a diploid set. A **trisomy** can occur as a result of nondisjunction, which occurs when a pair of chromosomes fails to separate during meiosis in the formation of an egg or sperm cell.

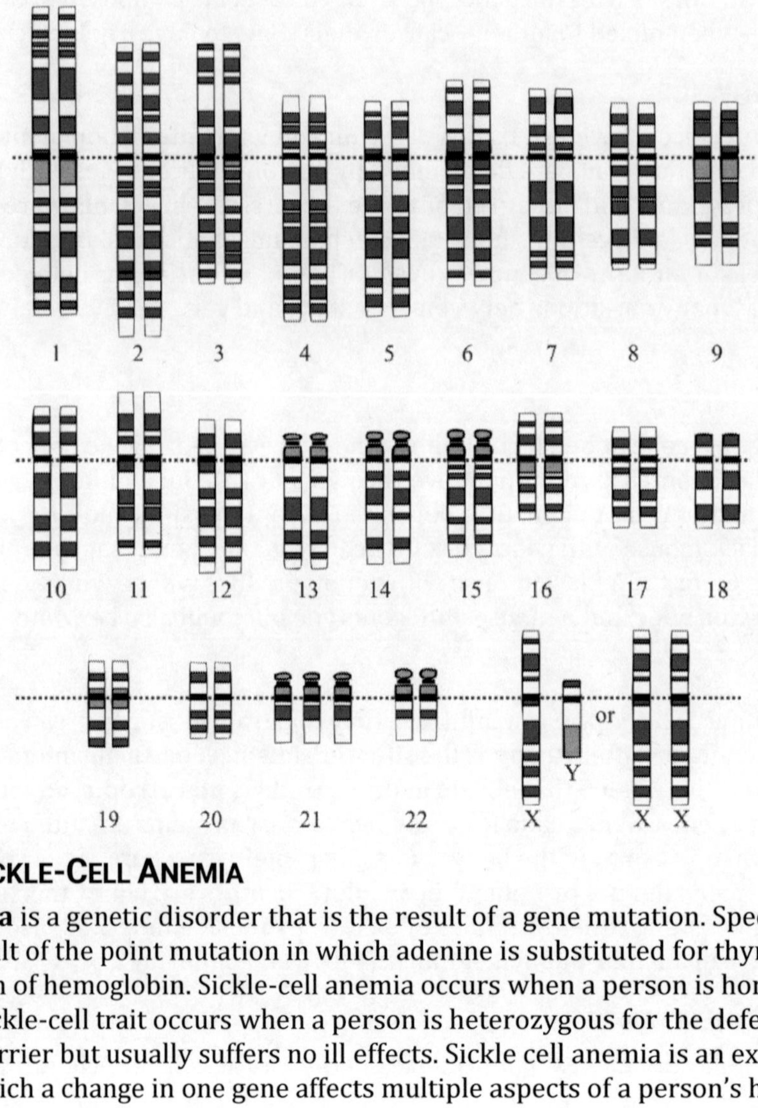

Genetics of Sickle-Cell Anemia

Sickle cell anemia is a genetic disorder that is the result of a gene mutation. Specifically, sickle cell anemia is the result of the point mutation in which adenine is substituted for thymine. This results in a defective form of hemoglobin. Sickle-cell anemia occurs when a person is homozygous for the defective gene. Sickle-cell trait occurs when a person is heterozygous for the defective gene, and this person is a carrier but usually suffers no ill effects. Sickle cell anemia is an example of **pleiotropy**, in which a change in one gene affects multiple aspects of a person's health. These health problems are due to the abnormally sickle-shaped red blood cells that block the flow of blood, damaging tissues and organs. The sickle-shaped cells tend to rupture, leading to anemia.

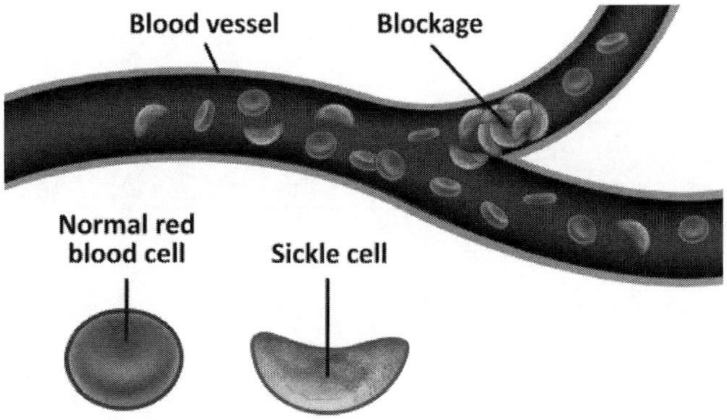

Sources of Genetic Variation

Genetic Variation

Mutations

Mutations are changes in DNA. Mutations are one of the main sources of genetic variation and can introduce new genetic information into the genome. The changes can be gene mutations such as the **point mutations** of substitution, addition, or deletion, or the changes can be on the chromosomal level such as the chromosomal aberrations of translocations, deletions, inversions, and duplications. Mutations are random and can benefit, harm, or have no effect on the individual. **Somatic mutations** do not affect inheritance and therefore do not affect genetic variation with regard to evolution. **Germline mutations** that occur in gametes (eggs and sperm) can be passed to offspring and therefore are very important to genetic variation and evolution.

Crossing Over

Crossing over is a major source of genetic variation. **Crossing over** is the exchange of equivalent segments of DNA between homologous chromosomes. Crossing over occurs during meiosis in prophase I. During synapsis, a **tetrad** is formed when homologous chromosomes pair up. Also during synapsis, the chromatids are extremely close together and sometimes the chromatids swap genes. Because genes have more than one allele, this allows for an exchange of genetic information. Crossing over is that exchange of genes. Crossing over can occur several times along the length of the chromosomes. Although crossing over does not introduce new information, it does introduce new combinations of the information that is available. Without crossing over during meiosis, only two genetically different gametes can be formed. With just one instance of crossing over, four genetically different gametes can be formed. With crossing over, each gamete contains genes from both the father and the mother. Crossing over leads to variation in traits among gametes, which leads to variation in traits among offspring.

Independent Assortment During Sexual Reproduction

Independent assortment during sexual reproduction is a source of genetic variation. Mutations originally brought about changes in DNA leading to alleles or different forms of the same gene. During sexual reproduction, these alleles are "shuffled" or "independently sorted," producing individuals with unique combinations of traits. Gametes are produced during meiosis, which consists of two cell divisions: meiosis I and meiosis II. Meiosis I is a reduction division in which the diploid parent cell divides into two haploid daughter cells. During the metaphase of meiosis I, the homologous pairs (one from the mother and one from the father) align on the equatorial plane. The orientation of the homologous pairs is random, and each placement is independent of another's placement. The number of possible arrangements increases exponentially as the number of chromosomes increases. The independent assortment of chromosomes during metaphase in meiosis I provides a variety of gametes with tremendous differences in their combinations of chromosomes.

Review Video: Gene Mutation
Visit mometrix.com/academy and enter code: 955485

Chromosomal Aberrations

Chromosomal aberrations are changes in DNA sequences on the chromosomal level. These mutations typically involve many genes and often result in miscarriages. Chromosomal aberrations include translocations, deletions, inversions, and duplications. **Translocations** occur when a piece of DNA breaks off of one chromosome and is joined to another chromosome. **Deletions** occur when a piece of DNA breaks off on a chromosome and is lost without reattaching. **Inversions** occur when a piece of DNA breaks off of one chromosome and becomes reattached to that same chromosome but with an inverted or flipped orientation. **Duplications** occur when a piece of DNA is replicated and attached to the original piece of DNA in sequence.

Sources of Genetic Exchange

Genetic exchange, or the transfer of DNA from one organism to another, is a source of genetic variation. Three general types of genetic exchange are transduction, transformation, and conjugation. **Transduction** occurs when genetic material is transferred from one bacterium to another by a bacteriophage. A bacteriophage is a virus that infects a bacterium. As the new bacteriophages are replicated, some of the host bacteria DNA can be added to the virus particles. **Transformation** occurs when a cell obtains new genetic information from its environment or surroundings. Many bacteria take up DNA fragments such as plasmids from their surroundings to obtain new genes. **Conjugation** occurs when bacteria or single-celled organisms are in direct contact with each other. Genes can be transferred from one into the other while the two cells are joined.

Processes Affecting the Gene Pool

Genetic Drift

Genetic drift is a microevolutionary process that causes random changes in allele frequencies that are not the result of natural selection. Genetic drift can result in a loss of genetic diversity. Genetic drift greatly impacts small populations. Two special forms of genetic drift are the genetic bottleneck and the founder effect. A **genetic bottleneck** occurs when there is a drastic reduction in population due to some change such as overhunting, disease, or habitat loss. When a population is greatly reduced in size, many alleles can be lost. Even if the population size greatly increases again, the lost alleles represent lost genetic diversity. The **founder effect** occurs when one individual or a few individuals populate a new area such as an island. This new population is limited to the alleles of the founder(s) unless mutations occur or new individuals immigrate to the region.

Gene Flow

Gene flow is a microevolutionary process in which alleles enter a population by immigration and leave a population by emigration. Gene flow helps counter genetic drift. When individuals from one genetically distinct population immigrate to a different genetically distinct population, alleles and their genetic information are added to the new population. The added alleles will change the gene frequencies within the population. This increases genetic diversity. If individuals with rare alleles emigrate from a population, the genetic diversity is decreased. Gene flow reduces the genetic differences between populations.

Hardy-Weinberg Equilibrium

HW Equilibrium

Hardy–Weinberg (HW) equilibrium is a theoretical concept that uses a mathematical relationship to study gene frequencies. According to HW, if specific conditions are met, the proportions of genotypes in a population can be described by the equation: $p^2 + 2pq + q^2 = 1$, in which p is the frequency of the dominant allele and q is the frequency of the recessive allele. Also, p^2 is the frequency of the homozygous dominant genotype, $2pq$ is the frequency of the heterozygous genotype, and q^2 is the frequency of the homozygous recessive genotype. In addition, the sum of p and q must be equal to one. If the frequencies on the left side of the equation have a sum of one, then the population is in equilibrium, and evolution is not taking place. If the frequencies on the left side of the equation do not have a sum of one, then evolution is taking place. Therefore, the HW equation is only true for populations that are in equilibrium.

The HW equilibrium requires the following five conditions to be met:

1. The population must be very large.
2. Mating is random.
3. There are no mutations.
4. No immigration or emigration can occur.
5. All individuals of the population have an equal chance to survive and reproduce.

According to this concept, if all five conditions are met, the gene frequencies will remain constant. In reality, these five conditions are rarely met except in a laboratory situation.

Calculation of Allele Frequency

> Explain how to calculate allele frequencies of a simple genetic locus at which there are two alleles (A and a) in a population of 1,000 individuals given that the population consists of 120 individuals homozygous for the dominant allele (AA), 480 heterozygous individuals (Aa), and 400 individuals homozygous for the recessive allele (aa).

To calculate the frequency of an allele, divide the total number of those alleles in the population by the total number of alleles in the population for that locus as shown in the following equation:

$$\text{allele frequency} = \frac{\text{total \# of allelles in population}}{\text{total \# of alleles in the population for that locus}}$$

First, find the total number of each type of allele. The 120 AA individuals produce 240 A alleles. The 480 heterozygous individuals produce 480 A alleles and 480 a alleles. The 400 aa individuals produce 800 a alleles. Therefore, there is a total of 720 A alleles and 1,280 a alleles. Adding the 720 and 1,280 yields a total of 2,000 alleles in the population for that locus. The allele frequency for $A = \frac{720}{2{,}000}$ or 0.36. The allele frequency for $a = \frac{1{,}280}{2{,}000}$ or 0.64.

Chapter Quiz

Ready to see how well you retained what you just read? Scan the QR code to go directly to the chapter quiz interface for this study guide. If you're using a computer, simply visit the online resources page at **mometrix.com/resources719/csetbiolifesci** and click the Chapter Quizzes link.

Biological Evolution: Unity and Diversity

Transform passive reading into active learning! After immersing yourself in this chapter, put your comprehension to the test by taking a quiz. The insights you gained will stay with you longer this way. Scan the QR code to go directly to the chapter quiz interface for this study guide. If you're using a computer, simply visit the online resources page at **mometrix.com/resources719/csetbiolifesci** and click the Chapter Quizzes link.

Mechanics of Evolution

Mechanisms of Evolution

Natural and Artificial Selection

Natural selection and artificial selection are both mechanisms of evolution. **Natural selection** is a process of nature in which a population can change over generations. Every population has variations in individual heritable traits and organisms best suited for survival typically reproduce and pass on those genetic traits to offspring to increase the likelihood of them surviving. Typically, the more advantageous a trait is, the more common that trait becomes in a population. Natural selection brings about evolutionary **adaptations** and is responsible for biological diversity. Artificial selection is another mechanism of evolution. **Artificial selection** is a process brought about by humans. Artificial selection is the selective breeding of domesticated animals and plants such as when farmers choose animals or plants with desirable traits to reproduce. Artificial selection has led to the evolution of farm stock and crops. For example, cauliflower, broccoli, and cabbage all evolved due to artificial selection of the wild mustard plant.

Sexual Selection

Sexual selection is a special case of natural selection in animal populations. **Sexual selection** occurs because some animals are more likely to find mates than other animals. The two main contributors to sexual selection are **competition** of males and **mate selection** by females. An example of male competition is in the mating practices of the redwing blackbird. Some males have huge territories and numerous mates that they defend. Other males have small territories, and some even have no mates. An example of mate selection by females is the mating practices of peacocks. Male peacocks display large, colorful tail feathers to attract females. Females are more likely to choose males with the larger, more colorful displays.

Coevolution

Coevolution describes a rare phenomenon in which two populations with a close ecological relationship undergo reciprocal adaptations simultaneously and evolve together, affecting each other's evolution. General examples of coevolution include predator and prey, or plant and pollinator, and parasites and their hosts. A specific example of coevolution is the yucca moths and the yucca plants. Yucca plants can only be pollinated by the yucca moths. The yucca moths lay their eggs in the yucca flowers, and their larvae grow inside the ovary.

Adaptive Radiation

Adaptive radiation is an evolutionary process in which a species branches out and adapts and fills numerous unoccupied ecological niches. The adaptations occur relatively quickly, driven by natural selection and resulting in new phenotypes and possibly new species eventually. An example of adaptive radiation is the finches that Darwin studied on the Galápagos Islands. Darwin recorded 13 different varieties of finches, which differed in the size and shape of their beaks. Through the process of natural selection, each type of finch adapted to the specific environment and specifically the food sources of the island to which it belonged. On newly formed islands with many unoccupied ecological niches, the adaptive radiation process occurred quickly due to the lack of competing species and predators.

Evidence Supporting Evolution

Molecular Evidence

Because all organisms are made up of cells, all organisms are alike on a fundamental level. Cells share similar components, which are made up of molecules. Specifically, all cells contain DNA and RNA. This should indicate that all species descended from a **common ancestor**. Humans and chimpanzees share approximately 98% of their genes in common, while humans and bacteria share approximately 7% of their genes in common suggesting that bacteria and humans are not closely related. Biologists have been able to use DNA sequence comparisons of modern organisms to reconstruct the "root" of the tree of life. The fact that RNA can store information, replicate itself, and code for proteins suggests that RNA could have could have evolved first, followed by DNA.

Homology

Homology is the similarity of structures of different species based on a similar anatomy in a common evolutionary ancestor. For instance, the forelimbs of humans, dogs, birds, and whales all have the same basic pattern of the bones. Specifically, all of these organisms have a humerus, radius, and ulna. They are all modifications of the same basic evolutionary structure from a common ancestor. Tetrapods resemble the fossils of extinct transitional animal called the *Eusthenopteron*. This would seem to indicate that evolution primarily modifies preexisting structures.

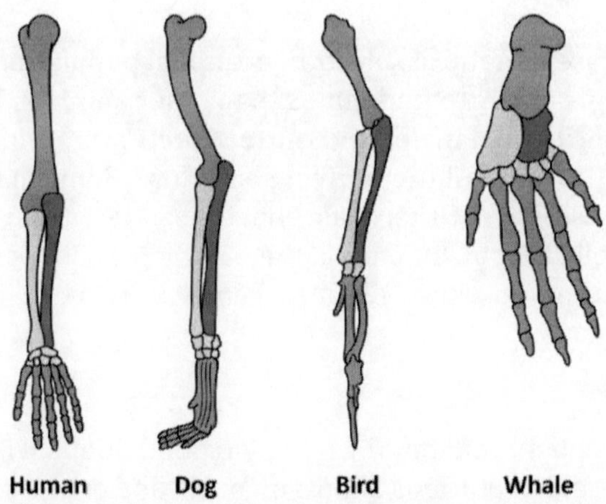

Review Video: Homologous vs Analogous Structures
Visit mometrix.com/academy and enter code: 355157

Embryology

The stages of **embryonic development** reveal homologies between species. These homologies are evidence of a **common ancestor**. For example, in chicken embryos and mammalian embryos, both include a stage in which slits and arches appear in the embryo's neck region that are strikingly similar to gill slits and gill arches in fish embryos. Adult chickens and adult mammals do not have gills, but this embryonic homology indicates that birds and mammals share a common ancestor with fish. As another example, some species of toothless whales have embryos that initially develop teeth that are later absorbed, which indicates that these whales have an ancestor with teeth in the adult form. Finally, most tetrapods have five-digit limbs, but birds have three-digit limbs in their wings. However, embryonic birds initially have five-digit limbs in their wings, which develop into a three-digit wing. Tetrapods such as reptiles, mammals, and birds all share a common ancestor with five-digit limbs.

Endosymbiosis Theory

The endosymbiosis theory is foundational to evolution. Endosymbiosis provides the path for prokaryotes to give rise to eukaryotes. Specifically, **endosymbiosis** explains the development of the organelles of mitochondria in animals and chloroplasts in plants. This theory states that some eukaryotic organelles such as mitochondria and chloroplasts originated as free living cells. According to this theory, primitive, heterotrophic eukaryotes engulfed smaller, autotrophic bacteria prokaryotes, but the bacteria were not digested. Instead, the eukaryotes and the bacteria formed a symbiotic relationship. Eventually, the bacteria transformed into mitochondrion or chloroplasts.

Supporting Evidence

Several facts support the endosymbiosis theory. Mitochondria and chloroplasts contain their own DNA and can both only arise from other preexisting mitochondria and chloroplasts. The genomes of mitochondria and chloroplasts consist of single, circular DNA molecules with no histones. This is similar to bacteria genomes, not eukaryote genomes. Also, the RNA, ribosomes, and protein synthesis of mitochondria and chloroplasts are remarkably similar to those of bacteria, and both use oxygen to produce ATP. These organelles have a double phospholipid layer that is typical of engulfed bacteria. This theory also involves a secondary endosymbiosis in which the original eukaryotic cells that have engulfed the bacteria are then engulfed themselves by another free-living eukaryote.

Convergent Evolution

Convergent evolution is the evolutionary process in which two or more unrelated species become increasingly similar in appearance. In convergent evolution, similar adaptations in these unrelated species occur due to these species inhabiting the same kind of environment. For example, the mammals shown below, although found in different parts of the world, developed similar appearances due to their similar environments.

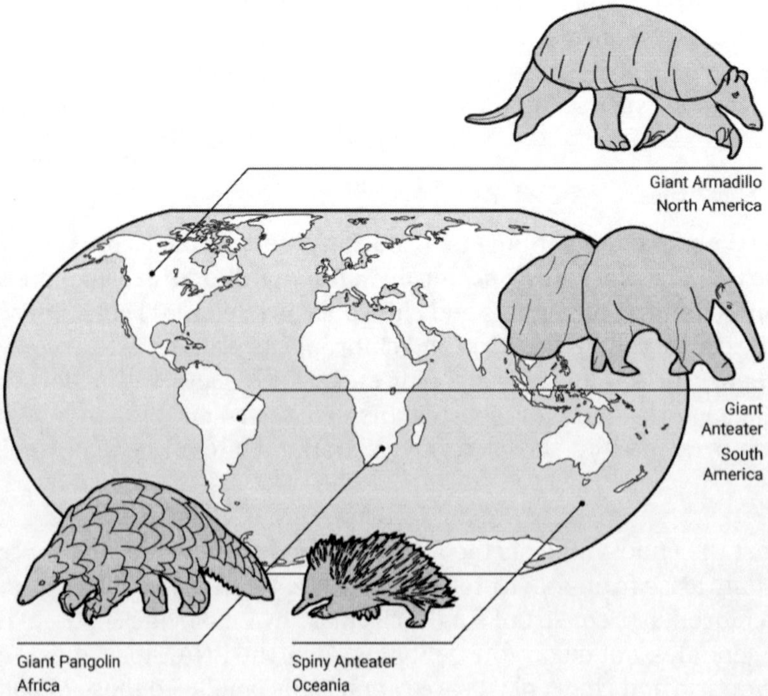

Divergent Evolution

Divergent evolution is the evolutionary process in which organisms of one species become increasingly dissimilar in appearance. As several small adaptations occur due to natural selection, the organisms will finally reach a point at which two new species are formed, also known as **speciation**. Then, these two species will further diverge from each other as they continue to evolve. Adaptive radiation is an example of divergent evolution. Another example is the divergent evolution of the wooly mammoth and the modern elephant from a common ancestor.

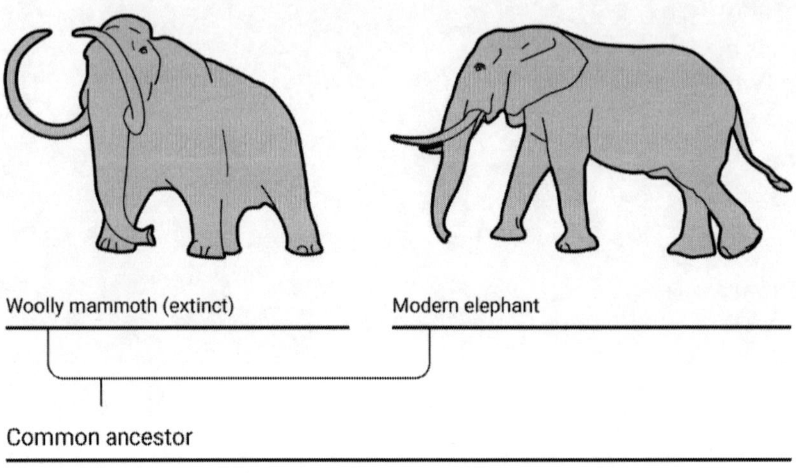

Fossil Record

The **fossil record** provides many types of support for evolution including comparisons from rock layers, transition fossils, and homologies with modern organisms. First, fossils from rock layers from all over the world have been compared, enabling scientists to develop a sequence of life from simple to complex. Based on the fossil record, the **geologic timeline** chronicles the history of all living things. For example, the fossil record clearly indicates that invertebrates developed before vertebrates and that fish developed before amphibians. Second, numerous transitional fossils have been found. **Transitional fossils** show an intermediate state between an ancestral form of an organism and the form of its descendants. These fossils show the path of evolutionary change. For example, many transition fossils documenting the evolutionary change from fish to amphibians have been discovered. In 2004, scientists discovered *Tiktaalik roseae*, or the "fishapod," which is a 375-million-year-old fossil that exhibits both fish and amphibian characteristics. Another example would be *Pakicetus,* an extinct land mammal, that scientists determined is an early ancestor of modern whales and dolphins based on the specialized structures of the inner ear. Most fossils exhibit homologies with modern organisms. For example, extinct horses are similar to modern horses, indicating a common ancestor.

Cephalization and Multicellularity

Cephalization is the evolutionary trend that can be summarized as "the evolution of the head." In most animals, nerve tissue has been concentrated into a brain at one end of an organism over many generations. Eventually, a head enclosing a brain and housing sensory organs was produced at one end of the organism. Many invertebrates, such as arthropods and annelids and all vertebrates, have undergone cephalization. However, some invertebrates, such as echinoderms and sponges, have not undergone cephalization, and these organisms literally do not have a head.

Another evolutionary trend is **multicellularity**. Life has evolved from simple, single-celled organisms to complex, multicellular organisms. Over millions of years, single-celled organisms gave rise to biofilms, which gave rise to multicellular organisms, which gave rise to all of the major phyla of multicellular organisms present today.

Genetic Basis of Speciation

Speciation

Significance of Reproductive Isolation

A biological species is a group of similar organisms that can breed and produce viable offspring. If gene flow between two groups of a species is hindered or stopped completely through **reproductive isolation**, more significant genetic differences between the two groups can accumulate and a new species may originate. This process is known as **speciation**. For the two incipient species to completely split, one of two things must occur: either successful mating between the incipient species cannot occur or the offspring must be nonviable or sterile. **Prezygotic barriers** occur before fertilization and stop or hinder species from mating. These barriers include, but are not limited to, habitat isolation, behavioral isolation, or temporal isolation. For instance, a change in the mating location or a change in the mating rituals can keep mating from occurring. **Postzygotic barriers** occur after fertilization but prevent the offspring or hybrid from living or being fertile. Some examples of postzygotic barriers include differences in chromosome numbers or the arrangement of genes on certain chromosomes. Various modes of geographic and population isolation may occur, but the key to speciation in each type is still the reduced gene flow.

MODES

Speciation has various modes that bring about the reduced gene flow needed for incipient species to fully separate. **Allopatric speciation** occurs between two incipient species that become geographically isolated populations. This would include if, for some geographic reason, two or more groups within a species cannot mate with each other due to a barrier like a desert or river. Some may still mate, but the gene flow is greatly reduced. Peripatric speciation is a more specific type of allopatric speciation. **Peripatric speciation** occurs when an extremely small group is geographically isolated at the edge of the rest of the population. This small population size brings about genetic drift relatively quickly, with unique characteristics of the smaller group getting passed on to future generations of that group and further diffientiating them from their original population. **Parapatric speciation** occurs within a population that is distributed over a large geographic area, thus creating "barrier" of space to distance. Individuals in the population simply choose to mate with close neighbors in their specific region, leading to a reduced gene flow. Natural selection in the range of those individuals brings about further differentiation among members of the species spread out across the population. **Sympatric speciation** occurs when a new species develops in a population, even though there is no geographic isolation or physical barrier separating or preventing this species from mating. Sympatric speciation is uncommon but may occur when a species inhabits a new niche.

Models of Evolutionary Rates

GRADUALISM

Gradualism is a model of evolutionary rates that states that evolutionary changes occurred slowly or gradually by a divergence of lineages due largely to natural selection. These accumulated changes occurred over millions of years at a slow and consistent rate. Many transitional forms occurred between ancestors and modern descendants. Although not all of these transitional forms were preserved in the fossil record, the fossil record clearly supports gradualism. Many transition fossils show adaptations as organisms evolve. The geologic time scale describes this gradual change from simple to complex organisms over millions of years.

PUNCTUATED EQUILIBRIUM

Punctuated equilibrium is a model of evolutionary rates that states that in some instances, evolutionary changes occurred in relatively short bursts that "punctuate" long periods of equilibrium of little or no change. These "short" periods would still consist of hundreds of thousands of years, but include one or more substantial changes. Most scientists believe that punctuated equilibrium occurred along with gradualism. The fossil record supports punctuated equilibrium for many organisms. Punctuated equilibrium provides an explanation for the supposed numerous "missing links" in the fossil record. If punctuated equilibrium is validated, then there actually are no missing links.

Scientific Explanations for the Origin of Life on Earth

Explanations for the Origin of Life on Earth

Panspermia

The word *panspermia* is a Greek work that means "seeds everywhere." **Panspermia** is one possible explanation for the origin of life on Earth that states that "seeds" of life exist throughout the universe and can be transferred from one location to another. Three types of panspermia based on the seed-dispersal method have been proposed. **Lithopanspermia** is described as rocks or dust transferring microorganisms between solar systems. **Ballistic panspermia** is described as rocks or dust transferring microorganisms between planets within the same solar system**. Directed panspermia** is described as intelligent extraterrestrials purposely spreading the seeds to other planets and solar systems. The panspermia hypothesis only proposes the origin of life on Earth. It does not offer an explanation for the origin of life in the universe or explain the origin of the seeds themselves.

Abiotic Synthesis of Organic Compounds

Scientists have performed sophisticated experiments to determine how the first organic compounds appeared on Earth. First, scientists performed controlled experiments that closely resembled the conditions similar to an early Earth. In the classic **Miller–Urey experiment** (1953), the Earth's early atmosphere was simulated with water, methane, ammonia, and hydrogen that were stimulated by an electric discharge. The Miller–Urey experiment produced complex organic compounds including several amino acids, sugars, and hydrocarbons. Later experiments by other scientists produced nucleic acids. Recently, Jeffrey Bada, a former student of Miller, was able to produce amino acids in a simulation using the Earth's current atmospheric conditions with the addition of iron and carbonate to the simulation. This is significant because in previous studies using Earth's current atmosphere, the amino acids were destroyed by the nitrites produced by the nitrogen.

Atmospheric Composition

The early atmosphere of Earth had little or possibly no oxygen. Early rocks had high levels of iron at their surfaces. Without oxygen, the iron just entered into the early oceans as ions. In the same time frame, early photosynthetic algae were beginning to grow abundantly in the early ocean. During photosynthesis, the algae would produce oxygen gas, which oxidized the iron at the rocks' surfaces, forming an iron oxide. This process basically kept the algae in an oxygen-free environment. As the algae population grew much larger, it eventually produced such a large amount of oxygen that it could not be removed by the iron in the rocks. Because the algae at this time were intolerant to oxygen, the algae became extinct. Over time, a new iron-rich layer of sediments formed, and algae populations reformed, and the cycle began again. This cycle repeated itself for millions of years. Iron-rich layers of sediment alternated with iron-poor layers. Gradually, algae and other life forms evolved that were tolerant to oxygen, stabilizing the oxygen concentration in the atmosphere at levels similar to those of today.

Development of Self-Replication

Several hypotheses for the origin of life involve the self-replication of molecules. In order for life to have originated on Earth, proteins and RNA must have been replicated. Hypotheses that combine the replication of proteins and RNA seem promising. One such hypothesis is called **RNA world**. RNA world explains how the pathway of DNA to RNA to protein may have originated by proposing the reverse process. RNA world proposes that self-replicating RNA was the precursor to DNA. Scientists have shown that RNA can actually function both as a gene and as an enzyme and could therefore have carried genetic information in earlier life stages. Also, RNA can be transcribed into DNA using reverse transcription. In RNA world, RNA molecules self-replicated and evolved through recombination and mutations. RNA molecules developed the ability to act as enzymes. Eventually, RNA began to synthesize proteins. Finally, DNA molecules were copied from the RNA in a process of reverse transcription.

Extinction of Species

Causes of Extinction of Species

Lack of Genetic Diversity

Genetic diversity provides a mechanism for populations to adapt to changing environments or even human impacts. With a diverse genome, individuals possessing genes making them better suited for the environment are more likely to exist. Without genetic diversity, populations cannot develop adaptations. Populations cannot resist diseases or adapt to changes in the habitat. As the populations of endangered species decrease, genetic diversity decreases even further. Normally, specific genes that resist disease or help the organism to adapt to changes in the habitat and therefore increase survivability are passed on to future generations. However, if those genes have drifted out of the population, the population cannot evolve with their changing environment and may become extinct. A small gene pool does not provide much variety for selection. For example, tigers in India are now in danger of extinction. Studies show that more than 90% of the genome has been lost largely due to a period when tigers were heavily killed by British officials and Indian royalty. With fewer than 2,000 tigers in the world and these in small populations, the genetic diversity can continue to decrease, possibly leading to extinction if much effort is not made to preserve the remaining genetic diversity.

Environmental Pressures

A changing environment may lead to the extinction of a species. If an animal has a small tolerance range to food sources and habitat needs or if a population is small, it is less likely to adapt to changes in the environment. For example, the giant panda feeds almost exclusively on bamboo. Bamboo is being threatened by global warming. Due to the dwindling of their food source, giant pandas are less able to adapt to a changing environment. **Climate change** and global warming can affect an ecosystem and some species may not be able to adapt to even seemingly minor temperature changes especially if their populations are small. If possible, animals needing cooler climates may need to move to cooler habitats. Melting ice caps and glaciers and rising sea levels can seriously disrupt many ecosystems and affect numerous species. For example, the polar bear may become extinct due to global warming as the polar bears' habitat is destroyed. Sea turtles may become extinct as the rising sea levels destroy the beaches needed for laying eggs. Even if the beaches are not destroyed, increasing temperatures affect the incubation process and the number of offspring being produced.

Human Impacts

Humans are responsible for impacting the environment in ways that endanger or harm species, which may even lead to those species' extinction. Humans destroy habitats directly through deforestation and clearing land for agriculture, logging, mining, and urbanization. Humans also threaten or endanger species through overfishing and overhunting. Pollution can destroy a habitat, and if a species is unable to relocate, this can eventually cause extinction if the effects cause drastic impacts. The intentional or unintentional introduction of an invasive species allows a new predator or competitor into the ecosystem, and it can threaten native species in that specific ecosystem if they cannot outcompete the invasive species. An example of human impacts leading to the extinction of a species is the case of the passenger pigeon. Millions of passenger pigeons were killed for meat from around 1850 to 1880. Because passenger pigeons only laid one egg at a time, huge flocks were destroyed. The last passenger pigeon died in 1914.

INTERSPECIFIC COMPETITION

Interspecific competition is competition between individuals of different species for the same limited resources such as food, water, sunlight, and living space. This is especially threatening if the two species share a limiting resource and that resource is not in abundant supply. Interspecific competition can limit the population size of a species. With reduced population size, there is less genetic variation. The species may not be able to adapt to environmental changes. For example, firs and spruces compete for resources in coniferous forests. Cheetahs and lions compete for prey in savannas.

Chapter Quiz

Ready to see how well you retained what you just read? Scan the QR code to go directly to the chapter quiz interface for this study guide. If you're using a computer, simply visit the online resources page at **mometrix.com/resources719/csetbiolifesci** and click the Chapter Quizzes link.

CSET Practice Test #1

Want to take this practice test in an online interactive format?
Check out the online resources page, which includes interactive practice questions and much more: **mometrix.com/resources719/csetbiolifesci**

1. A population of pea plants has 25% dwarf plants and 75% tall plants. The tall allele, *T* is dominant to the dwarf allele, *t*. What is the frequency of the *T* allele?

a. 0.75
b. 0.67
c. 0.5
d. 0.25

2. Which of the following mutations is most likely to have a dramatic effect on the sequence of a protein?

a. A point mutation
b. A missense mutation
c. A deletion
d. A silent mutation

3. Which of the following ideas most aligns with Darwin's work in *On the Origin of Species*?

a. If an organism changes during its life in order to adapt to its environment, those changes are passed on to its offspring.
b. The geological processes that alter the earth are uniform through time.
c. Human populations will rapidly increase unless kept in check by limits in food supply.
d. Nature selects the best-adapted varieties to survive and reproduce.

4. Darwin's idea that evolution occurs by the gradual accumulation of small changes can be described as:

a. Punctuated equilibrium
b. Phyletic gradualism
c. Convergent evolution
d. Adaptive radiation

5. Which of the following describes the physical or non-biological part of the carbon cycle?

a. Phytoplankton use carbon dioxide and other nutrients to produce carbohydrates and oxygen.
b. Cold water dissolves atmospheric carbon dioxide, stores it, and releases it back out to the atmosphere as needed.
c. Carbon dioxide is dissolved in sea water and is broken up to free carbon for use by marine life.
d. Warm, surface water dissolves carbon dioxide where it is converted to nitrogen and phosphorus for use by marine life.

6. Which of the following sentences is true?

a. All organisms begin life as a single cell
b. Animal cells begin life as multicellular embryos, while plants begin as single cells
c. Some organisms begin life as a single cell and others as multicellular
d. None of the above

7. The synaptonemal complex is present in which of the following phases of the cell cycle?

a. Metaphase of mitosis
b. Prophase of meiosis I
c. Telophase of meiosis I
d. Metaphase of meiosis II

8. Which of the following is NOT a mechanism that contributes to cell differentiation and development in embryos?

a. Asymmetrical cell division
b. Asymmetrical cytoplasm distribution
c. Organizer cells
d. Location of cells on the lineage map

9. Which of the following would not be used as evidence for evolution?

a. Fossil record
b. DNA sequences
c. Anatomical structures
d. Reproductive habits

10. Which enzyme in DNA replication is a potential source of new mutations?

a. DNA ligase
b. Primase
c. DNA gyrase
d. DNA polymerase

11. Which of the following is NOT a product of respiration?

a. Carbon dioxide
b. Water
c. Glucose
d. ATP

12. In the development of genetic traits, one gene must match to one __________ for the traits to develop correctly.

a. codon
b. protein
c. amino acid
d. chromosome

13. Which of the following is the substrate for DNA ligase?

a. Okazaki fragments
b. RNA primer
c. Single-strand binding protein
d. Leading strand

14. Which of the following correctly describes the genotype Ll, if "L" represents tallness and "l" represents shortness?

a. Heterozygous genotype and tall phenotype
b. Heterozygous phenotype and tall genotype
c. Homozygous genotype and short phenotype
d. Homozygous phenotype and short genotype

15. Most of the energy in a food chain is concentrated in the level of the

a. primary producers.
b. primary consumers.
c. secondary consumers.
d. tertiary consumers.

16. Pollination involves which plant parts?

a. Xylem and petiole
b. Apical meristem and floral meristem
c. Anther and stigma
d. Root hairs and stroma

17. The main function of ______ is to reduce the number of chromosomes to half the number of parent cells.

a. mitosis
b. telophase
c. meiosis I
d. meiosis II

18. Which of the following of Lamarck's evolutionary ideas turned out to be true?

a. Natural selection
b. Organisms naturally transform into increasingly complex organisms
c. Inheritance of acquired characters
d. Body parts develop with increased usage and weaken with disuse

19. Which of the following ecosystems is most likely to have an inverted biomass pyramid?

a. Forest ecosystem
b. Tundra ecosystem
c. Desert ecosystem
d. Aquatic ecosystem

20. Which of the following has a simple life cycle without a metamorphosis?

a. Frog
b. Newt
c. Grasshopper
d. Human being

21. Which organ system includes the spleen?

a. Endocrine
b. Lymphatic
c. Respiratory
d. Digestive

22. Which statement best explains the Biological Species Concept (BSC)?

a. It states that the status of species is based on the ability to pass on the most successful traits to their offspring.
b. It states that the status of species is based on the reproductive isolation of populations.
c. It states that the status of species is based on the ability of populations to mix and produce fertile hybrids.
d. It states that the status of a species is due to the theory of natural selection.

Refer to the following for question 23:

Let B represent the dominant allele for a full head of hair, and let b represent the recessive allele for male-pattern baldness. The following Punnett square represents the offspring of two people with recessive genes for baldness.

	B	**b**
B	Possibility 1	Possibility 2
b	Possibility 3	Possibility 4

23. According to the Punnett square, which possibility would produce an offspring with a full head of hair?

a. Possibility 1
b. Possibility 2
c. Possibility 3
d. All of the above

24. Which of the following molecules is thought to have acted as the first enzyme in early life on earth?

a. Protein
b. RNA
c. DNA
d. Triglycerides

25. Which part of a flower collects pollen?

a. Style
b. Stigma
c. Petals
d. Sepals

26. Which of the following is a trait that results from disruptive selection?

a. Insecticide resistance
b. Only male peacocks having colorful plumage
c. Some birds having significantly large bills than others within the same species
d. Human height

27. Which biome is most likely to support the growth of epiphytes?

a. Deserts
b. Tropical rain forests
c. Temperate deciduous forests
d. Taigas

28. How do animals of the phylum Mollusca respire?

a. Through gills
b. Through a trachea
c. Through book lungs
d. Through muscle contraction

29. Which of the following is an example of a density-dependent limiting factor?

a. Air pollution by a factory
b. The toxic effect of waste products
c. Nearby volcanic eruptions
d. Frosts

30. Evidence that humans share a common ancestor with other primates includes all of the following EXCEPT:

a. DNA sequence
b. Fossil evidence of intermediate species
c. Analogous structures
d. Homologous structures

31. What do all animals belonging to the Echinodermata phylum have in common?

a. They use multiple appendages for locomotion.
b. They use tube feet for locomotion and feeding.
c. They have an exoskeleton made of chitin.
d. They must shed their outer layer of skin to grow.

32. Plants begin to break down the products of photosynthesis through respiration. What is the result of respiration?

a. Water
b. Oxygen and glucose
c. Carbon dioxide and sugar
d. Carbon dioxide and water

33. Genetic engineering:

a. Is a form of human reproduction
b. Always involves using restriction enzymes to cut DNA
c. Always involves transient expression of genes
d. Often involves using nucleases to cut DNA

34. In which taxonomic group are organisms MOST alike?

a. Phylum
b. Family
c. Class
d. Order

35. How does meiosis differ from mitosis?

a. Meiosis is used to repair the body. Mitosis is used to break down the body.
b. Meiosis is used for asexual reproduction of single-celled organisms. Mitosis is used for sexual reproduction of multicellular organisms.
c. Meiosis only occurs in humans. Mitosis only occurs in plants.
d. Meiosis produces cells that are genetically different. Mitosis produces cells that are genetically identical.

36. In a strenuously exercising muscle under anaerobic conditions, NADH begins to accumulate in high concentration. Which of the following metabolic processes will be activated to reduce the concentration of NADH?

a. Glycolysis
b. The Krebs cycle
c. Lactic acid fermentation
d. Oxidative phosphorylation

37. What is the name of the structure that prevents food from entering the airway?

a. Trachea
b. Esophagus
c. Diaphragm
d. Epiglottis

38. Which of the following animals displays the greatest fitness?

a. A male wolf that dies young but has 4 cubs that are raised by an unrelated female
b. A female wolf that has 3 cubs and lives to be quite old
c. A male wolf that lives to old age and has 1 cub
d. A female wolf that dies young after raising 3 cubs

39. Which of the following extraembryonic membranes is an important source of nutrition in many nonhuman animal species but NOT in humans?

a. Amnion
b. Allantois
c. Yolk sac
d. Chorion

40. A prairie ecosystem is described below. Farmers treat fields surrounding the prairie with pesticides that kill part of the beetle population. What effect would the pesticides have on the rest of the ecosystem?

Grass is eaten by grasshoppers, rabbits, and crickets
Corn is eaten by squirrels and beetles
Grasshoppers, beetles, and crickets are all eaten by birds
Squirrels, birds, and rabbits are all eaten by both foxes and coyotes

a. There would be a decrease in the cricket population.
b. There would be an increase in the population of birds.
c. The population of rabbits would decrease.
d. The population of foxes would increase.

41. Which of the following cell types has a peptidoglycan cell wall?

a. Algae
b. Bacteria
c. Fungi
d. Land plants

42. What is the most likely reason that cells differentiate?

a. Cells differentiate to avoid looking like all the cells around them.
b. Cells differentiate so that simple, non-specialized cells can become highly specialized cells.
c. Cells differentiate so that multicellular organisms will remain the same size.
d. Cells differentiate for no apparent reason.

43. Which of the following metabolic compounds is composed of only carbon, oxygen, and hydrogen?

a. Phospholipids
b. Glycogen
c. Peptides
d. RNA

44. Which of the following best describes one of the roles of RNA?

a. Manufacturing the proteins needed for DNA
b. Creating the bonds between the elements that compose DNA
c. Sending messages about the correct sequence of proteins in DNA
d. Forming the identifiable "*double helix*" shape of DNA

45. How did Jean Baptiste Lamarck's theory of evolution compare to Darwin's theory of natural selection?

a. He expanded Darwin's theory of natural selection by stating that some genes allow for better survival than others.
b. He proposed an earlier theory stating that favorable traits developed due to environmental conditions and the desire and needs of the organisms.
c. He provided evidence to Darwin's belief that the desires and needs of organisms affected the evolution of populations.
d. He opposed Darwin's view that evolution was predetermined and believed that the selection of traits was more random.

Refer to the following for question 46:

A biome featuring scrubby plants and small evergreen trees has a hot, dry summer followed by a wetter winter. The following food chain exists in the biome:

$$tree \rightarrow caterpillar \rightarrow frog \rightarrow snake \rightarrow hawk \rightarrow vulture \rightarrow worm$$

46. Which biome is this?

a. Taiga
b. Coniferous forest
c. Chaparral
d. Savanna

47. Plant A undergoes C4 photosynthesis. What type of environment would the plant most likely live in?

a. Plant A lives in a very cold environment.
b. Plant A lives in a very hot environment.
c. Plant A lives in a marine environment.
d. Plant A lives in a dark environment that lacks solar energy.

48. Which of the following habitats would provide an opportunity for secondary succession?

a. A retreating glacier
b. Burned cropland
c. A newly formed volcanic island
d. A 500-year-old forest

49. Two companion models, gradualism and punctuated equilibrium, dominate evolutionary theory. Which of the following statements is most consistent with the theory of punctuated equilibrium?

a. Fossils show changes over large periods of time.
b. Fossils showing intermediate characteristics may not necessarily be found.
c. Speciation occurs gradually.
d. Evolution is a slow, steady process.

50. This organelle contains digestive enzymes that break down food and unneeded substances. They are also thought to be linked to the aging process. What part of a cell does this describe?

a. Lysosomes
b. Chromatin
c. Plastids
d. Golgi apparatus

Answer Key and Explanations for Test #1

1. C: According to Hardy-Weinberg equilibrium, $p + q = 1$ and $p^2 + 2pq + q^2 = 1$. In this scenario, $q^2 = 0.25$, so $q = 0.5$, and p must also be 0.5.

2. C: Insertions and deletions cause frameshift mutations. These mutations cause all subsequent nucleotides to be displaced by one position, and thereby cause all the amino acids to be different than they would have been if the mutation had not occurred.

3. D: Darwin introduced his idea of natural selection in *On the Origin of Species*, in which he stated that nature selects the best-adapted varieties to survive and reproduce. Lamarck wrote *Philosophie Zoologique*, in which he proposed a theory of inheritance of acquired characteristics. This theory states that if an organism changes during its life to adapt to its environment, those changes are passed on to its offspring. Lyell wrote *Principles of Geology*, in which he introduced his idea of uniformitarianism, which states that the geological processes that alter the earth are uniform through time. Malthus wrote *An Essay on the Principle of Population*, in which he stated that human populations will rapidly increase unless kept in check by limits in food supply.

4. B: Phyletic gradualism is the view that evolution occurs at a more or less constant rate. Contrary to this view, punctuated equilibrium holds that evolutionary history consists of long periods of stasis punctuated by geologically short periods of evolution. This theory predicts that there will be few fossils revealing intermediate stages of evolution, whereas phyletic gradualism views the lack of intermediate-stage fossils as a deficit in the fossil record that will resolve when enough specimens are collected.

5. B: Cold water dissolves atmospheric carbon dioxide, stores it, and releases it back out to the atmosphere as needed. This describes the physical or non-biological part of the carbon cycle. The carbon and nutrient cycles of the ocean are processed in part by the deep currents, mixing, and upwelling that occurs. Carbon dioxide (CO_2) from the atmosphere is dissolved into the ocean at the higher latitudes and distributed to the denser deep water. When upwelling occurs, CO_2 is brought back to the surface and emitted into the tropical air.

6. A: All organisms begin life as a single cell, which usually reproduce with mitosis or meiosis to further expand.

7. B: The synaptonemal complex is a multi-protein complex that serves to line up and connect homologous chromatids during prophase of meiosis I. It facilitates the exchange of genetic material between non-sister chromatids (i.e., crossing over) by ensuring that the chromatids are perfectly aligned and exchange equivalent segments. It is often described as a "molecular zipper." The points at which the homologous chromatids cross one another to exchange genetic material are known as chiasmata (singular: chiasma). The synaptonemal complex is disassembled once the crossovers have resolved, at which point prophase of meiosis I is complete.

8. D: A lineage map describes the fates of cells in the early embryo; in other words, it tells which germ layer different cells will occupy. In some small organisms such as the nematode *Caenorhabditis elegans*, all of the adult cells can be traced back to the egg. A lineage map is not a mechanism of embryo development, but rather a tool for describing it.

9. D: Reproductive habits would not be considered evidence for evolution. Usually, how a species reproduces does not support nor add to the body of evidence for the theory of evolution.

Reproductive habits might exemplify how any given organism can adapt to changes in its environment as a way to survive. This does not necessarily show evolution. Fossil record is evidence for evolution as it shows evolutionary change of organisms over time. DNA sequences show that organisms that are related evolutionarily also have related gene sequences. Anatomical structures such as having an internal bony structure provide evidence of descent from a common ancestor.

10. D: DNA polymerase does not match base pairs with 100% fidelity. Some level of mismatching is present for all DNA polymerases, and this is a source of mutation in nature. Cells have mechanisms of correcting base pair mismatches, but they do not fix all of them.

11. C: In respiration, food is used to produce energy as glucose and oxygen that react to produce carbon dioxide, water and ATP

12. B: Each gene must match to a protein for a genetic trait to develop correctly.

13. A: DNA synthesis on the lagging strand forms short segments called Okazaki fragments. Because DNA polymerase can only add nucleotides in the $5' \rightarrow 3'$ direction, lagging strand synthesis is discontinuous. The final product is formed when DNA ligase joins Okazaki fragments together.

14. A: The genotype Ll describes the genotype of the person or the traits for the genes they carry. It is heterozygous because it contains a dominant gene and a recessive gene. Tallness is the phenotype of the person or the physical expression of the genes they carry, because L for tallness is the dominant gene.

15. A: A food chain shows how energy is transferred from one organism to another. A producer uses the energy from the sun to make its own food. Most of the energy in a food chain is in the level of the producer.

16. C: Pollination is the transfer of pollen from the anther, the male part of the flower, to the stigma, the female part of the flower. This transfer can be accomplished either by wind, animals, or water. None of the other choices are involved in pollination: the xylem and petiole are structural and transport tissues; the apical and floral meristems are growth regions; root hairs absorb water and stroma is part of the chloroplast.

17. C: In humans, diploid cells are those that contain 46 chromosomes. There are 23 pairs of chromosomes each made up of one chromosome from the father and one from the mother. In meiosis I, each chromosome replicates itself and lines up, or synapses, with its homologous chromosome, and each of the daughter cells ends up with one copy of each of the chromosomes. The two daughter cells at the end of meiosis I are haploid because they contain half of the chromosomes of the parent cell. In humans, this would be 23 chromosomes. However, each of these chromosomes are made of two sister chromatids. In meiosis II, the sister chromatids in the daughter cells separate and result in the production of the gametes. These are also haploid cells because they contain one copy of half of the genetic material of the parent cell. Four haploid cells result from meiosis. Choice A, mitosis, can be eliminated as it refers to the process of cell division where each daughter cell contains exactly the same genetic material as the parent cell. Choice B, telophase, refers to phases of both mitosis and meiosis, during which chromosomes move toward the opposite ends of the cell.

18. D: Natural selection was Darwin's idea, not Lamarck's. Mendel discovered that genes are the basic units of inheritance. Lamarck's observation about use and disuse is true, although he did not connect it with the underlying mechanism of natural selection.

19. D: Biomass pyramids are graphical representations of the total amount of organic matter present within an ecosystem. Most terrestrial ecosystems have the traditional pyramid presentation with the smallest point at the top. In aquatic ecosystems however, the pyramid is often inverted with the major producer within the system having a smaller biomass than the consumers above it. This is generally because the producers, often phytoplankton in these cases, produce multiple generations quickly while having shorter individual lives. These are then quickly devoured by the substantially larger mass of zooplankton.

20. D: Human beings, like other mammals, birds, fish, reptiles, and spiders, have simple life cycles in that they are either born live or hatched from eggs, and then grow to adulthood. Frogs (A), newts (B), and grasshoppers (C) undergo metamorphoses wherein their forms change. Frogs and newts are amphibians; they begin life underwater, breathing through gills, but breathe through lungs by adulthood and move from the water to live on the land. Grasshoppers hatch from eggs into larvae, wormlike juvenile forms that do most of the feeding they need; then they progress to adulthood.

21. B: The lymphatic system includes the spleen.

22. B: The Biological Species Concept (BSC) states that the status of "species" is based on the natural reproductive isolation of populations. Populations that could potentially interbreed and produce fertile offspring but do not do so in nature are considered different species under the BSC. This species concept does not consider the ability to interbreed under artificial conditions: if two groups do not breed with one another for any reason (in nature), they are reproductively isolated and therefore different species according to the BSC. The isolation may be due to geography, behavior, appearance, or other factors. For example, the Eastern and Western meadowlark look very similar and have overlapping territories, but they have different songs. Individual meadowlarks identify others by their songs and only breed with those with the same song. Because the two populations are reproductively isolated from one another, they are considered different species under the BSC. If individuals with different songs did interbreed and produce fertile offspring, they would be considered the same species.

23. D: Refer to the complete Punnett square in the explanation for question 10. Because male-pattern baldness is recessive, the offspring would need the *bb* gene combination in order to inherit this trait. Therefore, any offspring with the *B* gene will have a full head of hair. Possibilities 1, 2, and 3 all have the *B* gene.

24. B: Some RNA molecules in extant organisms have enzymatic activity; for example, the formation of peptide bonds on ribosomes is catalyzed by an RNA molecule. This and other information have led scientists to believe that the most likely molecules to first demonstrate enzymatic activity were RNA molecules.

25. B: Flowers are the reproductive organs of a plant. Flowering plants reproduce by sexual reproduction where the gametes join to form seeds. Pollen is sperm. Pollinators help transfer the sperm to the ovule, by way of the stigma. The style is the part of the female reproduction system that transports the sperm between the stigma and the ovary, which are all parts of the pistil. The stigma is the sticky tip of the style on which the pollen lands. Sepals are usually small leaves between or underneath the petals and are not as obvious or as large and colorful as the petals.

26. C: Disruptive selection occurs when the environment favors alleles for extreme traits. In the example, seasonal changes can make different types of food available at different times of the year, favoring the large or small bills.

27. B: Epiphytes are plants that grow in the canopy of trees, and the tropical rain forest has a rich canopy because of its density and extensive moisture.

28. A: Animals of the phylum Mollusca or mollusks, respire (breathe) through gills. Respiration is the process of taking in oxygen and releasing carbon dioxide. Mollusca consists of several classes that include species as diverse as chitons, clams, land and marine snails, and squid. This represents a diverse range of body structures. Many mollusks have a mantle that includes a cavity that is used for both breathing and excretion. Within the mantle are gills (ctenidia). Mollusks do not have tracheas. Some land snails have a respiratory cavity that is often called a lung but is not a true lung. Spiders, which are not mollusks (they are arachnids), have a type of lungs called book lungs. Muscle contraction is not required for the gills to function. Other structures, such as cilia, work to pass water over the gills.

29. B: Density-dependent limiting factors on population growth are factors that vary with population density. Pollution from a factory, volcanic eruptions, frosts, and fires do not vary as a function of population size. Waste products, however, increase with population density and could limit further population increases.

30. C: Analogous structures do not reveal anything about common ancestors between species. They are simply features that arise due to adapting to similar ecological conditions.

31. B: Animals belonging to the phylum Echinodermata have tube feet for locomotion and feeding. About 7,000 species are extant in this phylum, including starfish and sand dollars. Tube feet are an organ system that provides locomotion, respiration, feeding, and sensory functions. Not all echinoderms have appendages. Having an exoskeleton made of chitin is characteristic of arthropods. Not all echinoderms shed their outer layer of skin to grow.

32. D: Respiration produces carbon dioxide and water. The net equation of respiration is the reverse of the equation for photosynthesis. Respiration is a series of reactions that consume glucose and oxygen to release energy and produce carbon dioxide and water. Oxygen and glucose are the substances that are broken down in respiration.

33. D: *Genetic engineering* is a general term to describe altering DNA sequences through adding or removing pieces of DNA from a native sequence. In the earliest genetic engineering processes, restriction enzymes were used to perform this "clipping" function, but other methods have been devised and are in use today. Current technologies include those using nucleases (such as CRISPR-Cas9, zinc-finger nucleases, or TALENs) or site-specific recombinases.

34. B: Organisms that belong to the same taxonomic group of family are most alike. In biological taxonomy, the ranks in descending order are Domain, Kingdom, Phylum, Class, Order, Family, Genus, and Species. The ranks become more exclusive and specific as the classification descends. Phylum, class, and order are all higher than the family group. The higher the rank, the fewer requirements it takes to be a member. Two mnemonics for taxonomy are Dashing Kings Play Cards On Fat Green Stools or Dear King Philip Cuts Open Five Green Snakes.

35. D: Meiosis produces cells that are genetically different, having half the number of chromosomes of the parent cells. Mitosis produces cells that are genetically identical; daughter cells have the exact same number of chromosomes as parent cells. Mitosis is useful for repairing the body while meiosis is useful for sexual reproduction.

36. C: Lactic acid fermentation converts pyruvate into lactate using high-energy electrons from NADH. This process allows ATP production to continue in anaerobic conditions by providing NAD^+ so that ATP can be made in glycolysis.

37. D: The epiglottis covers the trachea during swallowing, thus preventing food from entering the airway. The trachea, also known as the windpipe, is a cylindrical portion of the respiratory tract that joins the larynx with the lungs. The esophagus connects the throat and the stomach. When a person swallows, the esophagus contracts to force the food down into the stomach. Like many other structures in the digestive and respiratory systems, the esophagus secretes mucus for lubrication.

38. A: Evolutionary fitness is a measure of the ability to transmit genes to subsequent generations. As such, it is characterized by the ability to produce offspring. Although the male wolf described in choice A died young, he lived long enough to produce 4 offspring, more than any of the animals described in the other choices. Therefore, his genes have the greatest chance of being passed on. It is important to realize that evolutionary "success," or fitness, simply requires an organism to live long enough to reproduce, and is measured exclusively by reproductive success.

39. C: In birds and reptiles, the yolk sac contains the yolk, the main source of nutrients for the embryo. In humans, the yolk sac is empty and embryos receive nutrition through the placenta. However, the yolk sac forms part of the digestive system and is where the earliest blood cells and blood vessels are formed.

40. A: In the ecosystem described, birds eat beetles, crickets, and grasshoppers. If a pesticide were to kill off part of the beetle population, birds would be forced to consume more crickets and grasshoppers to meet their energy needs. As a result, there would be a decrease in the cricket population.

41. B: Bacteria and cyanobacteria have cell walls constructed from peptidoglycans—a polysaccharide and protein molecule. Other types of organisms with cell walls, for instance, plants and fungi, have cell walls composed of different polysaccharides. Plant cell walls are composed of cellulose, and fungal cell walls are composed of chitin.

42. B: Cells differentiate so that simple, less specialized cells can become highly specialized cells. For example, humans are multicellular organisms who undergo cell differentiation numerous times. Cells begin as simple zygotes after fertilization and then differentiate to form a myriad of complex tissues and systems before birth.

43. B: Glycogen is a polysaccharide, a molecule composed of many bonded glucose molecules. Glucose is a carbohydrate, and all carbohydrates are composed of only carbon, oxygen, and hydrogen. Most other metabolic compounds contain other atoms, particularly nitrogen, phosphorus, and sulfur.

44. C: RNA has several roles, one of which is to act as a messenger and deliver information about the correct sequence of proteins in DNA. The ribosomes do the actual manufacturing of the proteins. Hydrogen, oxygen, and nitrogen work to create the bonds within DNA. And far from having a double helix shape, RNA has what would be considered a more two-dimensional shape.

45. B: Jean Baptiste Lamarck's theory of acquired characteristics predated Darwin's book about theory of natural selection. Lamarck explained evolution as occurring when individual organisms of a species changed as a response to environmental conditions. Contrast this with Darwinism, which states that individuals with more successful characteristics are more likely to survive to breed and pass on those traits. Since Lamarck died in 1829 and Darwin published *On the Origin of Species* in

1859, the other answers that Lamarck "expanded," "provided evidence for," or "opposed" Darwin's theories are not likely.

46. C: The chaparral biome features scrubby plants and small evergreen trees and also has a hot, dry summer followed by a wetter winter. This biome is mainly found around the Mediterranean Sea, though there are also chaparrals in Australia, South Africa, and the American Southwest. The taiga is a colder biome found primarily in northern Europe and Asia. The vegetation of the taiga is mainly scattered stands of coniferous trees. A coniferous forest, meanwhile, is a warmer forest composed of trees that have needles and cones rather than leaves. These trees are better suited for a cold climate than are deciduous trees. A savanna is a tropical grassland with only a few trees. Savannas are clustered around the equator.

47. B: Photosynthesis converts carbon dioxide into sugars that plants use. Three types of photosynthesis are C3, C4, and CAM. C3 is used by most plants. C4 plants live in areas with high temperatures and high light exposure. C4 first forms a four-carbon sugar instead of the three-carbon sugar formed by C3. Also, the stomata of C4 plants are faster at absorbing carbon dioxide and do not have to open as long, so less water is lost by transpiration. A C4 plant, such as saltbush, corn, or some grasses, would live in a very hot environment rather than a cold, marine, or dark environment. Plants that use the CAM (Crassulacean Acid Metabolism) type of photosynthesis also use water more efficiently as their stomata are closed during the day and open at night. Desert cacti are examples.

48. B: Secondary succession occurs when a habitat has been entirely or partially disturbed or destroyed by abandonment, burning, storms, etc.

49. B: Gradualism states that evolution occurs slowly, with organisms exhibiting small changes over long periods of time. According to gradualism, the fossil record should show gradual changes over time. Punctuated equilibrium states that evolution occurs in spurts of sudden change. According to punctuated equilibrium, the fossil record should have large gaps.

50. A: A lysosome is an organelle that is thought to be linked to the aging process and contains digestive enzymes that break down food and unneeded substances. Chromatin is the structure created by DNA and various proteins in the cell's nucleus during interphase and condenses to form chromosomes. Plastids are found in plants and algae. They often contain pigments and usually help make chemical compounds for the plant. The Golgi apparatus prepares macromolecules like proteins and lipids for transport.

CSET Practice Test #2

1. In insects whose life cycles include an incomplete metamorphosis, which stage of the metamorphosis does not take place?

a. The egg
b. The larva
c. The imago
d. The pupa

2. Which hormone is NOT secreted by the placenta throughout pregnancy?

a. Human chorionic gonadotropin (hCG)
b. Gonadotropin-releasing hormone (GnRH)
c. Estrogen
d. Progesterone

3. A horse is an example of a(n) ________.

a. omnivore
b. carnivore
c. decomposer
d. herbivore

4. A dihybrid cross is made between the dominant genes for brown eyes (B) and blonde hair (S), and the recessive genes for blue eyes (b) and red hair (s). What fraction of offspring would have the genotype BbSs in the F2 generation?

a. $\frac{1}{16}$
b. $\frac{3}{16}$
c. $\frac{4}{16}$
d. $\frac{9}{16}$

5. In humans, more than one gene contributes to the trait of hair color. What is this an example of

a. Pleiotropy
b. Polygenic inheritance
c. Codominance
d. Linkage

Refer to the following for question 6:

A biome featuring scrubby plants and small evergreen trees has a hot, dry summer followed by a wetter winter. The following food chain exists in the biome:

$$tree \rightarrow caterpillar \rightarrow frog \rightarrow snake \rightarrow hawk \rightarrow vulture \rightarrow worm$$

6. What trophic level contains the greatest amount of energy?

a. Tree
b. Caterpillar
c. Hawk
d. Worm

7. Which of the following conditions would promote evolutionary change?

a. Random mating
b. A large population
c. An isolated population
d. Gene flow

8. Which of the following structures is *not* involved in translation?

a. tRNA
b. mRNA
c. Ribosome
d. DNA

9. Which of the following processes is an example of positive feedback?

a. High CO_2 blood levels stimulate respiration which decreases blood CO_2 levels
b. High blood glucose levels stimulate insulin release, which makes muscle and liver cells take in glucose
c. Increased nursing stimulates increased milk production in mammary glands
d. Low blood oxygen levels stimulate erythropoietin production which increases red blood cell production by bone marrow

10. When an animal takes in more energy than it uses over an extended time, the extra chemical energy is stored as:

a. Fat
b. Starch
c. Protein
d. Enzymes

11. Transfer of DNA between bacteria using a narrow tube called a pilus is known as:

a. Transformation
b. Transduction
c. Operation
d. Conjugation

Refer to the following for question 12:

A teacher in Arizona takes her class on a walk through a nearby park to study the flora and fauna of their local desert ecosystem. The students see cacti, snakes, and even evidence of coyote activity.

12. How should the teacher explain to students how these organisms are able to survive in harsh desert conditions?

a. Over thousands of years, these organisms have developed adaptations to survive in arid climates.
b. These organisms migrate out of the desert during the summer months, only living in the desert for a portion of the year.
c. Snakes, cacti, and coyotes work together to find sources of food and water.
d. Snakes, cacti, and coyotes are all aquatic species that live in ponds and rivers during the hot day.

Refer to the following for question 13:

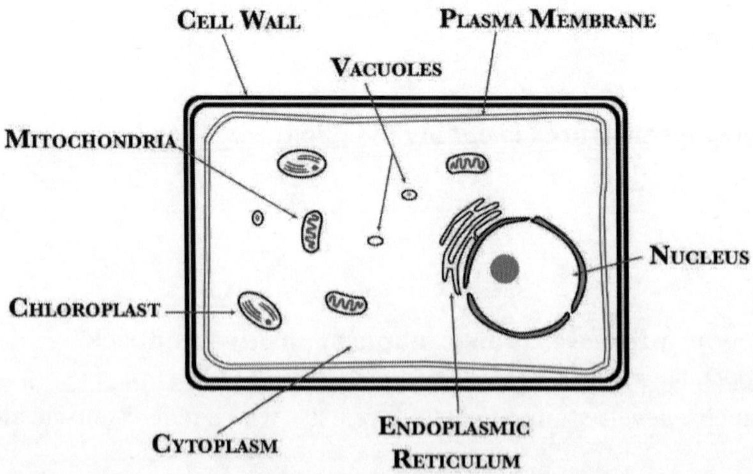

13. Which of the following structures contains DNA?

a. Cytoplasm
b. Vacuole
c. Endoplasmic reticulum
d. Nucleus

14. Which of the following human cell types has no nucleus?

a. Megakaryocyte
b. Red blood cell
c. White blood cell
d. Stem cells

15. What type of mutation is represented by the following sequence?

Original: 1 2 3 4 5 6
Mutated: 1 5 4 3 2 6

a. Breakage
b. Deletion
c. Insertion
d. Inversion

16. During primary succession, which species would most likely be a pioneer species?

a. Lichens
b. Fir trees
c. Mosquitoes
d. Dragonflies

17. Which of the following is the name for the study of the structure and shape of the human body?

a. Physiology
b. Anatomy
c. Biology
d. Genetics

18. Which of the following best describes the primary function of carbohydrates?

a. Provide energy
b. Aid in metabolism
c. Muscle tissue function
d. Prevents cell damage

19. The combination of DNA with histones is called

a. A centromere
b. Chromatin
c. A chromatid
d. Nucleoli

20. Which of the following does not help determine heart rate?

a. Body temperature
b. Physical activity
c. Concentration of ions
d. Anaerobic cellular metabolism

21. Which of the following parts of an angiosperm gives rise to the fruit?

a. Pedicel
b. Filament
c. Sepal
d. Ovary

22. A tropical flower is planted in a local garden. The garden is watered 2 to 3 times per week during all seasons. After only a few months, the tropical plant begins to droop and turn brown. How did environmental change most likely affect the tropical plant?

a. Being watered 2 to 3 times per week was not enough to sustain a tropical plant.
b. The new environment was too hot and burned the plant.
c. Insects attacked the plant causing it to wilt.
d. The new soil lacked the nutrients necessary to maintain the plant's health.

23. In plants and animals, genetic variation is introduced during

a. Crossing over in mitosis
b. Chromosome segregation in mitosis
c. Cytokinesis of meiosis
d. Prophase I of meiosis

Refer to the following for question 24:

B = alleles for brown eyes; **b** = alleles for green eyes

BB	**Bb**
Bb	**bb**

24. What is the possibility that the offspring produced will have brown eyes?

a. 25%
b. 50%
c. 75%
d. 100%

Refer to the following for question 25:

<u>*Protein Synthesis*</u>

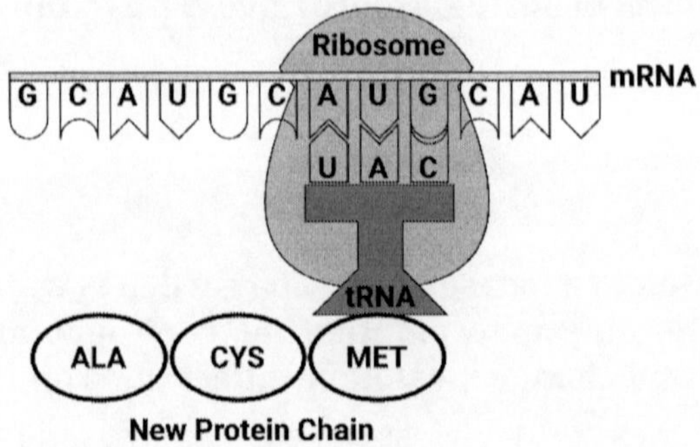

The Genetic Code

First	Second								Third
	U		C		A		G		
U	UUU	Phenylalanine	UCU	Serine	UAU	Tyrosine	UGU	Cysteine	U
	UUC	Phenylalanine	UCC	Serine	UAC	Tyrosine	UGC	Cysteine	C
	UUA	Leucine	UCA	Serine	UAA	STOP	UGA	STOP	A
	UUG	Leucine	UCG	Serine	UAG	STOP	UGG	Tryptophan	G
C	CUU	Leucine	CCU	Proline	CAU	Histidine	CGU	Arginine	U
	CUC	Leucine	CCC	Proline	CAC	Histidine	CGC	Arginine	C
	CUA	Leucine	CCA	Proline	CAA	Glutamine	CGA	Arginine	A
	CUG	Leucine	CCG	Proline	CAG	Glutamine	CGG	Arginine	G
A	AUU	Isoleucine	ACU	Threonine	AAU	Asparagine	AGU	Serine	U
	AUC	Isoleucine	ACC	Threonine	AAC	Asparagine	AGC	Serine	C
	AUA	Isoleucine	ACA	Threonine	AAA	Lysine	AGA	Arginine	A
	AUG	Methionine (START)	ACG	Threonine	AAG	Lysine	AGG	Arginine	G
G	GUU	Valine	GCU	Alanine	GAU	Aspartate	GGU	Glycine	U
	GUC	Valine	GCC	Alanine	GAC	Aspartate	GGC	Glycine	C
	GUA	Valine	GCA	Alanine	GAA	Glutamate	GGA	Glycine	A
	GUG	Valine	GCG	Alanine	GAG	Glutamate	GGG	Glycine	G

The genetic information for making different kinds of proteins is stored in segments of DNA molecules called genes. DNA is a chain of phosphoribose molecules containing the bases guanine (G), cytosine (C), adenine (A), and thymine (T). For DNA to be coded for a protein it must undergo two processes: transcription and translation. During transcription, a DNA molecule is copied into an RNA intermediary messenger RNA (mRNA) by complementary base pairing of DNA (i.e. G pairs with C and A pairs with T). However, RNA molecules do not contain thymine, but uracil (U) instead. Just like thymine, uracil binds to adenine. The mRNA then moves from the nucleus to the cytoplasm, where it locks onto a piece of protein-RNA machinery called a ribosome. The ribosome moves along the RNA molecule, reading the code three bases at a time, also known as a codon, to translate the mRNA into proteins. Each codon, as shown in the table, represents a specific amino acid and some are special codons for starting a protein chain (methionine) or stopping it. The ribosome relies on molecules of transfer RNA (tRNA) to help link the mRNA to specific amino acids and string the amino acids together to form a protein.

25. Which of the following is NOT part of a gene?

a. Codon
b. Cytosine
c. Ribosome
d. Phosphoribose

26. Remoras are fish that attach themselves to sharks and feed on the food particles left over by the larger fish. The shark is neither harmed nor helped by the remora's actions. This type of symbiotic relationship is best described as:

a. Parasitism
b. Commensalism
c. Mutualism
d. Passive transport

27. Which of the following is an example of the alternation of generations life cycle?

a. Asexual reproduction of strawberries by runners
b. Annual plants that live through a single growing season
c. Ferns that have a large diploid and a diminutive haploid stage
d. Insects that have distinct larval and adult stages

28. DNA electrophoresis accomplishes which of the following?

a. Breaking DNA into fragments
b. Separating DNA fragments by size and reactivity
c. Extracting DNA from evidence
d. Identifying key genetic codes with radioactive markers

29. In an ecosystem, its abiotic factors:

a. Are alive.
b. Are not alive.
c. Do not affect living organisms.
d. Include some microorganisms.

30. Which of the following could be an end product of transcription?

a. rRNA
b. DNA
c. Protein
d. snRNP

31. In DNA replication, which of the following enzymes is required for separating the DNA molecule into two strands?

a. DNA polymerase
b. Single-strand binding protein
c. DNA gyrase
d. Helicase

32. Scientists suggest that ______ has occurred through a process called ______.

a. evolution... differentiation
b. evolution... natural selection
c. natural selection... homeostasis
d. homeostasis... reproduction

33. Animals exchange gases with the environment in all of the following ways EXCEPT

a. Direct exchange through the skin
b. Exchange through gills
c. Exchange through stomata
d. Exchange through tracheae

34. A(n) ____________ is the physical and visible expression of a genetic trait.

a. phenotype
b. allele
c. gamete
d. genotype

35. Which of the following chemical moieties forms the backbone of DNA?

a. Nitrogenous bases
b. Glycerol
c. Amino groups
d. Pentose and phosphate

36. Which organisms depend most on light to survive?

a. Undersea plants
b. Mammalians
c. Land plants
d. Humans

37. Before they can be used by the body as fuel, complex carbohydrates must be converted into:

a. Glucose
b. Amino acids
c. Lipids
d. Folic acid

38. Which of the following statements describes the function of smooth muscle tissue?

a. It contracts to force air into and out of the lungs.
b. It contracts to move blood through large arteries.
c. It contracts to support the spinal column.
d. It contracts to assist the stomach in the mechanical breakdown of food.

39. When a population reaches its carrying capacity:

a. Other populations will be forced out of the habitat.
b. Density-dependent factors no longer play a role.
c. Density-independent factors no longer play a role.
d. The population growth rate approaches zero.

40. Which of the following would create the greatest amount of genetic variation for a diploid species in a single generation?

a. Crossing over
b. Mutation
c. Hybridization
d. Independent assortment of homologs

41. The behaviors of living organisms are changed and shaped by:

a. Primarily internal stimuli
b. Primarily external stimuli
c. Preset genetic programs
d. Internal and external cues

42. What is the second part of an organism's scientific name?

a. Species
b. Phylum
c. Population
d. Kingdom

43. Which of the following statements correctly compares prokaryotic and eukaryotic cells?

a. Prokaryotic cells have a true nucleus, eukaryotic cells do not.
b. Both prokaryotic and eukaryotic cells have membrane-bound organelles.
c. Prokaryotic cells do not contain membrane-bound organelles, eukaryotic cells do.
d. Prokaryotic cells are more complex than eukaryotic cells.

44. What does a food chain show?

a. The flow of energy between organisms
b. Every type of species living in a habitat
c. The population of each species in a habitat
d. The number of offspring a species will produce in a year

45. The energy flow through an ecosystem is represented by an energy pyramid. In the energy pyramid for a terrestrial ecosystem, the producers utilize 6,000 kilocalories per square meter per year. What approximate amount of energy is transferred to the third trophic level of this ecosystem?

a. 0.6 kilocalories per square meter per year
b. 6 kilocalories per square meter per year
c. 60 kilocalories per square meter per year
d. 600 kilocalories per square meter per year

46. When both parents give offspring the same allele, the offspring is ______ for that trait.

a. Heterozygous
b. Homozygous
c. Recessive
d. Dominant

47. Which of the following divisions of plants produces seeds for reproduction?

a. Anthophyta
b. Lycophyta
c. Sphenophyta
d. Pterophyta

48. Which of the following is a protein?

a. Cellulose
b. Hemoglobin
c. Estrogen
d. ATP

49. A length of DNA coding for a particular protein is called a(n)

a. Allele
b. Genome
c. Gene
d. Transcript

50. How is meiosis similar to mitosis?

a. Both produce daughter cells that are genetically identical.
b. Both produce daughter cells that are genetically different.
c. Both occur in humans, other animals, and plants.
d. Both occur asexually.

Answer Key and Explanations for Test #2

1. D: A complete metamorphosis, as butterflies undergo, includes the stages of egg (A), larva (B), pupa (D), and imago (C) or adult form. Insects such as mosquitos, grasshoppers, dragonflies, and cockroaches undergo an incomplete metamorphosis: they do not go through the stage of a pupa, which is typically inactive, does not feed, and stays hidden until the adult (imago) stage. The butterfly pupa, protected by a cocoon, is called a chrysalis. The mosquito pupa is called a tumbler.

2. B: The placenta secretes progesterone and estrogen once a pregnancy is established. The placenta secretes hCG early in pregnancy and in small doses throughout the pregnancy.

3. D: Horses eat plants but do not eat meat, so they are herbivores. Omnivores (A) eat plants and meat, while carnivores (B) eat meat but do not eat plants. Decomposers (C) consume only dead plants and animals, as they break down remains as a source of energy.

4. C: The fraction of offspring that that have the genotype BbSs is $\frac{4}{16}$. A dihybrid cross considers two traits at a time, in this case, eye color and hair color. In the parent (P) generation, a parent with the genotype BBSS would be crossed with a parent with the genotype bbss. The offspring are considered the F1 generation and all would have the genotype BbSs. This question asks about the F2 generation, which is the offspring between a cross of the F1 generation. Therefore, the parent genotypes in this question would be BbSs. To solve, develop a Punnet square of 16 cells. Each parent will produce the following gametes: BS, Bs, bS, bs. Place these across the top and the side. After completing the square, the resulting offspring show that four would have the genotype BbSs.

P → F1

	BS
bs	BbSs

F1 → F2

	BS	**Bs**	**bS**	**bs**
BS	BBSS	BBSs	BbSS	BbSs
Bs	BBSs	BBss	BbSs	Bbss
bS	BbSS	BbSs	bbSS	bbSs
bs	BbSs	Bbss	bbSs	bbss

5. B: When more than one gene contributes to a trait, inheritance of that trait is said to be polygenic. This type of inheritance does not follow the rules of Mendelian genetics. Pleiotropy is the opposite, which one gene contributes to two or more unrelated traits. Codominace is a non-Mendelian inheritance where both alleles are expressed in a heterozygote individual, rather than the dominant allele being expressed and the recessive being masked. Gene linkage occurs between two genes that are located near each other on a chromosome and are usually inherited together.

6. A: In the food chain of tree → caterpillar → frog → snake → hawk → worm, the tree is at the trophic level with the greatest amount of energy. Trophic level refers to the position of an organism in a food chain. Energy is lost according to the laws of thermodynamics as one moves up the food chain because it is converted to heat when consumers consume. Primary producers, such as autotrophs, are organisms who are at the base and capture solar energy. Primary consumers are herbivores that feed on the producers. Secondary consumers consume primary consumers and so on. Decomposers get their energy from the consumption of dead plants and animals.

7. D: Random mating (A) or a large (B) or isolated (C) population describe conditions that would lead to genetic equilibrium, where no evolution would occur. Gene flow, which is the introduction or removal of alleles from a population, would allow natural selection to work and could promote evolutionary change.

8. D: Deoxyribonucleic acid (*DNA*) is not involved in translation. *Translation* is the process by which messenger RNA (*mRNA*) messages are decoded into polypeptide chains. Transfer RNA (*tRNA*) is a molecule that moves amino acids into the ribosomes during the synthesis of protein. Messenger RNA carries sets of instructions for the conversion of amino acids into proteins from the RNA to the other parts of the cell. *Ribosomes* are the tiny particles in the cell where proteins are put together. Ribosomes are composed of ribonucleic acid (RNA) and protein.

9. C: In a positive feedback loop, an action intensifies a chain of events that, in turn, intensify the conditions that caused the action beyond normal limits. Nursing stimulates lactation, which promotes nursing. Contractions during childbirth and sexual orgasm are examples of positive feedback.

10. A: Long-term energy storage in animals takes the form of fat. Animals also store energy as glycogen, and plants store energy as starch, but these substances are for shorter-term use. Fats are a good storage form for chemical energy because fatty acids bond to glycerol in a condensation reaction to form fats (triglycerides). This reaction, which releases water, allows for the compacting of high-energy fatty acids in a concentrated form.

11. D: Conjugation is direct transfer of plasmid DNA between bacteria through a pilus. The F plasmid contains genes that enable bacteria to produce pili and is often the DNA that is transferred between bacteria.

12. A: Many organisms, especially organisms that live in harsh conditions such as deserts or frozen icy areas, have developed specific adaptations that allow them to survive. For example, cacti are able to expand to store large amounts of water, coyotes absorb some water from their food, and snakes can escape the heat by hiding within rocks.

13. D: The nucleus houses the chromosomes, which are made of both DNA and a protein component. The chromosomes contain the genetic code in the form of the particular sequence of bases that make up the DNA chain.

14. B: Red blood cells do not have a nucleus. This limits their lifespan, but makes more room for hemoglobin (the protein responsible for carrying oxygen). The other three types of cells are nucleated. Megakaryocytes produce platelets to contribute to blood clotting. White blood cells, otherwise known as leukocytes, help the body fight disease. Stem cells are undifferentiated cells that divide and specializing into other cell types.

15. D: An inversion mutation is represented in the sequence 1 5 4 3 2 6. An inversion error is a type of mutation where an entire sequence of DNA is reversed. In this case, 2 3 4 5 has been reversed to 5 4 3 2. Answer A, breakage, in a gene can mess up its function entirely or lead to a translocation of genetic information. Answer B, deletion, is when a section of DNA is omitted or lost. Answer C, insertion, is when an extra base pair is added to a DNA sequence. Deletions and insertions can lead to a frameshift effect where entire sequences are thrown off because one nucleotide is wrong. This could result in coding for the wrong amino acid and non-functioning proteins.

16. A: Pioneer species colonize vacant habitats, and the first such species in a habitat demonstrate primary succession. Succession on rock or lava often begins with lichens. Lichens need very little organic material and can erode rock into soil to provide a growth substrate for other organisms.

17. B: Anatomy is the study of the structure and shape of the body.

18. A: Carbohydrates are the primary source of energy for the body. Proteins and lipids also provide energy, but are not as readily digestible to use actively. The Dietary Guidelines for Americans recommend that 45-65% of food intake consist of carbohydrates. Vitamins and minerals aid in metabolism and allow for cellular repair. Fats and proteins are available for energy if the body needs them, but the primary function of fats is to support cell growth and regulation of bodily functions, while the primary function of proteins is to help repair and build muscle tissue and to regulate chemical balances in the body.

19. B: DNA wrapped around histone proteins is called chromatin. In a eukaryotic cell, DNA is always associated with protein; it is not "naked" as with prokaryotic cells.

20. D: Anaerobic cellular metabolism refers to processes of breaking things down and converting them to other substances (metabolites) in the body's cells. Anaerobic means these processes do not use or require oxygen. Metabolic processes not involving oxygen do not affect heart rate. Increases in body temperature and physical activity increase the heart rate as the heart works harder to pump blood-supplying oxygen to the body. The concentrations of calcium, sodium, and potassium ions do affect heart rate. These ions, known as electrolytes, must stay in balance to regulate heart rate. If they are balanced, heart function is not affected, but with imbalance, cardiac function will be elevated (excess calcium) or depressed (excess potassium or sodium). Sodium deficiency causes cardiac fibrillation.

21. D: The ovary houses the ovules in a flower. Pollen grains fertilize ovules to create seeds, and the ovary matures into a fruit.

22. A: Tropical environments typically receive rain 5 to 6 times per week, even if it is only a brief afternoon shower. In its new environment, the tropical plant is not receiving enough water to survive.

23. D: In prophase I, homologous chromosomes pair up and form tetrads. The arms of the chromosomes can break and recombine to create new genetic variations, a process called crossing over. At the end of meiosis, in telophase I and cytokinesis, the tetrads split up. The cell divides into two daughter cells that each contain one chromosome from each pair. Each daughter cell contains a unique combination of chromosomes that is different from both the mother cell and its cognate daughter cell.

24. C: Dominant genes are always expressed when both alleles are dominant (BB) or when one is dominant and one is recessive (Bb). In this case, ¾ or 75% will have brown eyes.

25. C: Phosphoribose gives the backbone of the DNA chain which makes up genes. In this area, bases like cytosine and guanine are strung together. Then, they are organized into triplets known as codons. These codons encode the protein to be made. The protein itself will be put together far away from the gene that is in the cell's nucleus. The ribosome is in the cytoplasm of the cell and will help to build the protein, but is not part of a gene.

26. B: Commensalism is a relationship between two organisms in which one organism is benefited and the other is neither harmed nor helped. Parasitism is a relationship in which one organism benefits but the other is harmed. Mutualism is a relationship in which both organisms benefit. Passive transport is a process such as osmosis by which materials are absorbed into cells.

27. C: Alternation of generations means the alternation between the diploid and haploid phases in plants.

28. B: DNA evidence is useful in criminal investigations. Once the DNA is collected, the DNA is extracted or isolated from the sample. Then the DNA is broken into fragments. After that comes DNA electrophoresis, in which the fragments are separated according to size and reactivity by placing them in a gel and applying a voltage across it. After that, key genetic codes are identified with radioactive markers, and a visual profile is developed. Finally, in DNA profiling, this profile is compared to possible suspects at a crime scene.

29. B: The abiotic factors of an ecosystem are not alive; hence (A) is incorrect. Abiotic factors include such things as the atmosphere, water, soil, sunlight, temperatures, nutrient cycles, etc. While not living themselves, abiotic factors *do* affect the living organisms (C) in the ecosystem. Living organisms are biotic factors, including humans, other animals, plants, *and* microorganisms; hence abiotic factors do NOT include microorganisms (D).

30. A: Transcription is the process of creating an RNA strand from a DNA template. All forms of RNA—for example, mRNA, tRNA, and rRNA—are products of transcription.

31. D: The enzyme helicase unwinds DNA. It depends on several other proteins to make the unwinding run smoothly, however. Single-strand binding protein holds the single-stranded DNA in place, and topoisomerase helps relieve tension at the replication fork.

32. B: Scientists suggest that evolution has occurred through a process called natural selection.

33. C: Plants exchange gases with the environment through pores in their leaves called stomata. Animals exchange gases with the environment in many different ways: small animals like flatworms exchange gases through their skin; insects use tracheae; and many species use lungs.

34. A: The physical expression of a gene—such as hair color—is the phenotype. The genotype is the basic genetic code.

35. D: DNA is composed of nucleotides joined together in long chains. Nucleotides are composed of a pentose sugar, a phosphate group, and a nitrogenous base. The bases form the "rungs" of the ladder at the core of the DNA helix, and the pentose-phosphates are on its outside, or backbone.

36. C: Plants growing on land depend on sunlight to perform photosynthesis, the process whereby they convert sunlight's energy to chemical energy as fuel for their life functions. Undersea plants (A) need water and nutrients like land plants; they do not need all gases in the atmosphere but need the gases in the water, and they need less light than land plants, or no light at all, to survive. Mammals (B) need air, water, and nutrients; some mammals need more or less light, but none need light for photosynthesis as land plants do. Humans (D) are also mammals.

37. A: The body's main fuel is the simple sugar glucose. Complex carbohydrates provide the body with sustained energy by slowly breaking down into glucose.

38. D: Smooth muscle tissue involuntarily contracts to assist the digestive tract by moving the stomach and helping with the breakdown of food.

39. D: Within a habitat, there is a maximum number of individuals that can continue to thrive, known as the habitat's carrying capacity. When the population size approaches this number, population growth will stop.

40. C: Hybridization between two different species would result in more genetic variation than sexual reproduction within a species.

41. D: Living organisms change their behaviors according to internal cues, such as hunger, thirst, need for sunlight, need to reproduce, etc., and external cues like environmental changes, such as changes in temperature, amounts of water, availability of nutrients, etc. Their behavior is shaped NOT primarily by one or the other of these (A, B) but by both. It is not controlled solely by genetic programming (C), but it consists of adaptations to intrinsic needs and extrinsic changes in the environment.

42. A: The second part of an organism's scientific name is its species. The system of naming species is called binomial nomenclature. The first name is the *genus*, and the second name is the *species*. In binomial nomenclature, species is the most specific designation. This system enables the same name to be used all around the world, so that scientists can communicate with one another. Genus and species are just two of the categories in biological classification, otherwise known as taxonomy. The levels of classification, from most general to most specific, are domain, kingdom, phylum, class, order, family, genus, and species. As you can see, binomial nomenclature only includes the two most specific categories.

43. C: Prokaryotic cells are simpler cells that do not have membrane-bound organelles, whereas eukaryotic cells have several membrane-bound organelles.

44. A: A food chain shows how energy flows from one consumer to another. The arrows point in the direction that energy moves. For example, if an arrow points from a flower to a bee, then the energy from the flower flows to the bee as the bee eats the nectar of the flower.

45. C: Producers always form the base of an energy pyramid as the first trophic level. Each successive level receives about 10% of the energy from the previous level. In this energy pyramid, the second trophic level receives 10% of 6,000 or 600 kilocalories per square meter per year. The third trophic level receives 10% of 600, or 60 kilocalories per square meter per year.

46. B: When both parents give offspring the same allele, the offspring is homozygous for that particular trait.

47. A: Anthophyta is a division of plants that produces seeds as part of reproduction. Spermatopyta is the broader group that includes all plants that produce seeds for reproduction, which includes gymnosperms and angiosperms (the same group as anthophyta). Anthophyta are also known as the group that contains flowering plants. It is the largest and most diverse grouping of plants and includes many food, clothing, and medicinal uses for humans. Grains, beans, nuts, fruits, vegetables, spices, tea, coffee, chocolate, cotton, linen, and aspirin are all derived from plants from anthophyta. Lycophyta is a small group of plants including club mosses and scale trees. Sphenophyta contains about thirty species including horsetails, foxtails, or scouring rushes. Pterophyta contains non-seed plants like ferns. Lycophyta, sphenophyta, and pterophyta all use spores to reproduce sexually.

48. B: *Hemoglobin* is a protein. Proteins contain carbon, nitrogen, oxygen, and hydrogen. These substances are required for the growth and repair of tissue and the formation of enzymes. Hemoglobin is found in red blood cells and contains iron. It is responsible for carrying oxygen from the lungs to the various body tissues. *Adenosine triphosphate* (ATP) is a compound used by living organisms to store and use energy. *Estrogen* is a steroid hormone that stimulates the development of female sex characteristics. *Cellulose* is a complex carbohydrate that composes the better part of the cell wall.

49. C: Genes code for proteins, and genes are discrete lengths of DNA on chromosomes. An allele is a variant of a gene (different DNA sequence). In diploid organisms, there may be two versions of each gene.

50. C: Both meiosis and mitosis occur in humans, other animals, and plants. Mitosis produces cells that are genetically identical, and meiosis produces cells that are genetically different. Only mitosis occurs asexually.

How to Overcome Test Anxiety

Just the thought of taking a test is enough to make most people a little nervous. A test is an important event that can have a long-term impact on your future, so it's important to take it seriously and it's natural to feel anxious about performing well. But just because anxiety is normal, that doesn't mean that it's helpful in test taking, or that you should simply accept it as part of your life. Anxiety can have a variety of effects. These effects can be mild, like making you feel slightly nervous, or severe, like blocking your ability to focus or remember even a simple detail.

If you experience test anxiety—whether severe or mild—it's important to know how to beat it. To discover this, first you need to understand what causes test anxiety.

Causes of Test Anxiety

While we often think of anxiety as an uncontrollable emotional state, it can actually be caused by simple, practical things. One of the most common causes of test anxiety is that a person does not feel adequately prepared for their test. This feeling can be the result of many different issues such as poor study habits or lack of organization, but the most common culprit is time management. Starting to study too late, failing to organize your study time to cover all of the material, or being distracted while you study will mean that you're not well prepared for the test. This may lead to cramming the night before, which will cause you to be physically and mentally exhausted for the test. Poor time management also contributes to feelings of stress, fear, and hopelessness as you realize you are not well prepared but don't know what to do about it.

Other times, test anxiety is not related to your preparation for the test but comes from unresolved fear. This may be a past failure on a test, or poor performance on tests in general. It may come from comparing yourself to others who seem to be performing better or from the stress of living up to expectations. Anxiety may be driven by fears of the future—how failure on this test would affect your educational and career goals. These fears are often completely irrational, but they can still negatively impact your test performance.

Elements of Test Anxiety

As mentioned earlier, test anxiety is considered to be an emotional state, but it has physical and mental components as well. Sometimes you may not even realize that you are suffering from test anxiety until you notice the physical symptoms. These can include trembling hands, rapid heartbeat, sweating, nausea, and tense muscles. Extreme anxiety may lead to fainting or vomiting. Obviously, any of these symptoms can have a negative impact on testing. It is important to recognize them as soon as they begin to occur so that you can address the problem before it damages your performance.

The mental components of test anxiety include trouble focusing and inability to remember learned information. During a test, your mind is on high alert, which can help you recall information and stay focused for an extended period of time. However, anxiety interferes with your mind's natural processes, causing you to blank out, even on the questions you know well. The strain of testing during anxiety makes it difficult to stay focused, especially on a test that may take several hours. Extreme anxiety can take a huge mental toll, making it difficult not only to recall test information but even to understand the test questions or pull your thoughts together.

Effects of Test Anxiety

Test anxiety is like a disease—if left untreated, it will get progressively worse. Anxiety leads to poor performance, and this reinforces the feelings of fear and failure, which in turn lead to poor performances on subsequent tests. It can grow from a mild nervousness to a crippling condition. If allowed to progress, test anxiety can have a big impact on your schooling, and consequently on your future.

Test anxiety can spread to other parts of your life. Anxiety on tests can become anxiety in any stressful situation, and blanking on a test can turn into panicking in a job situation. But fortunately, you don't have to let anxiety rule your testing and determine your grades. There are a number of relatively simple steps you can take to move past anxiety and function normally on a test and in the rest of life.

Physical Steps for Beating Test Anxiety

While test anxiety is a serious problem, the good news is that it can be overcome. It doesn't have to control your ability to think and remember information. While it may take time, you can begin taking steps today to beat anxiety.

Just as your first hint that you may be struggling with anxiety comes from the physical symptoms, the first step to treating it is also physical. Rest is crucial for having a clear, strong mind. If you are tired, it is much easier to give in to anxiety. But if you establish good sleep habits, your body and mind will be ready to perform optimally, without the strain of exhaustion. Additionally, sleeping well helps you to retain information better, so you're more likely to recall the answers when you see the test questions.

Getting good sleep means more than going to bed on time. It's important to allow your brain time to relax. Take study breaks from time to time so it doesn't get overworked, and don't study right before bed. Take time to rest your mind before trying to rest your body, or you may find it difficult to fall asleep.

Along with sleep, other aspects of physical health are important in preparing for a test. Good nutrition is vital for good brain function. Sugary foods and drinks may give a burst of energy but this burst is followed by a crash, both physically and emotionally. Instead, fuel your body with protein and vitamin-rich foods.

Also, drink plenty of water. Dehydration can lead to headaches and exhaustion, especially if your brain is already under stress from the rigors of the test. Particularly if your test is a long one, drink water during the breaks. And if possible, take an energy-boosting snack to eat between sections.

Along with sleep and diet, a third important part of physical health is exercise. Maintaining a steady workout schedule is helpful, but even taking 5-minute study breaks to walk can help get your blood pumping faster and clear your head. Exercise also releases endorphins, which contribute to a positive feeling and can help combat test anxiety.

When you nurture your physical health, you are also contributing to your mental health. If your body is healthy, your mind is much more likely to be healthy as well. So take time to rest, nourish your body with healthy food and water, and get moving as much as possible. Taking these physical steps will make you stronger and more able to take the mental steps necessary to overcome test anxiety.

Mental Steps for Beating Test Anxiety

Working on the mental side of test anxiety can be more challenging, but as with the physical side, there are clear steps you can take to overcome it. As mentioned earlier, test anxiety often stems from lack of preparation, so the obvious solution is to prepare for the test. Effective studying may be the most important weapon you have for beating test anxiety, but you can and should employ several other mental tools to combat fear.

First, boost your confidence by reminding yourself of past success—tests or projects that you aced. If you're putting as much effort into preparing for this test as you did for those, there's no reason you should expect to fail here. Work hard to prepare; then trust your preparation.

Second, surround yourself with encouraging people. It can be helpful to find a study group, but be sure that the people you're around will encourage a positive attitude. If you spend time with others who are anxious or cynical, this will only contribute to your own anxiety. Look for others who are motivated to study hard from a desire to succeed, not from a fear of failure.

Third, reward yourself. A test is physically and mentally tiring, even without anxiety, and it can be helpful to have something to look forward to. Plan an activity following the test, regardless of the outcome, such as going to a movie or getting ice cream.

When you are taking the test, if you find yourself beginning to feel anxious, remind yourself that you know the material. Visualize successfully completing the test. Then take a few deep, relaxing breaths and return to it. Work through the questions carefully but with confidence, knowing that you are capable of succeeding.

Developing a healthy mental approach to test taking will also aid in other areas of life. Test anxiety affects more than just the actual test—it can be damaging to your mental health and even contribute to depression. It's important to beat test anxiety before it becomes a problem for more than testing.

Study Strategy

Being prepared for the test is necessary to combat anxiety, but what does being prepared look like? You may study for hours on end and still not feel prepared. What you need is a strategy for test prep. The next few pages outline our recommended steps to help you plan out and conquer the challenge of preparation.

Step 1: Scope Out the Test

Learn everything you can about the format (multiple choice, essay, etc.) and what will be on the test. Gather any study materials, course outlines, or sample exams that may be available. Not only will this help you to prepare, but knowing what to expect can help to alleviate test anxiety.

Step 2: Map Out the Material

Look through the textbook or study guide and make note of how many chapters or sections it has. Then divide these over the time you have. For example, if a book has 15 chapters and you have five days to study, you need to cover three chapters each day. Even better, if you have the time, leave an extra day at the end for overall review after you have gone through the material in depth.

If time is limited, you may need to prioritize the material. Look through it and make note of which sections you think you already have a good grasp on, and which need review. While you are studying, skim quickly through the familiar sections and take more time on the challenging parts.

Write out your plan so you don't get lost as you go. Having a written plan also helps you feel more in control of the study, so anxiety is less likely to arise from feeling overwhelmed at the amount to cover.

STEP 3: GATHER YOUR TOOLS

Decide what study method works best for you. Do you prefer to highlight in the book as you study and then go back over the highlighted portions? Or do you type out notes of the important information? Or is it helpful to make flashcards that you can carry with you? Assemble the pens, index cards, highlighters, post-it notes, and any other materials you may need so you won't be distracted by getting up to find things while you study.

If you're having a hard time retaining the information or organizing your notes, experiment with different methods. For example, try color-coding by subject with colored pens, highlighters, or post-it notes. If you learn better by hearing, try recording yourself reading your notes so you can listen while in the car, working out, or simply sitting at your desk. Ask a friend to quiz you from your flashcards, or try teaching someone the material to solidify it in your mind.

STEP 4: CREATE YOUR ENVIRONMENT

It's important to avoid distractions while you study. This includes both the obvious distractions like visitors and the subtle distractions like an uncomfortable chair (or a too-comfortable couch that makes you want to fall asleep). Set up the best study environment possible: good lighting and a comfortable work area. If background music helps you focus, you may want to turn it on, but otherwise keep the room quiet. If you are using a computer to take notes, be sure you don't have any other windows open, especially applications like social media, games, or anything else that could distract you. Silence your phone and turn off notifications. Be sure to keep water close by so you stay hydrated while you study (but avoid unhealthy drinks and snacks).

Also, take into account the best time of day to study. Are you freshest first thing in the morning? Try to set aside some time then to work through the material. Is your mind clearer in the afternoon or evening? Schedule your study session then. Another method is to study at the same time of day that you will take the test, so that your brain gets used to working on the material at that time and will be ready to focus at test time.

STEP 5: STUDY!

Once you have done all the study preparation, it's time to settle into the actual studying. Sit down, take a few moments to settle your mind so you can focus, and begin to follow your study plan. Don't give in to distractions or let yourself procrastinate. This is your time to prepare so you'll be ready to fearlessly approach the test. Make the most of the time and stay focused.

Of course, you don't want to burn out. If you study too long you may find that you're not retaining the information very well. Take regular study breaks. For example, taking five minutes out of every hour to walk briskly, breathing deeply and swinging your arms, can help your mind stay fresh.

As you get to the end of each chapter or section, it's a good idea to do a quick review. Remind yourself of what you learned and work on any difficult parts. When you feel that you've mastered the material, move on to the next part. At the end of your study session, briefly skim through your notes again.

But while review is helpful, cramming last minute is NOT. If at all possible, work ahead so that you won't need to fit all your study into the last day. Cramming overloads your brain with more information than it can process and retain, and your tired mind may struggle to recall even previously learned information when it is overwhelmed with last-minute study. Also, the urgent nature of cramming and the stress placed on your brain contribute to anxiety. You'll be more likely to go to the test feeling unprepared and having trouble thinking clearly.

So don't cram, and don't stay up late before the test, even just to review your notes at a leisurely pace. Your brain needs rest more than it needs to go over the information again. In fact, plan to finish your studies by noon or early afternoon the day before the test. Give your brain the rest of the day to relax or focus on other things, and get a good night's sleep. Then you will be fresh for the test and better able to recall what you've studied.

Step 6: Take a Practice Test

Many courses offer sample tests, either online or in the study materials. This is an excellent resource to check whether you have mastered the material, as well as to prepare for the test format and environment.

Check the test format ahead of time: the number of questions, the type (multiple choice, free response, etc.), and the time limit. Then create a plan for working through them. For example, if you have 30 minutes to take a 60-question test, your limit is 30 seconds per question. Spend less time on the questions you know well so that you can take more time on the difficult ones.

If you have time to take several practice tests, take the first one open book, with no time limit. Work through the questions at your own pace and make sure you fully understand them. Gradually work up to taking a test under test conditions: sit at a desk with all study materials put away and set a timer. Pace yourself to make sure you finish the test with time to spare and go back to check your answers if you have time.

After each test, check your answers. On the questions you missed, be sure you understand why you missed them. Did you misread the question (tests can use tricky wording)? Did you forget the information? Or was it something you hadn't learned? Go back and study any shaky areas that the practice tests reveal.

Taking these tests not only helps with your grade, but also aids in combating test anxiety. If you're already used to the test conditions, you're less likely to worry about it, and working through tests until you're scoring well gives you a confidence boost. Go through the practice tests until you feel comfortable, and then you can go into the test knowing that you're ready for it.

Test Tips

On test day, you should be confident, knowing that you've prepared well and are ready to answer the questions. But aside from preparation, there are several test day strategies you can employ to maximize your performance.

First, as stated before, get a good night's sleep the night before the test (and for several nights before that, if possible). Go into the test with a fresh, alert mind rather than staying up late to study.

Try not to change too much about your normal routine on the day of the test. It's important to eat a nutritious breakfast, but if you normally don't eat breakfast at all, consider eating just a protein bar. If you're a coffee drinker, go ahead and have your normal coffee. Just make sure you time it so that the caffeine doesn't wear off right in the middle of your test. Avoid sugary beverages, and drink enough water to stay hydrated but not so much that you need a restroom break 10 minutes into the test. If your test isn't first thing in the morning, consider going for a walk or doing a light workout before the test to get your blood flowing.

Allow yourself enough time to get ready, and leave for the test with plenty of time to spare so you won't have the anxiety of scrambling to arrive in time. Another reason to be early is to select a good seat. It's helpful to sit away from doors and windows, which can be distracting. Find a good seat, get out your supplies, and settle your mind before the test begins.

When the test begins, start by going over the instructions carefully, even if you already know what to expect. Make sure you avoid any careless mistakes by following the directions.

Then begin working through the questions, pacing yourself as you've practiced. If you're not sure on an answer, don't spend too much time on it, and don't let it shake your confidence. Either skip it and come back later, or eliminate as many wrong answers as possible and guess among the remaining ones. Don't dwell on these questions as you continue—put them out of your mind and focus on what lies ahead.

Be sure to read all of the answer choices, even if you're sure the first one is the right answer. Sometimes you'll find a better one if you keep reading. But don't second-guess yourself if you do immediately know the answer. Your gut instinct is usually right. Don't let test anxiety rob you of the information you know.

If you have time at the end of the test (and if the test format allows), go back and review your answers. Be cautious about changing any, since your first instinct tends to be correct, but make sure you didn't misread any of the questions or accidentally mark the wrong answer choice. Look over any you skipped and make an educated guess.

At the end, leave the test feeling confident. You've done your best, so don't waste time worrying about your performance or wishing you could change anything. Instead, celebrate the successful completion of this test. And finally, use this test to learn how to deal with anxiety even better next time.

Review Video: Test Anxiety
Visit mometrix.com/academy and enter code: 100340

Important Qualification

Not all anxiety is created equal. If your test anxiety is causing major issues in your life beyond the classroom or testing center, or if you are experiencing troubling physical symptoms related to your anxiety, it may be a sign of a serious physiological or psychological condition. If this sounds like your situation, we strongly encourage you to seek professional help.

Online Resources

Due to our efforts to try to keep this book to a manageable length, we've created a link that will give you access to all of your online resources:

mometrix.com/resources719/csetbiolifesci

It's Your Moment, Let's Celebrate It!

Share your story @mometrixtestpreparation